THE GREAT IMPEACHER:
A POLITICAL BIOGRAPHY OF JAMES M. ASHLEY

BY
ROBERT F. HOROWITZ

PUBLISHED BY BROOKLYN COLLEGE PRESS
DISTRIBUTED BY COLUMBIA UNIVERSITY PRESS
NEW YORK

1979

Robert F. Horowitz is an Assistant Professor of History
at Rutgers University, Camden

BROOKLYN COLLEGE
OF
THE CITY UNIVERSITY OF NEW YORK
SCHOOL OF SOCIAL SCIENCE

STUDIES ON SOCIETY IN CHANGE, No. 9

BROOKLYN COLLEGE STUDIES ON SOCIETY IN CHANGE

—EDITOR IN CHIEF BÉLA K. KIRÁLY—

To the Memory of My Mother

ESTHER HOROWITZ

CONTENTS

EDITOR'S INTRODUCTION

"Brooklyn College Studies on Society in Change" was launched originally to publish the proceedings of scholarly conferences held by the School of Social Science of our college alone, or jointly with the Center for European Studies, Graduate School CUNY. From the inception of this series, however, we intended to publish monographs also. The precondition has been original archival research, innovative interpretations, revision of obsolete conceptions, and pioneering endeavors in fields not yet plowed by the Academy. Professor Robert F. Horowitz's present monograph meets these standards. Professor Donald M. Jacobs of Northeastern University wrote, "I sincerely feel that Professor Horowitz has done a solid job of bringing Ashley to life." Professor LaWanda Cox of Hunter College and the Graduate School CUNY wrote, "there is need of a modern biography to understand and evaluate his[Ashley's] role within the context of our changing perception of the issues at stake in the 1860s. Professor Horowitz's study fills that need." I wish to thank both these colleagues for helping us assess the manuscript.

"Brooklyn College Studies on Society in Change" is pleased to offer this book to the Academy and the literate reading public.

Highland Lakes, New Jersey
June 1, 1978

Béla K. Király
Editor in Chief

J. M. Ashley

PREFACE

In 1929, Claude G. Bowers described James M. Ashley as "low and corrupt," "depraved," and "disreputable." For years Ashley has been portrayed as a self-seeking, vituperative, fanatical, and impractical radical Republican. As recently as 1974, C. Vann Woodward called the Ohio Republican a "nut with an *idée fixe*."[1] These descriptions are unjust and erroneous.

The main reason for the persistence of this one-sided picture of Ashley (although historians Hans L. Trefousse, Michael Les Benedict, and Herman Belz have presented more balanced portraits in their studies on the Civil War and Reconstruction), has been the lack of a modern full-length study of his political career. Ashley's only published biographer is his son Charles S. Ashley, whose work appeared in 1907. The destruction of the Ohioan's personal papers, which were burnt during his lifetime, may account for the lack of attention to him. But the discovery of various Ashley letters and of an autobiographical memoir has made a reappraisal of his public career possible.

This book is a political biography. Since Ashley's personal papers were destroyed it is difficult to recapture more than the barest outline of his private life. In his political letters, which were found in collateral manuscript collections, Ashley very rarely discussed himself or his family. The only known piece of writing in which he opened his private self to the world was his "Memoir," and this unpublished work is important not for its literal description of his early life, but for its ability to recreate the milieu in which he grew up and to convey the forces of the environment which influenced his development. Yet, it is not Ashley's personal life which makes him interesting and worth studying, but his contributions to the political history of some of the most exciting and fascinating decades in American history.

This book tries to give a balanced and realistic interpretive portrayal of a significant and controversial politician. In one way or another, Ashley was connected with almost every seminal political event in American history from 1852 to 1872. As a young man he played a leading role in forming the Ohio Republican party and the national Republican organization. Ashley later successfully guided the Thirteenth Amendment to passage in the United States House of Representatives. He was an early and unceasing advocate of Negro suffrage, and of full political and civil rights for blacks. Unlike many Republicans, he was a principled fighter for equalitarian legislation for black Americans in the North as well as the South. Ashley was at the center of the controversy concerning Reconstruction. In fact, his March 12, 1862, reconstruction bill set the tone for much of the future debate on this complex subject.

And historians cannot truly comprehend what may well have been the most important executive-legislative conflict of the nineteenth century—the impeachment of President Andrew Johnson—without a full understanding of Ashley's much disputed, and at times bizarre, role in the struggle.

I intend to explain his motives and his reasoning, but I shall not try to hide Ashley's faults, his tendency to be rash and impetuous, or the political misjudgments of his career.

Ashley was an independent, intelligent, highly principled, determined, but not uncompromising man, who had a deep feeling for his country and a sense of compassion for the oppressed. This book endeavors to explain why he was honored by his black contemporaries and why he should be given credit for the many positive contributions he made to a dynamic political era.

I would like to take this opportunity to thank all those who helped in the writing of this book. My gratitude is due first to Hans L. Trefousse, who directed an earlier version of this work, and who over the years has been a devoted friend and faithful critic. The late John A. Carpenter, Jerome L. Sternstein, Gerald S. Henig, Stanley P. Hirshson, and the late John H. Cox, all read various versions of the manuscript and made many valuable suggestions. I would also like to thank my friend and colleague at Rutgers University-Camden, Rodney P. Carlisle, for his support and encouragement.

John M. Morgan, of the University of Toledo Library, kindly allowed me to use the Ashley "Memoir," for which I am most appreciative. Congressman Thomas L. Ashley of Toledo has been both kind and helpful. I owe an especially large debt of gratitude to the editor of this series, Béla K. Király, for his patience, knowledge, and generosity.

Finally, I wish to thank my wife Louise K. Horowitz, for her intelligent criticism, never-ending support, and for being such an extraordinary person.

CHAPTER I

EARLY LIFE

The young boy stood proudly on a table in the home of a staunch anti-slavery man. When he finished reading selections from the speeches of Cassius M. Clay and other abolitionists, the members of the household broke into loud applause. The scene was often repeated when the youngster visited the home of the abolitionist family.[1] Approximately thirty years later, on January 31, 1865, a six-foot tall, handsome, heavy-set man with dark brown, curly hair stood triumphantly by his desk in the United States House of Representatives. People were cheering, yelling, waving handkerchiefs, hugging, and kissing; Congress had just passed the Thirteenth Amendment to the Constitution, and the large man had guided it successfully through the House. Slavery, the institution which James M. Ashley had long viewed as a violation of natural law, Biblical injunctions, and the Constitution, was now on its way to extinction.[2]

Born in Allegheny, Pennsylvania, on November 14, 1824, James was the first child of John Clinton Ashley and Mary Ann Kirkpatrick Ashley.[3] There were four other sons in the family—John, Benjamin, William, and Eli—all of whom lived into adulthood. Unhappily for the Ashley family, two of James's sisters did not live beyond infancy; the third, Mary Jane, died when she was only eighteen.[4]

Ashley's paternal ancestors can be traced to Captain John Ashley of London, a signer of the Second Virginia Charter in 1609. Captain Ashley's descendants came to the area around Norfolk, Virginia, in 1635 and lived there for almost two hundred years. Not until early in the nineteenth century did one branch of the family move to western Pennsylvania, near Pittsburgh. James Ashley's great-grandfather, William Ashley, was a master's

mate in the Virginia state navy during the Revolutionary War; his grand-
father, Benjamin Ashley, was a Baptist minister in Portsmouth and
Norfolk.[5]

John Clinton Ashley, James's father, was born in Norfolk in 1800. At
seventeen he moved with his family to Pittsburgh, where he became an
apprentice and later a journeyman bookbinder. An extremely religious
man, John C. Ashley often spent many hours a day studying the Bible.
Shortly after his arrival in Pennsylvania, John joined with seven others
(one of whom was to become his future wife) to form the first Campbellite
(later Disciples of Christ) Church in Pittsburgh. Founded by Thomas
Campbell and his son Alexander in southwestern Pennsylvania in the early
eighteen hundreds, the church believed in simple, evangelical Christianity,
based on the concept of a union of all Christians, with the Bible serving as
the constitution of the religion. Salvation was impossible without baptism,
and baptism by immersion was only for adults who had made a simple
confession of faith in Christ. The sect spread rapidly and became quite
strong in the Ohio Valley.[6]

In 1820 John Ashley married twenty-year-old Mary Ann Kirkpatrick
of Allegheny, Pennsylvania.[7] Of Scotch-Irish lineage, Mary Ann would
come to provide a moral and spiritual contrast to her Southern-born husband, particularly for her eldest son, James.

James's family was exceedingly poor, since his father had trouble
choosing his vocation. In 1826, John Ashley moved his family to Portsmouth, Ohio, on the Ohio River, where during the next decade he engaged
in a variety of occupations. First he became involved in a bookbinding
concern, but since very few books were bought in this frontier region,
there was little call for his skill. To earn more, John soon began hauling
and selling ice in the community. A failure in this venture, too, in 1831 he
established the first soap and candle concern in Portsmouth, which was
fairly successful.[8]

But John Ashley's real passion was religion, and during his spare time
he studied for the ministry. In February, 1830, he was instrumental in
drafting the bylaws for the Scioto County Bible Society. A short time later
he became an itinerant Campbellite preacher with a circuit in southeastern
Ohio and the border counties of Kentucky and western Virginia. In 1842,
John C. Ashley obtained letters of ordination as an elder and evangelist,
and he faithfully followed this profession in Ohio and Illinois until his death
thirteen years later.[9]

His first-born, James, was deeply marked by the religious atmosphere
which enveloped the Ashley household. It was largely from this source
that the future congressman drew his vehement opposition to slavery.

There is little material available about James Ashley's boyhood. The lack of personal papers is a decided handicap in working toward an understanding of the motivating factors in his life. But fortunately, the discovery of an autobiographical manuscript has greatly reduced one's bewilderment in dealing with this dedicated, but enigmatic, figure.

Obviously a memoir—in this case, one written in 1896, when Ashley was seventy-one years old—can never be taken completely at face value. Such material inevitably suffers from conscious or unconscious bias. Nevertheless, from this, the one manuscript where Ashley significantly shows his private self, the reader can get a general sense of the forces which operated on the boy and the man to create his intense aversion to slavery.

It is, furthermore, this part of the self—the commitment to abolishing slavery—which Ashley especially seeks to illuminate in his memoir. Unquestionably, he does not want to discuss personal matters unrelated to his eventual stand on slavery and on other major political issues. In the first sections of his memoir (those most directly related to intimate questions), Ashley focuses on four essentially interrelated motivational patterns: hatred of his father coupled with adoration of his mother; the particular religious atmosphere in which he grew up; his own first-hand experiences in witnessing the practices of slavery; and his relationship with a Quaker abolitionist family.[10] The illuminating aspect of the memoir is not its attempted literal recounting of events, but rather its ability to recreate the religious milieu in which Ashley lived as a youth. How this milieu influenced him, how it defined and colored his relationship with his parents, and how it permeated the whole climate of opinion regarding slavery which surrounded a boy growing up on the Ohio-Kentucky border—these are the fundamental issues clarified by the memoir.

Most aspects of life in Portsmouth—social, political, and economic—were discussed, defined, and carried out within the framework of the Campbellite faith. Ashley lived among a sect which encouraged independent reading of the Bible, and as often happens in such cases, the religious conclusions he reached were in many ways diametrically opposed to the views of his father and the Campbellites.

In discussing religion and antislavery, Ashley supplies a fascinating portrayal of his parents. Although the congressman wrote more than forty years after his father's death, his recollections are filled with hostile references to John C. Ashley as a man, to his religious beliefs, and to his views on slavery. Ashley shows an animosity toward his father which bordered on hatred. As an elderly man, he appears to be still psychologically scarred by his adolescent relationship with his father. On the other hand, he maintained a feeling of deep love and respect for his mother. Ashley portrays his parents, with strikingly different personalities—the father authoritarian and dogmatic, the mother open-minded and tolerant. This opposition obviously created tension in the family and influenced Ashley's relationship with his parents and his feelings for them. These two interrelated factors—the sentiments for his parents and the Campbellite religion espoused so fervently by the father—make Ashley's eventual growth into a radical Republican more understandable.

At the core of Ashley's development was an educational process which provided a solid foundation for an inquisitive, critical mind. The youth became a voracious reader, having acquired the basic skills under the direction of his mother. Mother and son together studied the Bible and various scriptural commentaries. Ashley also developed an interest in political tracts and philosophy, as well as a lifelong love of poetry. But the initial, most lasting experience, the one to which he referred so often in his memoir and in many of his political stump speeches, was scriptural study.[11] His appetite for learning, however, was not satisfied by books alone. An undeveloped community offered many occasions for a boy to observe life at first hand. In southeastern Ohio, James had ample opportunity to witness directly the practices of American Negro slavery.

Between the age of nine and thirteen, Ashley often accompanied his father on the preaching circuit in Kentucky and western Virginia where he observed slavery's harsh realities. Chained and shackled gangs of slaves, being driven on the road to the Deep South, passed before his eyes. He saw the whipping post. On one occasion he encountered a man who refused to allow his cattle to drink from a stream in which Ashley's father was baptizing slaves. During these trips, the boy also listened with curiosity to the slave songs "whose trembling melodies could not fail to touch all unperverted human hearts."[12]

Ashley could never comprehend how Christians and especially the leaders of the Campbellite church, could condone the brutalities of slavery. The Disciples believed that, according to the Bible, slaveholding was permissible to Christians, since the relation of master and servant was not a sin. In the region where Ashley lived, this view was quickly converted into a proslavery interpretation of the Bible. In the memoir and other reminiscences, Ashley tells how one day he was reading to his mother from the *Millenium Harbinger* (Alexander Campbell's magazine) in which it was stated that slavery per se could exist without sin. He did not understand the meaning of the term *per se*, so his mother explained it to him. (Ashley always claimed that "in her heart" she rebelled against this position and had only contempt for the proslavery interpretation of the Bible.) Distressed by the church's position, James questioned this statement. "While at home in my earliest

youth," Ashley later wrote, "the preaching of the gospel as I heard it expounded in behalf of slavery bewildered me, but could not banish from
my mind and heart the brutality which I had repeatedly witnessed when
slaves were beaten and tortured."[13]

Exhibiting a streak of independence which would characterize his life,
Ashley soon rebelled against his church's proslavery interpretation, and as
he grew older, decided to study the Bible for himself. His analysis gave him
a clear picture of the immorality of slavery, and he came to believe that
proslavery churchmen had deliberately misinterpreted the Bible and the
Golden Rule. The Disciples of Christ believed that each individual must interpret the Bible as his understanding allowed. Since Ashley came from a
family in which Bible reading and discussion were an everyday occasion,
his analysis soon brought him into conflict with his father. James was outraged because his father was an elder in a religious organization which upheld slavery.[14]

Increasingly, Ashley began to question the hypocrisy which surrounded
him. Both at home and at church meetings, slavery was a major topic of
discussion. Once a friend told his father, with a knowing look, how the
wife of a young preacher was given some slaves by the members of his
church, to tie the minister to the institution of slavery. Ashley's father
accepted this story without protest or concern. At various times, people
talked about the social and religious behavior of the family's Kentucky
neighbor, the future Vice President of the United States, Richard M.
Johnson. Johnson was condemned for allowing the mail to be delivered on
the Sabbath and for living in concubinage with one of his slave women, on
whom he fathered two girls and a boy. But the real scandal was Johnson's
recognizing the children as his own, educating them rather than treating
them as slaves. Later in life, Ashley maintained that the attitudes exhibited
by the Campbellites disgusted him as a youth and alienated him from his
father and the church.[15]

At the time these events occurred, James did not always readily understand their full meaning. He turned to his mother, and she supplied ex-
planations. While Mary Ann was educating her son, she also told him abolitionist stories which Ashley always said had an enormous influence on
him.[16] Growing up in a household where the father was often absent on
his ministerial rounds, James looked to his mother for intellectual and
moral sustenance. Sensitive and humane, she had abolitionist friends and
was committed to temperance. As a grown man, Ashley would strive to
emulate and please her.

But Mary Ann Ashley's presence was not a sufficiently mitigating influence to maintain family harmony. During a Disciples' revival meeting, a

notorious slave catcher made a confession of faith and asked to be baptized. Some members of the congregation did not want to grant this request. But since the elders could not in good conscience refuse any sinner who desired redemption, the unsavory individual was duly immersed. Campbellites discussed the new convert's past during the next few months, but although it was generally conceded that he was guilty of kidnapping and then selling free Negroes into slavery, few church members became overly upset. Some months later the slave catcher was accused of stealing a horse, and it was suggested that he be dismissed from the church. Upon hearing this James said, "if he had stolen a man, nothing would have been said about it; but as he was simply suspected of stealing a horse, he must be churched [sic] and expelled from the communion of saints."[17] James was severely punished for what his father considered an imprudent remark.

From early youth, Ashley showed a tendency to be outgoing, outspoken, and inquisitive; his father was a strict dogmatist who did not like his children to differ with him. When he was home, duty rather than love seems to have been his watchword. James could not accept his father's theology nor his method of imparting it. As Ashley grew to young manhood, he came to distrust the concept of a single creed, which contained all religious wisdom. A religious person, who believed in God, he nevertheless refused to accept any theological doctrine as the one and only truth.[18]

Soon after the horse-stealing incident, when his father began to insist that James attend a Campbellite college to further his religious education, the young man decided to leave home. The combination of his growing disenchantment with the Campbellites and his animosity toward John C. Ashley drove James from the family hearth; at fourteen, he went out to make his way in the world. Ashley did not speak or write to his father until he was twenty-one. He did write his mother often, however; and years later he described her letters to him as "a never failing source of comfort and strength." Nonetheless, he went without seeing her for seven years. This was obviously painful to both of them. But James would not return home, even for a visit, until he felt he could deal with his father on equal terms; and Mary Ann could do little more than beseech her husband to go after their son and bring him home. He tried but was unsuccessful.[19] In leaving home to earn his own living, James clearly demonstrated an independent spirit, strength of will, vitality, and a determination to stand up for what he believed. These personality traits remained fundamental to his character.

Ashley went directly to the farm of Joshua Nurse, a Quaker abolitionist who lived in the western part of Scioto County, Ohio. Mrs. Nurse was one of his mother's friends; and he felt confident that she would take him in. The Nurses understood why James had left home, and they agreed to help him. He stayed with them for a short time, but when he learned that his father was coming after him, he left.[20]

Securing a ride on a river raft, Ashley made his way down the Ohio to Cincinnati. Unable to find a job in a printing office or on a newspaper, as he would have liked, the young adventurer began working as a cabin boy on a steamboat. Once, when the boat docked at Nashville, he went ashore hoping to see his boyhood hero, General Andrew Jackson at the Hermitage. With the brashness only a boy of fourteen could possess, James went out to the mansion, obtained admission, and had a brief but warm conversation with the former President.[21] Throughout his later political career, Ashley always maintained that Jackson and Thomas Jefferson were the statesmen he most admired.

During the next two years, Ashley worked on several steamboats, gathering valuable experience of human nature. One of Ashley's sons would later write that his father's detestation of slavery was increased during this period by the way he saw free blacks and slaves treated on the boats and in the ports of southern rivers.[22]

The effort to explain the growth of Ashley's antislavery views has required consideration of several factors: his experiences witnessing slavery as a boy; his work on river boats; his study of the Bible; his hatred of his father; his deep love for his mother; and finally his friendship with the Nurses. The last four of these are connected and most important. As a young member of a church group which gave the individual the freedom to interpret the Bible for himself, Ashley, with the help and understanding of his mother, came to believe that slavery was not condoned by the Scriptures. As a grown man, Ashley, like many other radical Republicans, focused on the moral aspect of the antislavery movement: slavery was a sin. This conviction created tension between father and son, a tension obviously so great that sixty years later, although Ashley could write about his mother in the most glowing terms, he still could not speak of John Ashley except in a most derogatory manner.

After James left home he came under the direct influence of the antislavery Nurse family. For the next decade these Quaker abolitionists became, in effect, his second parents. In their household he heard and took part in innumerable antislavery discussions. Ashley respected and trusted the Nurses, and he listened to their advice. At the same time he was still corresponding with, and receiving guidance from his mother, who had originally encouraged his inquisitiveness and independence of spirit. The years in which Ashley was growing into manhood, in which his ideas were forming definite patterns, were the years when his closest friends were the Nurses, when he was intellectually deserting his father, establishing his individual religious beliefs, and trying to maintain his mother's approval. These four factors cannot be separated in any evaluation of Ashley; their influence in the development of his antislavery views is paramount.

After his two-year odyssey on river boats, Ashley returned to the Nurses to recover from an illness. During his stay he received a letter from his mother advising him to visit some relatives near Washington, D.C. She enclosed a letter of introduction from a family friend, the Reverend John T. Johnson, to his brother, the outgoing Vice President, Richard M. Johnson. After discussing the matter with Mr. and Mrs. Nurse, Ashley decided to write Johnson, indicating that as a young Democrat interested in politics, he wished to come to Washington to see the great men of the nation and to be present at the inauguration of a President of the United States. Within a few weeks, Ashley received an affirmative answer, and he immediately left for Washington. Upon his arrival, Ashley went directly to Johnson's residence.

During the course of the next two weeks, the Vice President introduced his young visitor to a number of distinguished men. Ashley also witnessed the inauguration of President William Henry Harrison and Vice President John Tyler. The sixteen-year-old was highly impressed by both the people and the events he saw. Ashley was still in Washington when Harrison died on April 4, 1841. He stayed in the capital until John Tyler was sworn in as the new chief of state. Ashley's trip had taken place at an historic time; he was naturally affected by what he saw, and he soon returned to his friends in Scioto County, his mind full of new ideas.[23]

Extremely determined to make something of himself, Ashley resolved to seek permanent employment, and he quickly secured a position as clerk and bookkeeper with a general drygoods store, Waller and McCabe of Portsmouth, Ohio. While working in the store, Ashley became friendly with William P. Camden, the publisher of a Democratic newspaper, the *Scioto Valley Republican*. Always interested in the printing business and being ambitious, he began helping Camden at nights and on Sundays, while continuing to work in the drygoods store. Ashley's association with Camden's newspaper, and later on with other Democratic journals, especially with the powerful Ohio Democrat Samuel Medary's *Ohio Statesman*, was important in the growth of the young man's early anti-bank, hard money, moderate tariff, and equitable taxation beliefs.[24] Like many young Democrats at the time, Ashley favored opening the avenues of social advancement to all laborers, and he believed in the rights of property and in the value of economic individualism. While working on various newspapers, Ashley also became acquainted with a number of politicians, and gained an education in the art and game of politics.

When on August 16, 1841, President Tyler vetoed Henry Clay's Bank bill, Ashley and Camden immediately started to set the message in type and published an extra. Ashley made a wood engraving showing Andrew Jackson congratulating Tyler for his stand, which was printed in the newspaper. A copy of this edition, along with a letter of praise from Camden, was sent to the President. Tyler acknowledged receipt of these compliments and thanked Camden for his support. At a Democratic meeting called in the office of the *Scioto Valley Republican*, Camden was chosen to be chairman and Ashley to serve as secretary. The meeting drafted resolutions applauding Tyler's veto and sent them off to the White House. In return for that support Tyler appointed Camden the new postmaster of Portsmouth. Tyler meetings were then organized all over the county, but office seekers constituted most of the attendance. At first Ashley thought this was funny, but he soon became disgusted with these job hunters and ashamed of his part in the movement. When it became evident that Camden was approving every act and decision that Tyler made, regardless of the consequences, Ashley, a good Democrat, severed his ties with the eager editor.[25] He was standing on principle, as he would so often do in the future. Although Ashley was a practical man, flexible and capable of compromise in order to move toward specific goals, he also had a true moralistic fervor, which caused him to stick by certain basic principles of behavior. On this occasion he also learned a valuable lesson in how politics often worked.

Like many self-educated young men, Ashley was striving hard to find some great opportunity. Through the next six or seven years he searched for a profession in which he would be happy and could obtain some success. His main employment during this period was working as a printer and editor for various newspapers associated with the Democracy. He also began studying law with Ohio attorney Charles O. Tracy. Ashley was admitted to the bar in 1849, but rarely practiced his profession since he found it dull.[26]

In 1848, Ashley and Edward Jordan, later solicitor of the Treasury Department under Salmon P. Chase, bought William Camden's old printing equipment. The two ambitious young men began a weekly newspaper, the *Democratic Inquirer*. Neither Ashley nor Jordan had money enough to sustain the enterprise. It soon collapsed and they then sold the journal to Captain Francis Cleveland, a transplanted New Englander, who continued to publish it as a Democratic paper. For a while, Ashley stayed with the newspaper as a printer and editor, and spent much of his time at the Cleveland home. A voracious reader, James greatly increased his knowledge of literature and political philosophy by much reading in the Captain's large library.[27]

During the next few years, Ashley, now in his mid-twenties, continued searching for a way to advancement, but made little progress. The year 1850 found him in western Virginia, involved in boatbuilding and the transport of farm produce and pig iron at stops along the Ohio River. Although the project was somewhat successful, it was, unfortunately for Ashley, short-lived.[28]

Since his experiences in Washington and from the beginning of his association with newspapers, Ashley had shown an interest in public affairs. On April 7, 1851, he made his first attempt to win elective office. He ran as a Democrat for mayor of Portsmouth, but was defeated by the incumbent Benjamin Ramsey, a Whig, by a vote of 261 to 201. It was fast becoming clear to Ashley that there was no real future for him in southern Ohio.[29]

His views on slavery found small welcome in Portsmouth, a generally proslavery area. Southern Ohio, with its close commercial ties to the South, and its numerous tobacco farms, was very southern in outlook. Ashley had always maintained that an individual should speak his mind and stand up for what he believed was right. A man of ardent temperament and physical courage, he began attacking the Fugitive Slave Law of 1850. Regardless of the personal consequences, he forcefully declared that he would never obey such an infamous law.[30]

Ashley had also been involved with the Underground Railroad between 1839 and 1841 when he helped two groups of slaves escape to freedom. He continued to help runaway slaves and after one incident in 1851, in which he helped some fugitive slaves across the Ohio River, his activities became public knowledge in Portsmouth.[31] It was therefore growing dangerous for him to remain in this section of the state.

In the summer of 1851, Ashley realized that he would have to move, and after obtaining a letter of introduction from his old friend, Samuel Medary, who had previously introduced him to important Ohio politicians, he set out for the Northwest. He had planned to investigate the opportunities in St. Paul, Minnesota, but he stopped at Toledo. While looking around this rising Great Lakes city, he learned that there was a need for a new Democratic newspaper. Along with James B. Steedman, the future Civil War general, Ashley put out a prospectus for a newspaper, but nothing came of it. Although the project was not successful, Ashley liked the city, especially the economic opportunities it offered.[32]

Returning to southern Ohio to settle his affairs, he married Emma J. Smith of Portsmouth in November, 1851. The Ashleys were a handsome couple. Emma was a graceful, spirited woman, with light brown hair, and fine features. James, now in his late twenties, was tall and powerfully built. Alert, deep-set blue eyes in a broad face, a prominent nose, a firm aggressive chin, a straight mouth all bespoke the alert mind, the strong will. A slight upward tilt to the corners of the lips told of the warmth and humor that won him friends.

It is difficult to say anything about Emma's background since there is no accurate information on her early years. As an adult she was an intelligent woman with firm opinions of her own. She and her husband often discussed politics together. They were intellectually compatible, able to share one another's views on racial and religious issues; both finally became Unitarians. Emma Ashley was a strong advocate of women's suffrage and undoubtedly influenced her husband's readiness to support a demand that contemporaries considered so outrageous. In her, Ashley found a competent helpmate, capable of independent action when the situation called for it. Rearing their four children—James, Jr., born 1854; Henry, born 1856; Charles, born 1864; and Mary, born 1866—was largely her responsibility, for James was frequently away on business or political trips. Ashley developed full trust in his wife's judgment. On every level, the two were congenial and all the available evidence points to a happy marriage.[33]

Shortly after the wedding the couple left for Toledo, eager to establish themselves in their new community. Ashley and a partner bought out Z.S. Stocking and set up a drug store on the west side of Summit Street. Ashley's business was more a general store than a pharmaceutical enterprise. The firm sold medicines, paints, oils, dyestuffs, chemicals, perfumes, clothing, coffee, sugar, tobacco, fruits, raisins, medicinal wines and liquors, glassware, and all kinds of fancy articles. In February, 1853, Ashley dissolved his partnership for unspecified reasons but continued to run the business by himself. A month later he opened a larger store on the corner of Summit and Jefferson Streets, in what was known as the Morris Block. In April, he began publishing, along with Church Hughes and Company, a paper called the *Monthly Visitor*. Both firms used the paper for advertising, and it featured fiction as well as general news items. But this enterprise had a short life, as there was no real market for it in the community.[34]

Ashley's younger brother Eli moved to Toledo in 1854 and entered the drug business. Two years later, Ashley, in need of funds, took in another partner, John G. Howard, a Toledo businessman. The store burnt down in 1857 and though it was rebuilt, it was never again really profitable. By this time Ashley was deeply involved in politics, and Eli was running the firm. Ashley was a rather unorthodox businessman. His accounts were disorganized; sometimes, he forgot the details of the business deals in which he was involved. Always short of money, he was often in debt, and his drug business was never more than moderately successful.[35] Clearly his mind was on other matters.

Ashley's real passion was politics. His work on newspapers and his business dealings in Toledo brought him into contact with Ohio politicians, and the art and strategy of the political game fascinated him. As an entrepreneur he never managed to accomplish much, but in the political arena he would find the success which had previously eluded him. From his mother he had acquired idealism and a belief in trying to improve the state of humanity; politics and public service were ways to fulfill his real desire to serve the people. Outgoing, blessed with an ebullient personality and a sense of humor, Ashley felt intensely alive in the atmosphere of rallies, campaigns, and elections. Possessed of a fine speaking voice he loved the intellectual excitement of addressing large groups of people. Ambitious, aggressive, and immensely energetic by nature, but not overly astute as a merchant, Ashley saw politics as the avenue for obtaining the type of power he could never have had in business. Thus, almost from the moment he settled in Toledo he became involved in local and state politics. In 1858 he finally decided to sell his business to his brother Eli and another man. He planned to return to practicing law, then, if everything worked out to his satisfaction, to run for Congress.[36]

Ashley had at last found the profession which would bring him the happiness, the self-esteem, and the opportunity for success and power he so desperately wanted. During the 1850s Ashley's hatred for slavery, his tendency to question the status quo and rebel against conventional political wisdom, his sharp mind, his instinctive political shrewdness, and his desire to get ahead, would bring him to the forefront of radical Republicanism.

CHAPTER II

TOLEDO POLITICIAN

When Ashley and his wife arrived in Toledo, northwestern Ohio was reverberating with political excitement over such issues as prohibition, bank laws, internal improvements, and the extension of slavery into the federal territory. Intensely interested in politics, Ashley hoped to establish himself as a rising member of the Democratic party.[1]

Ashley was a Democrat of what he liked to call the Jefferson and Jackson school. He believed in strict regulation of banks, a specie currency, equitable tax laws, rigid economy in a government devoid of pomp and special privilege, a reformed federal judiciary, free labor, and free public schools. Although he was in favor of economic growth, he looked upon corporations as pernicious institutions.[2]

Eric Foner's analysis of typical Democrats who joined the Republican party portrays men whose beliefs were similar to Ashley's. For the most part these Democratic-Republicans were anti-southern and would not compromise on the issue of slavery in the territories. They felt that the Democratic party had deserted them. If they were from the Middle West they wanted government aid for internal improvements and a transcontinental railroad. Finally, the former Democrats in the party saw eye to eye with the radical Republicans, many of whom were ex-Whigs.[3] Ashley was too individualistic to fit strictly into any pattern. His positions on Democratic-Republican issues sometimes differed from the norm, but over the course of his political career, the ideas he expounded were generally within the framework just described.

Ashley had cast his first presidential vote for Lewis Cass, the Democratic candidate in 1848. Later in life he would claim that he voted in 1852 for the Free Soil candidates John P. Hale and George W. Julian, but the evidence on this matter is not clear. During the 1852 campaign, Ashley did make a few speeches in support of the Democratic presidential ticket, but he was also becoming disillusioned with Franklin Pierce; and it is quite possible that while he still thought of himself as a Democrat in 1852, he may very well have cast his ballot for Hale. In any event, Ashley never joined either the Liberty or Free Soil parties. He was a member of the anti-slavery faction of the Democratic party, and like many other young Democrats in the early 1850s he believed the Democracy could be made into an organization which would stand up against the "peculiar institution."[4] Ashley stayed with the Democrats until the early part of 1853, when his disenchantment with Pierce, his belief in temperance, and his realization that his old party would never become truly antislavery, drove him to Salmon P. Chase and the Independent Democrats.

During the year 1852, with the help of his friend Steedman, Ashley became a familiar figure in the Lucas County Democratic party. The yearly Democratic county convention was held in Maumee City, and the Toledoan took an active part in the proceedings. Resolutions were adopted condemning slavery and pledging delegates to support whatever candidate received the Democratic presidential nomination at Baltimore. Pierce was nominated and ran on a platform endorsing the entire Compromise of 1850. At first, believing that regardless of the platform, Pierce personally sympathized with the true ideas of the Democratic party as Ashley interpreted them, the young politician signed a call for a meeting of Lucas County voters favoring Young Hickory's election. Early in the campaign Ashley made a few speeches in support of the ticket; but he quickly became angered by some of Pierce's proslavery statements.[5]

The Whigs nominated General Winfield Scott on a platform which endorsed the finality of the Compromise of 1850. Thus both parties stood on practically the same ground with respect to sectional issues. The campaign in Ohio was bitterly fought, with both major parties importing well-known speakers to help their cause. The Democrats called upon the services of Sam Houston and Stephen A. Douglas; the Whigs brought in Horace Greeley and General Scott himself. Refusing to support either candidate, the Free Democrats or Free Soilers worked for the election of John P. Hale. Pierce won the national election easily. He carried Ohio, with 169,160 votes to 152,626 for Scott and 31,782 for Hale. Most of Hale's votes had come at the expense of Scott and the Ohio Whig party.[6]

Ashley soon discovered that he had been mistaken in his early 1852 assessment of Democratic national politics. The proslavery leanings of Pierce's inaugural address were a bitter disappointment to him and convinced him that Pierce "had sold us out . . . ." The news of Jefferson Davis's appointment to the Cabinet shocked Ashley. Realizing that the Democracy no longer had room for people with radical antislavery views, Ashley prepared to leave the party.[7]

During the early 1850s, the temperance agitation was one of the most volatile issues in Ohio politics. Because it offered a positive program for change, and because it involved cultural differences among ethnic and religious groups, temperance quickly became a matter for dispute. Initial concern with the issue developed when the members of the 1850-1851 Ohio constitutional convention, unwilling to jeopardize their work by tying the liquor question to the constitution, submitted a separate clause to the voters. The clause, which forbade the licensing of traffic in liquor, received an affirmative vote, as did the new constitution. Temperance advocates now started to demand statewide adoption of the Maine Law, which called for complete prohibition of the sale of liquor. The law soon became the object of political conflict, and the Democratic state legislature of 1852, in order to avoid dealing with the question directly, passed a mild regulatory bill which did not appease anyone. Having been reared in a temperance environment, Ashley did not drink as a young man. Although he had long been in favor of some sort of alcohol control, in 1852 Ashley was not yet a supporter of complete prohibition.[8]

By the following year the temperance organizations were determined to achieve passage of the Maine Law, and since it was a gubernatorial election year, the issue of prohibition was forced into the campaign. The Free Democrats, viewing prohibition as a moral issue, took a strong stand in favor of the law at their state convention in January. They nominated the well-known reformer Samuel Lewis for governor, and he endorsed the party's position. The Whigs and their candidate, Nelson Barrere, took no official stand on the question. A split occurred among the Democrats: the rural Democracy was in favor of temperance, but foreign-born citizens (German and Irish) were adamantly opposed to it. The state organization tried to keep the subject in the background, but local candidates were forced to take some position. Those Democrats who ran for the state legislature tended to be against temperance for the most part, but William Medill, the gubernatorial candidate, was silent on the issue. Temperance partisans decided to give their support to any candidate who stood for the law, and if none could be found, to put up independent candidates.[9]

As the year went on, the position of the Ohio Democratic party on temperance began to add to Ashley's growing disenchantment with the Democracy in general. By late summer he had decided to support the Maine Law drive, and he was actively urging John Fitch of Toledo to run as an Independent Democrat for the state senate from the Toledo district.[10]

On September 15, 1853, a temperance convention was held at Swanton, Lucas County. Ashley was appointed chairman of the resolutions committee, and he personally reported back to the convention. The preamble to the platform stated that temperance was "the greatest and most absorbing of all the questions of the age," and that the prohibition party must use "the protecting arm of the law, to shield and save us from . . . evils . . . in intoxicating liquors." Resolutions were then presented and carried which demanded the passage of the Maine Law and promised to oppose all candidates who were anti-prohibition. The convention nominated Sanford L. Collins, an antislavery Whig, as an independent candidate for the state legislature from the district.[11]

The Democratic party now began to put tremendous pressure on local Democrats to vote not as their conscience dictated, but as the party directed, that is, in opposition to the Maine Law. This was the final insult, and Ashley now boldly broke with the Democracy. On September 21, 1853, Ashley and nineteen others, including the future Republican Congressman Richard Mott, announced in favor of John Fitch as an independent candidate for the state senate. The local Democratic newspaper, the Toledo *Republican*, began blasting Ashley for his actions. He answered his critics on September 27 in an open letter to the Toledo *Blade*. Stating that his antialcohol activities had not been motivated by any selfish desire for personal or business gain, and that he had always been in favor of some form of temperance, he sent along an article from the *Ohio Life Boat*, a prohibition paper, which backed up his assertions. Ashley went on to indicate that he had always worked for the Democratic party in the past, but on this issue he had to lay aside party preference in favor of principle.[12] His store sold medicinal alcohol, which would have been illegal if the Maine Law had passed. Such legislation would have hurt his business, so his actions were evidently not taken out of mere self-interest.

Ashley, standing on the resolutions of the Swanton platform, campaigned for the independent gubernatorial candidate, Lewis, and for the local independents, Collins and Fitch. The prime issue of the contest was temperance; even Chase and Lewis stressed it rather than antislavery. Unfortunately, because of pressing personal problems, Fitch could not campaign for himself, and his absence hurt the cause. Fitch, Collins, and almost all the Independent candidates were defeated. A Democratic, anti-Maine Law, state legislature was elected, and William Medill easily won the race for governor. Even though the Free Democrats had lost they were not depressed, since the combination of prohibition and antislavery had given them their highest total vote so far.[13]

To say that Ashley became actively involved in the political aspects of the temperance movement out of a lust for power would be to call him a cynic, and that he was not. Yet it cannot be denied that he gained political contacts and influence from his association with the movement. His temperance background gave him a genuine interest in the cause, but he was never as dedicated to prohibition as he was to antislavery. In any event, after 1853 the prohibition issue became less important as the new excitement over nativism, Kansas-Nebraska, and slavery pushed it aside. In 1854, a mild temperance law was passed which made it illegal to drink liquor where it was bought. Ashley was one of the seventy-five people in the Toledo area who signed a manifesto pledging to enforce the new law.[14]

Ashley had always been ambitious, and since his move to Toledo in 1851, he had managed to realize some of his goals. Although true business success eluded him, he was becoming a man of influence in local politics. But if politics had captured his heart, he found himself in an awkward position as 1853 came to a close. Still believing in many principles of the Democracy, he supported Ohio's radical "crow bar law," which authorized county treasurers to break open vaults if banks refused to pay taxes on all forms of banking property. Yet his views on other matters had separated him from the party, and the independent group was not strong in northwestern Ohio. Like many future Democratic-Republicans, he believed that the Democratic party had deserted him, and not the other way around. The solution to the dilemma seemed to be an effort to solidify the antislavery men of Toledo into a viable third party.[15] If he had any doubts about his decision, the events of 1854 dispelled them. In terms of Ashley's future political life, 1854 was a year of major importance.

On January 4, 1854, Senator Stephen A. Douglas introduced a bill in the United States Senate which in its final form became the Kansas-Nebraska Act. Because of the repeal of the Missouri Compromise, the Kansas-Nebraska issue galvanized into concerted action all those who were dissatisfied with the national administration. It was in a very real sense both a blessing and a catalyst for the antislavery forces in Ohio, since the result was the formation of the Republican party. The Kansas-Nebraska Act united the radicals, disrupted the moderates, and fragmented the entire American political party structure.

In the process a number of ambitious young politicians came to the forefront. Ashley was one of them. As a staunch antislavery advocate he opposed the Kansas-Nebraska Act on principle, but it is also clear that he grasped the opportunity to get into the thick of the dispute. If Douglas had not acted as he did, it is quite possible that Ashley's political rise would have been much slower. The fragmented political situation gave Ashley a chance to prove his capabilities as a politician; on this occasion he did not fail.

During the resulting upheaval, Ashley established strong relationships with many of the leading antislavery men of the state and nation, and rose from being an obscure local politician to one with nation-wide influence and connections. Of the latter the most important would prove to be the close personal and political friendship he formed with the Cincinnati antislavery leader, Salmon P. Chase. The two men had first become acquainted during Chase's successful election to the United States Senate in 1849.[16] Ashley appears to have been attracted to Chase because of the latter's capacity to blend shrewd political instinct with intellectual brilliance. The two men were politically and intellectually compatible. Fully agreeing with Chase's antislavery interpretation of the Constitution, Ashley also endorsed Chase's desire to keep the moral wrong of slavery a central principle of the Republican party. It is also clear that, being eager for success and influence, Ashley followed Chase because he believed the antislavery leader was destined to be a man of enormous power and influence. Chase in turn admired Ashley's strong will, integrity, and political sagacity. The two politicians became close friends and confidants.

While the Kansas-Nebraska bill, with its popular sovereignty and its repeal of the Missouri Compromise, was being debated in Congress, a series of mass meetings was held in Ohio demanding its defeat. On January 28, 1854, there was an anti-Nebraska meeting in Cleveland, and on February 14, another took place in Columbus. From the latter, which led ultimately to the formation of the Ohio Republican party, a call went out for a state-wide anti-Nebraska convention on March 22. On February 24, a group of anti-Nebraska Germans held a meeting in Cincinnati where the bill was attacked as prejudiced against the foreign-born. In Toledo, Douglas was denounced as a Benedict Arnold for trying to repeal the Missouri Compromise; the South was castigated for seeking to spread slavery into the southwestern and western portions of the nation; Pierce and his administration of doughfaces were vilified.[17]

On March 22, those who opposed the Nebraska bill met in the Town Street Methodist Episcopal Church in Columbus. Although it had been raining for two days, a large number of delegates, including Ashley, attended the meeting. Ashley's growing importance in Ohio politics was indicated by his election as one of the vice-presidents of the convention and his appointment to its committee on resolutions. The committee reported out a series of strong resolutions, protesting the proposed repeal of the Missouri Compromise and stating that, if not impeded, slavery would definitely extend into the territories. The third resolution said that this was the exact purpose of the Nebraska bill and questioned the legitimacy of the popular sovereignty section of the legislation, since it denied the vote to foreigners who declared their intention to become citizens. Other resolutions stated that the North was determined not to allow slavery in the territories of Kansas and Nebraska, since they had to be kept open as areas for free laborers ("liberty is National, slavery is sectional"); approved the conduct of Ohio's two United States Senators; and urged Ohio's Representatives in Congress to vote against the measure. This platform was subsequently adopted and former Whigs, antislavery Democrats, and regular Democrats left with a feeling of harmony.[18]

There were other anti-Nebraska meetings in the next two months, but most people felt content to wait and see how Congress would deal with the issue. Chase, one of the leaders of the Ohio antislavery forces, was now quite willing to cooperate with any political element opposed to slavery, but as yet the movement lacked cohesion. On May 22, the Kansas-Nebraska bill passed the House of Representatives, and this created an immediate uproar in Ohio. A series of calls for a nominating convention was immediately issued, and on June 26, a formal call went out for a mass meeting on July 13, at Columbus.[19]

A movement for a new party was now firmly established, but as David Bradford has indicated, this was not owing to the Kansas-Nebraska Act alone. Ohioans were agitated about a Southern-controlled Democratic party which they felt was now running the country, and they were beginning to complain about the South in general. Pierce's veto of an internal improvements bill, which would have increased Ohio's canal and river trade, and Congress's defeat of a homestead bill, alienated many residents of the state. Thus by the middle of 1854, many people looked upon the passage of the Kansas-Nebraska Act as another effort by a Southern-controlled government to injure Northern laboring men.[20]

There was a general feeling of discontent in Lucas County. On June 23, Ashley, Mott, Fitch, and ninety-three others issued a call for a mass meeting on July 1 at Maumee City to pick delegates to the Columbus meeting, to discuss issues, and to help set up an organization "of a *true* and INDEPENDENT NATIONAL DEMOCRACY, worthy of the great Republic of the United States." At this gathering Ashley was appointed to the committee on resolutions, and along with Fitch and one Dr. D. Cook he was on a committee to draft an address to the electors of the congressional district. Ashley would later claim that he wrote both the address and the resolutions, but that they were modified by the more conservative members of the committee.[21] The resolutions were, even in their final form, so radical, and their language so forthright, so much in the style of Ashley's rhetoric, that there is no reason to doubt his assertion.

The resolutions were remarkable for their time, and a writer of Toledo history believes that it was "one of the most strikingly progressive documents ever framed in the history of Lucas County politics."[22] These resolutions not only indicate the past influences which had worked on Ashley, but they set forth many of the principles and ideals to which he would devote the rest of his political life.

In the preamble Ashley stated that there was a crisis in the country, which had been brought about by a conspiracy of slaveholders and doughfaces determined to nationalize slavery. "The liberties of the nation are doomed to inevitable destruction," he wrote, "unless the people are rallied to her rescue." Therefore, all party considerations must be relinquished and a new political organization entered into "for the purpose of establishing a true and reliable Independent National Democratic Party." Like many other future Republicans, including Salmon P. Chase, Ashley believed that a conspiratorial slave power was seizing the government.[23]

At the core of Ashley's political philosophy was a distrust of executive power (except in war time), a growing belief that Congress should be the dominant branch of government, and a real faith in the wisdom and intelligence of the common man. These ideas were expounded in resolutions where Ashley called for restrictions on the patronage power of the President and for granting Congress the right to appoint foreign ministers. In order for democracy to have any meaning Ashley advocated direct election of all officials, including the President, the end of the two-thirds rule at Democratic national conventions, and the people's right to recall senators and representatives.[24]

Ashley also opposed the distribution of public land to states and railroad companies, since he thought that granting large estates to individuals or to companies was dangerous for democracy. A homestead bill, he believed, embodied the idea that land should be sold only to actual settlers and only "in proportion to the number and wants of each family."[25] In the Middle West suspicion of corporations and economic concentration was still strong among men who, like Ashley, had Democratic backgrounds.

The fourth, fifth, and sixth planks of the platform dealt with the Kansas-Nebraska bill and slavery. Popular sovereignty was considered to be a fraud. Individuals who attended the meeting were asked not to support those who voted for the bill and who had bowed to a slave oligarchy "at the invitation of a weak, corrupt and imbecile President who is their mere tool." Ashley was extremely fond of colorful rhetoric when he believed he had been betrayed on political principles. The document stated that there should be no more slavery or slave territory in areas under national jurisdiction.

Ashley believed that the federal government should have no responsibility for slavery, but that it could not constitutionally interfere with it in the states. The best plan according to the Maumee proposals was to deny slavery "the sanction and protection of the National Government, either in the States, Territories or on the Seas" and to let it "support and protect itself as best it may, surrounded by a liberal and progressive civilization." These extremely radical concepts indicate how much Ashley was influenced by Chase, who had formulated similar ideas as early as 1841. In a blast at the Fugitive Slave Law, Ashley maintained that the general government had no right to interfere with trial by jury and habeas corpus.[26]

The importance of ex-Democrats in the party revolution was clearly evident in Ashley's resolutions calling for economy in government, repeal of unfair tax laws, and passage of a law taxing every person according to his actual wealth. Another axiom of Democratic ideology was the establishment of free nonsectarian public schools, and the platform at Maumee City supported this proposition.[27]

In addition, the platform dealt with the furor created by the nativist uproar over naturalization laws. The resolutions on this issue stated that all new immigrants should enjoy the full protection of the law and that the present naturalization laws, administered honestly, were all that was required.[28] There was to be no proscription of the foreign-born in Lucas County if Ashley could help it. Given the number of German-American and Irish-American voters in the area, this was a tactically wise stance for a young politician to take.

The convention endorsed these resolutions and chose twenty-six men— Ashley was one—to represent the county at the upcoming state-wide anti-Nebraska convention at Columbus. Ashley then made a speech in which he showed how radical he really was on the slavery issue. It was clear he said, "that justice demanded the emancipation of every slave within the limits of the republic, and that the true democratic idea recognized liberty as the birthright of the human race." By demanding the abolition of slavery in 1854, in no sense a popular idea, he placed himself in the ultraradical wing of the emerging new party. Until 1865 and the passage of the Thirteenth Amendment, this principle remained the focal point of Ashley's political philosophy; he never deviated or backed away from it. For radical Republicans slavery was the issue which shaped their political careers.[29] Ashley was no exception.

The Toledoan did not play any significant role at the Columbus convention. Judge Joseph Swan, an ex-Democrat, was nominated for the Ohio Supreme Court, and Jacob Blickensderfer, an ex-Whig, for the Board of Public Works. Both were running as anti-Nebraska candidates. A series of bland resolutions was passed as the more radical ones were buried in committee. The only important proposal called for the preservation of the free territory established by the Missouri Compromise and opposed any new slave states or slave territories. A committee of five was to be established to correspond with similar organizations in other states concerning the possibility of a national convention. No name was selected for the new party which was called the "People's Movement," the "Anti-Nebraska Movement," or the "Fusionist Movement."[30]

At the same time that the anti-Nebraska movement was gaining momentum, another organization was also being formed. For a time, this new group would join with the antiadministration forces, then split apart from them, and eventually disappear. The Know-Nothing, or American, party was an outgrowth of many years of nativist and anti-Catholic activity. Many Republicans were attracted to it, but most future radical Republicans were against nativism since they believed it diverted attention from true antislavery principles.[31] Ashley was one of the radicals who joined the organization, only to leave it shortly afterward.

Organized political nativism began in the Buckeye State in the spring of 1854, where its orientation was more anti-Catholic than antiforeign. Anti-Catholicism, always present to some degree in predominantly Protestant Ohio, was reignited by Catholic opposition to the 1853 school law establishing a special school tax of two mills. Catholics were against using their money for nonsectarian schools. The Know-Nothing organization grew rapidly in Ohio, and by October, 1854, it had approximately 50,000 members. Know-Nothingism in the state was always characterized by an antislavery attitude which often overshadowed nativism; and it never developed into the type of independent political organization set up in the East.[32]

The duration and depth of Ashley's affiliation with the Know-Nothings have often been misrepresented. Clark Waggoner, editor-publisher of the Toledo *Blade* and later of the Toledo *Commercial*, and Ashley's political enemy for over thirty years, always maintained that Ashley was a dedicated, thoroughgoing Know-Nothing. In 1890, when Ashley was again running for Congress, Waggoner presented all the old charges. He tried to show that Ashley was a true Know-Nothing, but he never quoted from any of Ashley's speeches or letters to support his accusations. Waggoner simply printed parts of the Know-Nothing platform as his proof. Randolph Downes believed that Ashley stayed with the nativists through 1855, but this is incorrect.[33] In a series of public debates in 1860, Ashley explained his connection with the Know-Nothings. Initially approached about joining the Toledo Know-Nothing group in 1854, Ashley at first refused the invitation, but accepted later in the year. He attended one Know-Nothing convention, at which he and his associates tried to have a friend nominated for a particular office. But his friend lost overwhelmingly, despite private assurances from others that he would win. Ashley then inquired how this result was possible, and the true principles of the group were explained to him. Quickly realizing that the proscriptive aspects of the Know-Nothings, besides being personally repugnant to him, were too strong to make the organization into an antiadministration party in which he would have power, Ashley discontinued his association with the group. He later readily admitted that his joining the Know-Nothings had been a blunder.[34]

The available contemporary evidence supports Ashley's assertion that his connection with the nativists was of short duration, and that he left them in 1854. The July 1, 1854, convention at Maumee City passed a resolution drawn up by Ashley stating that all new immigrants were entitled to the full protection of the law and that the present naturalization laws, honestly administered, were all that was required for citizenship. This is hardly the type of sentiment an individual still connected with the nativists would present publicly. In late September 1854, Ashley wrote to A. Shankey Latty, editor of the Paulding *Democrat*, maintaining that he was happy with the way old parties were breaking up. He suggested that the people should avoid a party if it "should compromise its honor, degrade its standing, by cowardly silence, ambiguity, and a Know-Nothing policy on great questions which affect the public heart. . . ."[35] At the 1855 Lucas County anti-Nebraska Convention, Ashley was on the resolutions committee, and he drafted a plan which stated:

> Resolved, That the present Naturalization laws, if honestly administered, are all that we require. We are opposed to the proscription of any man on account of birthplace or religious belief: and the only test of fitness for office that we recognize are honesty, capacity and uncompromising hostility to the extension of Slavery.[36]

It is thus obvious that Ashley had only a passing connection with the Know-Nothings. Becoming involved with them during the confusion of political parties in 1854, he left the organization almost immediately after the initial connection. Like most radical Republicans Ashley regarded slavery as the real danger to liberty in America, and he was not prepared to let nativism distract from the antislavery crusade.

The process of reforming or reorganizing Ohio's political parties was most evident during the 1854 election. During the anti-Nebraska meeting at Maumee City, a number of people approached Ashley about the possibility of his running for Congress. Though greatly flattered, he declined the honor on the ground that he had been in the district for only two years and was too young and inexperienced to lead such a fight. This, by the way, clearly puts to rest Waggoner's charge that Ashley switched parties solely to obtain political office. When the anti-Nebraska men continued to press the young merchant, Ashley finally agreed to find a suitable candidate (an antislavery man), and if he failed in this, to run himself. After much effort, he persuaded his Quaker friend Richard Mott to be a candidate.[37]

During the campaign Ashley continued setting forth the view that he was happy so many people were breaking away from political ties and exhibiting independence. Taking verbal swipes at the Democrats and the Pierce administration, he said, "acquiescence in the policy of the Slave Power is to us death. The demands of the Administration if acceded to, will prove fatal to the dearest hopes of the friends of freedom." Although damned by the Democrats for leaving the party, he stated that he would not waver and would vote for Mott.[38]

Campaigning vigorously for his friend, Ashley often made two or three speeches a day. The main issue of the canvass, both in Toledo and throughout the state, was the Nebraska question. The Independents or Fusionists attacked those members of Congress up for election, who either voted for the Kansas-Nebraska bill or refused to break with the President over it. Ashley took the offensive, calling the Kansas-Nebraska Act a declaration "that the People . . . have no right through a majority of their Representatives in Congress, to prohibit slavery there." It was a surrender to the slave power and "a base betrayal of the true theory of government." At first he thought that Mott would lose, since the district had been firmly Democratic for years. But as the day of the election drew near, Ashley came to believe that his friend would emerge victorious. His confidence was rewarded as the Quaker won by over 3,000 votes.[39]

Throughout the state the Fusionists won an incredible victory. They captured every congressional seat, and both Swan and Blickensderfer won their state-wide contests. With the election over, the real fight began: which faction would dominate the new party. On one side were the conservative Whigs and Know-Nothings who wanted to sacrifice antislavery ideals for nativism and anti-Catholicism in an effort to build a national rather than a sectional party. On the other side were the radical Democrats, Whigs, and Free Soilers who were determined to hold firmly to their antislavery principles and who were hostile to Know-Nothingism. The ex-Democrats were also afraid of a return to the generally more conservative economic thought of many Whigs.[40] In the next year there would be a gubernatorial election, and it was over the nomination for this office that the two wings of the Fusionist movement were to battle for domination.

After the 1854 elections, Ashley and other Chase supporters, such as E.S. Hamlin, editor of the Ohio *Columbian*, Joseph R. Williams, editor of the Toledo *Blade*, Dr. John Paul of Defiance, Mott, and Fitch began planning strategy for Chase's effort to obtain the gubernatorial nomination. These antislavery men were ready to juggle nominations and to make deals on certain matters, but they would not settle for anyone but Chase.[41] Ashley devoted most of the next eight months to this fight.

In January, 1855, after assessing the political situation, Ashley informed Chase of his opinions on how to win the nomination. He was against calling a separate Independent Democratic convention, as other Chase partisans advised. Arguing that the antislavery forces would gain nothing from such a course, he stated that he hoped the effort would be discouraged. Ashley wanted the Fusionist organization to continue as it had in 1854, since he believed that the Chase faction could control the next state convention. He really hoped to accomplish two things: the endorsement by ballot for a second time of the aims and principles of the antislavery forces and the destruction of the Hunker Democracy, which he feared would win if the Fusionists split. If the Hunkers were destroyed, "the young-doubting and aspiring in their ranks will at once leave them [the Hunkers] and join that party which gives them most assurances of success. If they believe it to be K-Ns—let them go there—better in their ranks with the old liners, so far as we are concerned." Ashley reported that by June 1 he would know exactly what to do. If everything did not work out, Chase's followers would still have time to call a separate convention, or attend the Fusionist meeting and withdraw if it appeared they were not in control.[42]

Yet, Ashley's real reason for fearing an open split within the Fusionist movement was that he was already looking ahead to the 1856 presidential election. He concluded that an open fight with friends both in Ohio and across the nation was inevitable, but at the moment they had to avoid this and keep the minds of the people on the issue they held most dear, antislavery. To him this was so paramount that he "could not conceive how men could wish . . . to endanger our success in so important a matter, by lending their names and influence to open or render worthless the advantages we gained last year by the fusion movement."[43]

The conservative Whig-Know-Nothing element wanted the nomination for Jacob Brinkerhoff of Mansfield, a former Democrat who had been a Free Soiler in 1848 and who had recently joined the Know-Nothings. This branch of the Fusionists was decidedly opposed to Chase. The two groups bickered all through the spring. By May, Chase was undecided about the correct course of action. He would not accept any lesser position as a compromise, but would support Brinkerhoff if the latter could prove that he was truly representative of antislavery opinion. If Brinkerhoff was forced on the Chase wing, however, and if this was seen as a triumph for the Whig-

Know-Nothing side, it would have a decided influence on the direction which antislavery men would take.[44]

By the end of May, Ashley believed that the radical forces could not control the July 13 convention, and he was now in favor of calling an Independent Democratic meeting at Columbus on July 4. He feared that if Chase lost the nomination it would be impossible for him to recover in time for the presidential contest in 1856. In any event, he felt that if the Independents nominated Chase on July 4, they would go into the Fusionist convention in a strong position. But if they could not obtain their candidates and their platform, they could either break up the convention or withdraw and resolve to stand by the July 4 ticket and resolutions. "This," he declared, "is the only feasible plan I can derive to draw off *the true friends of freedom* from the Know-Nothings. . . . If we wait until after the 13th of July, we will be *divided* . . . and *beaten* and *afterwards disheartened and inactive.*" He also urged Chase to take a strong public stand against the Know-Nothings, since he felt it would clarify the antislavery leader's position and help him in 1856. Ashley continued to take readings of the situation and as late as June 16 he still approved of calling a separate convention.[45]

The apprehensions of Ashley and other Chase supporters proved to be unfounded. The Independent Democratic convention never had to meet, since the Ohio Know-Nothings grew weaker as the year went on. Ohio nativists always had a strong degree of antislavery sentiment in their midst, and the radicals tried to draw on this opinion with the formation in January, 1855, of an organization called the *Know-Somethings*. In Ohio the Know-Somethings, seeking to attract antislavery Germans to the cause, became increasingly disenchanted with the nativists' sweeping denunciation of all foreigners and broke away from the Know-Nothing party. The Know-Somethings were really an antislavery group for whom nativism was a secondary consideration. The platform of the organization castigated slave power aggressions, praised free labor, and advocated that principles rather than place of birth be the test for citizenship. All that remained of the nativist influence was the statement, "we will repeal every ecclesiastical interference in political affairs by potentate, pontiff or priest, as destructive to the right to worship God according to the dictates of conscience and of liberty."[46]

By April the new organization had succeeded in winning over many Know-Nothings and thus had weakened the old order's strength. At the same time the Know-Nothings lost ground in various municipal elections. In June, the Ohio Know-Nothings repudiated the pro-Southern platform of the national convention.[47] Thus, when the Fusionist convention met in

July, the antislavery aspects of the secret society had taken precedence over nativism.

Because of their antislavery predilections, Ashley was associated with the Know-Somethings, whom he wanted to influence in Chase's favor. Attending the national Know-Something convention at Cleveland in mid-June, Ashley did all he could to protect Chase's interests. He came away with the belief that the organization was really dominated by "men of true anti Slavery convictions."[48]

At the Fusionist convention on July 13, 1855, after some argument, discussion, and a lot of dealing, Chase received the gubernatorial nomination and Brinkerhoff was nominated for Ohio supreme court judge. Eight other nominations went to the Know-Nothings, but the platform was strongly antislavery. The antislavery forces had won; they obtained the nomination and the platform they wanted, with no mention of Know-Nothing principles. This convention officially organized the Republican party in Ohio. It was not the Whig party in disguise, but as Ashley would later exclaim: "The leading radical and Jackson Democrats . . . were the first to organize the Republican party, especially in the West."[49]

At a convention on August 9, 1855, a group of Whig-Know-Nothings who could not support Chase, nominated former Governor Allen Trimble for the highest state office. The Democrats had renominated Governor William Medill on January 8, 1855.[50]

The election was hard fought. Medill and Trimble attacked Chase as an abolitionist and a disunionist. Chase, in an effort to win German voters, without at the same time offending his Know-Nothing supporters, stressed the Kansas issue. After initial strong returns for Medill, Chase emerged as the victor by 16,000 votes.[51]

The Ohio antislavery forces were jubilant over the results of the election. They were now the dominant faction in the Ohio Republican party, as the Know-Nothings had been pushed aside. Ashley was satisfied with the outcome.[52] The man for whom he had worked so hard was now governor-elect, and the antislavery crusade seemed to be well under way. In terms of his own life, the past four years had been the best Ashley had ever known. Starting out as a small city druggist, with radical Democratic ideas, he had risen to become a man of political influence and power in Ohio. Now a leader in the antislavery cause and in the emerging Republican party, he was ready to turn his attention to the national political arena. The following year a presidential election was to take place, and Ashley was convinced his candidate was a frontrunner.

CHAPTER III

PRESIDENTIAL POLITICS AND ELECTION TO CONGRESS

The anti-Nebraskans had increased their power and influence during 1855, and now they were preparing to try to obtain the presidency. Ashley, like other radical Republicans, believed that Chase could win the presidential nomination. Six feet in height, broad-shouldered, and handsome, with an intelligent face, Chase looked the statesman. A successful lawyer, an ambitious, tireless, and hardworking politician who refused to compromise with the slave power, he was greatly respected for his comprehensive antislavery interpretation of the Constitution. But if Chase was to gain the nomination, a strong national political organization and lots of hard work would be necessary. Ashley was prepared to do all he could for Ohio's new governor.

Throughout 1855, Ashley's advice to Chase was often more concerned with the future presidential contest than with the gubernatorial election. In January, he was afraid that a split in the Fusionist ranks would hurt the cause and hinder Chase's efforts for the nomination. But more importantly it would destroy Chase's chances for the presidential contest in 1856. By May, Ashley, Mott, and Williams had gone over a letter Chase had written to Dr. John Paul on December 28, 1854, which dealt with his refusal to endorse the Know-Nothing movement. Chase had said, "I cannot proscribe men on account of their birth. I cannot make religious faith a political test." But the letter had also shown a sympathetic feeling towards antislavery Know-Nothings. Ashley wanted Chase to have a revised edition (most likely eliminating the paragraph favorable to antislavery nativists) of this letter published, since he felt it was indispensable that something be done before William Seward or any other presidential aspirant came out against the Know-Nothings. Such action would indicate that Chase was not "solicitous as to what the public might say," and that those individuals who intended to support the antislavery leader could not later claim to have done so without understanding where he stood on the issue. Also, it would place him in the front line for the nomination in 1856 with those antislavery men who feared nativism, and this was of utmost importance.[1]

Chase eventually published the letter in June, but without the suggested revisions of Ashley and his friends. The Cincinnati antislavery leader believed that one had to work cautiously to moderate Know-Nothing influence in the People's movement, not attack it head on, since an open breach between the two branches of the fusion coalition would cause great harm to the antislavery movement.[2] On this matter Chase's analysis, and not Ashley's, would prove to be the correct one.

In June, 1855, Ashley attended the Know-Something convention at Cleveland (at the same time that a Know-Nothing gathering was breaking apart at Philadelphia), where he worked diligently for Chase. After three days of effort Ashley managed to obtain a resolution which set up a committee to correspond with the seceding Know-Nothings and other independent organizations in the Middle West. The committee was to contact all groups opposed to the Pierce administration and to the slave power who, regardless of party, wished to rally behind an anti-Nebraska presidential ticket in 1856. He was appointed chairman of the committee, which included among its members the antislavery leader James A. Briggs of Cleveland, future Congressman Schuyler Colfax of Indiana, and the Maine politician John A. Swayne. The committee was empowered to call a general mass meeting at Pittsburgh on September 10, or at any place it might choose to make preliminary arrangements for a national anti-Nebraska convention in 1856. Pittsburgh was selected because of its central location, but Ashley, who favored the city only as the site for an organizational meeting, wanted the nominating convention to be held in Cincinnati. This Ohio city was supposedly Chase territory. Ashley wrote to Chase and asked him for the names of those who might be interested in such a movement. The young man from Toledo was prepared to do all he could to secure the cooperation of their "friends throughout the Union." According to historian Andrew Crandall, this effort was the genesis of the first Republican national convention; the preliminary meeting, however, did not take place until February, 1856.[3]

What Ashley and Chase were trying to accomplish was the organization of a national political machine favorable to the governor-elect. To be specific, Ashley formulated the plan because he wanted "to be in advance of any movement that the 'organization' as such might make for Seward, or Hale or any other person." He was determined not to be caught napping while other prospective candidates were intensifying their efforts. At this time Ashley was extremely optimistic over Chase's chances for 1856. If enough of their friends took the initiative, he informed Chase, "we can easily nominate you and assume the name *Independent Democrat.*"[4] Since Chase had not yet received even the gubernatorial nomination, Ashley's statement was premature, to say the least.

On October 9, 1855, Ashley sat up all night, tending to his sick infant son James, Jr., and waiting for election returns. When he was certain that Chase had been elected, he began thinking about what the next political moves should be. Accordingly, he wrote to Thomas Spooner of Cincinnati. Thanking the head of the Ohio Know-Nothings for his help in the election, he asked him to resign his post and join the Republican party. Ashley argued that this would lead to the disintegration of the Ohio order, except for the Trimble proslavery wing, and clear the Republicans of the charge that they had joined with a group "whose principles were antagonistic to freedom." He concluded that if this course were followed, the Republicans would gain over half the foreign vote of Ohio and a large number of sincere old-line antislavery Democrats. It would also preserve the harmony vital to Republican interests and thus to Chase's success. To Ashley, as to other antislavery men, it was very important that the Republicans free themselves of the Know-Nothings by 1856, if they hoped to reach their goals. There is no firm evidence to indicate that Spooner explicitly adopted Ashley's suggestions, but he did break with the Ohio order, and with the national Know-Nothings. He also remained a strong Chase supporter. Many other Ohio Know-Nothings who followed Chase in 1855, also soon forgot nativism and readily accepted the antislavery concepts of the new Republican party.[5]

Since Chase had run on a platform free of nativist ideas, Ashley believed that the Cincinnatian's election was a step in the right direction, as it freed antislavery men from the charge that they secretly favored the Know-Nothing movement. Thus Ashley concluded that Chase's position was no longer open to misrepresentation. Nevertheless, Ashley was disturbed over other matters. Seward's speech at Albany, New York, on October 12, 1855 (in which he endorsed the new Republican party) was creating a nation-wide sensation and catapulting him into a position of leadership.[6] This only distracted attention from Chase. Ashley was most concerned, however, over the efforts of some Republicans to talk about the governor-elect as if he were a fanatic. He wrote Chase that he regretted,

> The New York Tribune in speaking of you should have used the term abolitionist. I am half inclined to think it done purposely and for effect. I hope it was not, but really it does you no good. Our Republican papers ought to call the attention of the Tribune to it, and ask it to make the distinction between an Abolitionist and a Republican.[7]

Ashley was also fearful of what the Democrats were thinking. He was convinced that they had decided to join the free state men (the antislavery forces) in Kansas, and to insist on the adoption of squatter sovereignty as part of their national platform. If this were to happen, he told Chase, "they would catch a great many of our votes."[8] His fears concerning the Democrats were unfounded, but they clearly showed how worried he was about any movement which might distract from the vote-getting power of Chase and the new party.

In the fall of 1855, after the gubernatorial election, a group of antislavery leaders met at Congressman Mott's home in Toledo. Among those present were Ashley, Chase, Hamlin, Dr. Paul, Williams, Fitch, future Congressman Fernando Beaman of Michigan, and Friedrich Hassaurek of Cincinnati, a German language newspaperman. The purpose of the conference was to discuss plans for securing the presidential nomination for Chase. All agreed on the definite necessity of holding a preliminary meeting to set up the machinery for a national convention. But the question was where to hold it. That it should be in the West was obvious. After considering Cincinnati, Chicago, and St. Louis, Ashley's original suggestion, Pittsburgh, was accepted. To try to gain support for this decision, the Ashley correspondence committee went into action.[9]

Ashley immediately sent letters and circulars to friends throughout the nation and also began traveling around the East. On November 16, he was in Pittsburgh discussing matters with Russell Errett of the Pittsburgh *Gazette*. Errett did not have encouraging news. He told Ashley that at present there was no real hope of uniting the Pennsylvania anti-Nebraska factions without sacrificing principles. But he did believe that David Wilmot, the Pennsylvania antislavery leader, would be in favor of holding an informal convention in Pittsburgh.[10]

By January 18, 1856, Ashley had received forty-one responses to his circular calling for a mass meeting in Pittsburgh on February 22. Only one reply was against the idea of such a meeting and only three opposed the date. Ashley was encouraged by this response, but while he was busy corresponding with antislavery men, a new organization, "The Republican Association of Washington," was set up. The new group, headed by Lewis Clephane (an aide to Dr. Gamaliel Bailey of the Washington *National Era*), was in favor of a later date for the preliminary meeting. In fact, Wilmot, Bailey, and other more conservative antislavery men preferred March 26 as the best time. In January, Ashley informed Chase that he had written twenty-five more letters urging insistence on February 22, believing that they would win this battle, since many in Washington under Mott's prodding were coming around to their point of view. He was correct in his assessment, for Bailey's group finally agreed to the February date.[11] Thus, Ashley was to a large degree responsible for the idea of the February convention, and he deserves credit for being one of the founders of the national Republican party.

While devoting most of his time to national politics, Ashley was still concerned with local matters. He became interested in patronage, as he attempted to build a strong Republican organization in Toledo, and his efforts stressed party harmony and loyalty. There can be little doubt that he was also trying to establish personal political support in Lucas County.[12]

On February 20, Ashley left Toledo to go to Pittsburgh. He meant to try, among other things, to persuade the preliminary convention to adopt the name Democratic-Republican, though a convention in his own district was against the idea. He had contacted other delegates about the matter and told Chase that "David Wilmot and several to whom I have written on the subject favor the name—and none oppose it but the most ultra Whigs—except to my surprise Doctor Bailey."[13] Ashley had also been in constant touch with Chase over the last month, and though no definite plan of action had been worked out, he knew what was expected of him.

The radical antislavery men dominated the Pittsburgh convention, with Ohio having the second largest delegation at the meeting. Chase was unable to attend, but his views were expressed by Ashley. Among the Chase supporters at the meeting were Alfred P. Stone (a future national committeeman who had worked hard to have the preliminary convention held on February 22) and the Ohio politician Francis D. Kimball. Other prominent radicals present were Joshua R. Giddings of Ohio, George W. Julian of Indiana, Owen Lovejoy of Illinois, and Zachariah Chandler of Michigan. The convention achieved its purpose and established the machinery necessary for a national nominating convention at Philadelphia on June 17, 1856. The basis for representation at the nominating convention was to be six at-large delegates from each state and three delegates from each congressional district. Ashley moved to amend this resolution by making it two at-large and one district delegate, but his proposal was tabled.[14] He was also unable to convince the gathering to adopt the name Democratic-Republican.

As soon as the Pittsburgh meeting was over, he sent Chase his analysis of what had happened. Pleased with the overall results of the convention, Ashley had been impressed by the quality and talent of those who attended. The gathering did not take as radical a stance as he desired, but on the whole Ashley was contented. Glad that he had insisted on holding the meeting on February 22, instead of in March, he informed Chase, "I am well satisfied and believe we shall triumph—let the KNs take what course they please." The sanguine Ashley also reported that if the nomination had been made at this convention, Chase would have received it.[15]

The Toledoan then tried to analyze the total political picture. He predicted that strong movements were going to be made in favor of the nomination of Nathaniel P. Banks of Massachusetts and of John C. Frémont of California. Of the two Ashley was more worried about Banks. He also believed there was some support for Wilmot, Seward, Hale, Preston King of New York, Cassius M. Clay of Kentucky, and Supreme Court Judge John McLean of Ohio. Since the Pittsburgh convention had been dominated by antislavery elements, Ashley tended to be overly optimistic, believing Chase could obtain a majority of the delegate votes from New York and Pennsylvania, all the votes from the West, and many from the South.[16]

He was so confident that Chase would receive the nomination that he began to talk about vice-presidential running mates. Among the possibilities mentioned at Pittsburgh were Francis P. Blair, Sr., of Maryland, Francis P. Blair, Jr., of Missouri, Frémont, and Banks. Believing that good politics indicated that the nomination should go to a man from a slave state, Ashley felt that Blair of Maryland was the best choice. (This is ironic considering the future hostility generated between Chase and the Blair family.) If the vice-presidential nomination was to come from the North, Ashley preferred Banks, since he would give strength and popularity to a ticket.[17]

Ashley's reasoning proved to be unrealistic. It soon became obvious that none of the leading antislavery radicals had a chance of securing the nomination. Chase simply could not overcome his background as a Free Soiler and his former close association with the Know-Nothings in Ohio. He also never managed to acquire sufficient support from the East. Ohio Republicans were split between Chase and Judge McLean, and at the state convention in May, no preference was established. The main criterion for obtaining the nomination became the ability to attract voters from all elements of the party, especially the conservatives. The man who had such a following seemed to be Frémont, and as the June convention drew near, many radical Republicans were ready to accept him, rather than a conservative.[18]

Ashley was chosen as a delegate from Ohio's Fifth Congressional District to the 1856 Republican national convention in Philadelphia. The Ohio delegation was still split, but a majority, including Ashley, favored Frémont as its second choice. Chase had instructed his emissaries to withdraw his name for consideration if the movement for Frémont became too strong; his orders were carried out. Frémont received the presidential nomination on the first ballot, with Ashley voting for the Pathfinder. William L. Dayton of New Jersey, a former Whig, was nominated for the vice-presidency. The chairman of the convention, Henry S. Lane of Indiana, acting on a motion made by Ashley, appointed a committee of nine, including Ashley, Thaddeus

Stevens of Pennsylvania, and Kingsley S. Bingham of Michigan to notify Frémont of his nomination.[19] The platform was all that Ashley and other radicals had hoped for. It condemned polygamy and slavery as the "twin relics of barbarism," asserted that neither Congress nor a territorial government could establish slavery in a territory, called for the admission of Kansas as a free state, came out in favor of a transcontinental railroad and internal improvements, and accepted Chase's idea that the federal government had the power to abolish slavery in areas under its jurisdiction. Ashley had also put forth this view. Chase and his followers were satisfied because these resolutions clearly called for "the denationalization of slavery."[20]

Upon returning to Toledo, Ashley was forced to devote a great deal of his time to his business, but in his spare moments he immersed himself in the campaign. In July, a large campaign meeting calling for "Freedom and Frémont" was held in Toledo. A Frémont Club was established, with Ashley as one of a three-man executive committee. At the district congressional nominating convention, Ashley served as presiding officer and helped renominate Mott.[21] As the campaign progressed Ashley made a few stump speeches for Mott's reelection and for the national ticket. Most of these speeches were typical election year efforts, but one given in September, in a grove near Montpelier, Williams County, was as daring and radical an oration as had ever been heard in that part of the country.

After answering a few questions from the audience, Ashley quickly informed his listeners where he stood on the question of slavery. He said, "I am opposed to the enslavement in any country on God's green earth, of any man or any race of men . . . and I do not admit that the Constitution of my country recognizes property in man."[22] Slavery to him was " 'the sum of all villainies' . . . the blackest of crimes . . . and . . . the most revolting infamy that ever afflicted mankind or cursed the earth." "This monster wrong," he roared, "this crime of centuries, has fastened its fangs into our national life, and . . . has demoralized and debauched a large part of the entire nation, north and south." There was, as far as he was concerned, no excuse or justification for the peculiar institution.[23]

As for who was responsible for this deplorable situation, Ashley, like Chase and other radical Republicans, placed the blame on a conspiracy of slaveholders and northern doughfaces. These men, he stated, had misinterpreted the Constitution, degraded religion, deliberately misconstrued the Bible, and gained control of the federal government. The conspirators, he said, who were committing,

> Crimes against humanity and our democratic government are at this very hour laying broad and deep the conditions which are certain to ultimate in a revolution of fire and blood that must end, either in the destruction of this Union and Government, or in the abolition of the institution of slavery which the slave barons are to-day madly attempting to fasten upon the nation for all time.[24]

Furthermore, Ashley believed that an accurate reading of the United States Constitution clearly proved that slavery could not legally exist in the nation for a single hour. He reiterated that the men who founded this country did not intend the Constitution to recognize property in men. If the document were properly interpreted "a slave could not breathe anywhere, on the land or on the sea beneath our starry flag."[25]

To Ashley the theory that the Bible sanctioned American slavery was blasphemy. The sight of churchmen defending this infamous falsehood was a revolting spectacle, as it had been since he was a boy. He vehemently denied "that the Bible anywhere authorizes or justifies . . . slavery," but that as he read it, slavery was "abolished and prohibited under the dispensation and teaching of Christ."[26]

In consonance with his constitutional theories, which had been greatly influenced by his close association with Chase, Ashley then turned to the Fugitive Slave Law. He was horrified and dismayed that the law was being readily obeyed. Those who practiced the profession of slave catching were "land-slave pirates." He presented a strong case for the position that no clause or section of the Constitution gave Congress the power to enact laws for the return of runaway slaves. The section of the Constitution dealing with fugitives, he maintained, was simply a compact stipulation between states, and no authority direct or indirect was delegated to Congress to enforce it by passing laws. Thus, anyone who claimed to find support for a fugitive slave act in the Constitution was guilty of a "forced interpretation and an outrage on the meaning of language and all known rules of law." Congress did not possess such power, and he was "confident that no such power was intended to be conferred."[27]

Though he was now a Republican, Ashley's stand on many economic and political matters was still basically Democratic. In his oration, he called corporations artificial, soulless institutions which had to be regulated and controlled if the individual's rights and liberties were to be protected. He desired "that all God's children shall have an even chance in the race of life."[28] Trusting in the wisdom of the common man, Ashley spoke out against magnifying the virtues of the rich and well-born. His hatred of privileged classes or élites was exemplified when he said, "we must . . . amend our national Constitution, so as to provide for the election of the President and United States Senators by a direct vote of the people."[29]

With deep feeling Ashley urged his audience to support Frémont. Millard Fillmore, the American party candidate, was nothing more than a "decoy duck" who was "simply being used by the slave barons to catch Northern doughface suckers and political eunuchs." As for the Democratic candidate James Buchanan, Ashley exclaimed, "all his life he has been a suave, putty-man, ready and willing to be molded and stamped with the brand of the slave barons." He was "the prince of all Northern Janus-faced politicians," and if he was elected the nation would be disgraced and dishonored.[30]

But the heart of Ashley's speech was the statement that slavery had to be eradicated:

> If this can be done in no other way, it will become our duty to amend our national Constitution and all our State constitutions, so as to secure to every living human soul within our gates, their right to life, liberty and property, and it must also be amended so as to secure to all States, representatives in Congress, and in State legislatures—in proportion to the votes cast in each, to the end that all people, white and colored, shall be fairly represented in State legislative assemblies and in the national Congress.[31]

In the year 1856, this was as radical a statement as an orator dared to make. Ashley had not only declared that he was an abolitionist, but more importantly he had come out for Negro suffrage and officeholding.[32]

He ended his stirring speech to great applause, citing, as he so often did, the abolitionist poet, John Greenleaf Whittier, and then saying, "It cannot be that this long, dark night of shame and crime will endure forever . . . . so I . . . close my speech to-day with the declaration, that come what may 'AMERICAN SLAVERY MUST BE DESTROYED.'"[33]

In this speech Ashley clearly showed where he stood on most of the major issues of the day, regardless of the consequences. He spoke with a passionate feeling for humanity and a deep moral earnestness. Taking bold, forthright positions, he proved that he was a man who possessed not only moral courage, but the fortitude to follow his beliefs. Ashley's moving oration proves the validity of David Potter's statement that Democrats who became Republicans had to be men "of stout conscience."[34] Above all Ashley's address showed how far in advance he was of Frémont and the majority of the Republican party.

At this point it seems appropriate to say a few words about Ashley's attitude toward black Americans. Although he was an outspoken and persistent antislavery man, like most radical Republicans he was affected by the prejudice of his time. Ashley always feared miscegenation; when he discussed the issue a tinge of repugnance crept into his writing. Because of his distaste for interracial marriage, and of his fear that white prejudice might make racial equality impossible, Ashley at times voiced skepticism about the idea of blacks assimilating into American society. In one speech he even talked about a final separation of the races through colonization of ex-slaves. Yet on other occasions he was relatively optimistic about the possibility of the two races living in harmony.

Ashley ardently believed in equality of opportunity for all, and he accepted in full the humanity of the black man. Nonetheless, he seems to have believed that the white race was superior. On the other hand, unlike many other antislavery men, he never pandered to racial prejudice to gain political points. Although Ashley was associated with a number of black abolitionists, and was honored by Negro groups during his lifetime, no evidence indicates that he ever established real friendship with any black American. Ashley simply was never able to reconcile his contradictory attitudes about social equality.

But if he had some social bias against Negroes, he did not let it hinder his actions. He consistently fought not only for emancipation, but for Negro land ownership, equal access to public education, Negro jury rights, and Negro suffrage. Ashley's courageous support of black suffrage in 1856 went against prevailing opinion, and was a risky issue for an ambitious young politician to espouse. It was a political liability to take constantly pro-Negro positions, yet Ashley did so throughout his political career; and his valiant fight for black suffrage in Ohio in 1867 was one of the main reasons he was not reelected to Congress in 1868. Whatever prejudice he may have held, Ashley had a true humanitarian interest in the Negro, and he fervently believed that all Americans, black or white, should have an equal chance at obtaining success in life. Given the intensity of racism in the United States in the 1850s, 1860s, and 1870s, Ashley's commitment to black freedom and rights was extraordinary.

The 1856 campaign in Ohio was hard fought and often quite bitter. Democrats and Know-Nothings charged the Republicans with radicalism, calling them fanatical abolitionists, believers in Negro equality, and disunionists. The Republicans played up the Kansas issue and the caning of Charles Sumner by Preston Brooks. They attacked the concept of popular sovereignty "as subterfuge for the advancement of slavery." The evangelical churches in Ohio, motivated by the moral issue of slavery, supported Frémont. In the October state and congressional elections, the Republicans in Ohio were successful, but by smaller pluralities than in 1854. Mott won in the Fifth Congressional District. In the November national elections, Frémont carried Ohio, but Fillmore votes in Pennsylvania, Indiana, and Illinois gave Buchanan the final victory.[35]

Although Frémont lost, Ashley does not appear to have been overly upset. The Republicans suffered a setback, but the future looked promising. Informing Chase that many of the state officials who had been elected with the governor were incompetent and no longer had the confidence of the people, Ashley advised the antislavery leader not to run for reelection. He argued that if Chase declined the nomination in 1857, McLean and the ex-Whigs would rally to the cause and offset the large Fillmore vote against them. Besides, if Chase decided to run and then lost, it would create great obstacles in the way of his obtaining the 1860 Republican presidential nomination. This would be tragic since Ashley believed that the Frémont movement would die out within six months, and that if Chase only maintained his present good standing there would be no great difficulty in nominating him.[36] Ashley wanted Chase to be President almost as much as the governor himself.

The Toledoan spent most of his time in 1857 running his store and only occasionally became involved in politics. Ohio was shocked that year by a $550,000 state treasury scandal which involved the Republican State Treasurer William H. Gibson and his Democratic predecessor, John G. Breslin. Chase forced Gibson to resign and managed to find funds to cover the loss. Because of this imbroglio, many of Chase's political friends echoed Ashley's sentiments and pleaded with the governor not to run again. But believing that the reputation of his administration and his party was at stake, Chase decided by June to seek reelection.[37]

Once the governor had made his decision, Ashley quickly lent his support, even though he did not approve of Chase's course. Disgusted with all the scandals and the frauds of Republicans acting for personal gain, Ashley feared they were ruining the party, and with it, the antislavery cause. He wished that Chase were doing anything, rather than running for reelection, since he believed it would be a losing effort. But if the Republicans were to have any chance of success, Ashley felt that the remaining Know-Nothings, who would never vote for Chase, must present a ticket; and he urged the state committee to try to arrange it. He feared that if there were no separate American party slate, at least two-thirds of the Know-Nothings would vote Democratic and ensure Chase's defeat.[38] On this matter Ashley's advice was sound.

Chase was renominated at the Ohio Republican convention on August 12. The Democrats put up Henry B. Payne of Cleveland. Philadelph Van Trump was the American party candidate. The campaign centered not on the treasury scandals, but on the Dred Scott decision, which legalized slavery in the territories. Republicans naturally condemned the decision; Democrats supported it. The Panic of 1857, which ushered in a period of financial demoralization, hurt the Republicans, since they were the party in power. Ashley with his usual vigor, stumped the Fifth Congressional District in Chase's behalf. The governor lost this area anyway, but he did manage to win reelection by 1,503 votes. Van Trump polled approximately 10,000 votes, which probably would have gone to Payne (most Fillmore Know-Nothings had joined the Democrats) if the nativists had not presented a candidate.[39]

Ashley was happy over the victory, but now he needed to reach some decisions concerning his own future. Thirty-three years old, he was the father of two children (a second son, Henry, was born in 1856) and the proprietor of an only moderately successful drug or general store. The next year was congressional election time, and Mott had previously indicated that he would not seek a third term.[40] Ashley therefore had to decide whether to run for political office or stay in business.

Before coming to any definite conclusions, Ashley, in the early part of 1858, went East on a political scouting trip for Chase. His travels took him to New York City and Albany, where he spoke to Horace Greeley, the eccentric editor of the New York *Tribune*, Governor Preston King, and other leading Republicans. Ashley was surprised to learn that Greeley opposed Seward for nomination in 1860. The editor was not yet committed to Chase, and Ashley felt that old Whigs, such as United States Senator Benjamin F. Wade and Joshua Giddings, should be encouraged to influence him. This was sound reasoning, but since Wade himself wanted the 1860 nomination, the advice was not well received. As for Governor King and the Albany Republicans, Ashley really had no idea where they stood, except that they were opposed to Seward. The Toledo politician was never able to talk to John Bigelow of the New York *Evening Post* or to newspaperman Hiram Barney. In fact, he was highly dissatisfied with the work Barney was doing in New York, and he suggested to Chase that another man ought to be sought for this area.[41]

The trip convinced Ashley that since all the true antislavery men in the nation knew where Chase stood on slavery, it would be wise for him to proceed more cautiously. Chase had to avoid scaring off the easily frightened conservative elements in the party, who were essential to any serious movement in 1860, "there being," Ashley said, "no sacrifice of principle in cautious and judicious silence."[42] Since Chase failed to obtain the nomination in 1860 at least partly because of his radical views, Ashley's judgment was sound.

During the first half of 1858, the Buchanan administration was involved in a political fight with Senator Douglas of Illinois over the admission of Kansas to the Union, under the proslavery Lecompton Constitution. Since Douglas refused to support the Democratic party line on this matter, many Republicans felt that this was an opportunity to make common cause with the Little Giant. During his trip to New York, Ashley discovered that Henry Raymond of the *New York Times* was thinking of forming an alliance with Douglas and forcing him on the Republicans in 1860. Both Ashley and Chase were appalled by this movement. At the same time, many radical Republicans did not know how to deal with the situation in Kansas. Ashley wanted the Free State settlers to put their own state government into operation, but this was too extreme a solution. In Congress, a compromise idea, the Crittenden-Montgomery amendment, calling for a referendum on the entire Lecompton Constitution was presented. If the constitution were approved, the proposal provided for the admission of Kansas as a slave state. The radicals in the House realized that the administration would not accept a compromise, and voted for the measure. Ashley was horrified at their action, since he considered it an intolerable sacrifice of principles. But events showed his horror to be unwarranted, as the administration refused to accept the amendment in the Senate, and the entire Lecompton proposal was then defeated in the House.[43]

By April, 1858, Ashley had made up his mind about his future. He would sell his business and return to the legal profession. Before the month ended he had sold his store, but there is no evidence to suggest that he established a law firm at this time. Ashley had also decided to make a swing around his district to test the political winds. If everything seemed encouraging, he intended to become a candidate for the Republican congressional nomination. In April, Ashley appeared to have no strong opposition, except for Judge Asher Cook of Wood County. But some arrangements were being planned which would enable the judge to withdraw and support Ashley.[44]

The Fifth Congressional District nominating convention was scheduled to be held at Defiance, on July 22. With the help of the Republican state committee, Chase, and his Toledo friend E.P. Bassett, Ashley won the nomination on the first ballot. He overcame the opposition of a powerful, conservative clique of ex-Whigs, who would continue to oppose him throughout his political career.[45]

Response to Ashley's nomination was favorable. The Sandusky *Register* praised him for being one of the first to break away from the Democrats; the Toledo *Blade* called him energetic and popular and promised to do all it could to get him elected. The Cleveland *Plain Dealer*, on the other hand, felt that any good Democrat could beat him easily. Ashley's friend, A.S. Latty of Paulding, pledged his personal support, but since the district had voted Democratic in 1857, he believed it was going to be an uphill battle.[46]

In order to overcome the Democratic majority in the district, Ashley and his supporters planned a great effort to get all Republican voters to the polls. Ashley intended to make fifty stops throughout the region, speaking twice a day. His Democratic opponent, William Munger, was a newspaperman connected with the Findlay *Courier*, and was a supporter of the Lecompton Constitution. In February, 1856, Ashley had been appointed to Governor Chase's militia staff, and the Toledo *Blade*, in an effort to lend prestige to his name, often referred to him as general, though actually he was only a colonel.[47] The tradition thus started was to last throughout Ashley's career.

As the campaign progressed, Ashley began to make hard-hitting, radical speeches which addressed themselves directly to the issues. Clearly re-emphasizing his desire for abolition and his distrust of machine politics, Ashley was determined that should he win the election, his constituents could not later claim that they did not know where he stood on the major controversies. In all he made ninety-nine speeches, most of them in Methodist churches.[48]

Campaigning in northern Ohio in the late 1850s was a rough-and-tumble affair at times. Ashley was often interrupted and heckled during his speeches. On one occasion, while talking from the pulpit of a church, he was struck on the head by a live goose thrown through an open window. Later on in the campaign, Ashley made a speech in the town of Leipsic in Putnam County. During his presentation he was constantly interrupted by a member of a rowdy gang who kept shouting, "that's a damn lie." Ashley attempted to quiet the heckler with gentle humor, but to no avail, as the young man, named Armstrong, continued to interrupt. Ashley asked him to be quiet or leave the church. Armstrong refused and dared Ashley to put him out. Realizing that the audience was waiting to see how he would handle himself in this situation, Ashley jumped off the stage, seized Armstrong by the collar, tapped him on the head with his cane, and threw him out the door. He then returned to continue his talk to loud cheers.[49]

The Democrats immediately started to flood the district with posters which accused Ashley of almost beating a helpless old man to death. As it turned out Armstrong was not seriously hurt, and he returned to his job the next day. The incident only increased the size of Ashley's audiences at his other stops, as many people wished to see the battling politician.[50] The fight probably helped him, since more than a few men voted for him because they respected this type of courage.

Towards the end of September, the *Blade* predicted that Ashley would win the October 12 election by fifteen hundred votes. He won but by a much smaller margin. His total vote was 10,532; Munger polled 9,986. As for Lucas County, Ashley won by 189 votes out of 3,303 cast.[51]

As soon as the election was over, he accompanied Chase to Illinois to help Abraham Lincoln in his senatorial campaign against Stephen Douglas. Ashley first met Lincoln at Alton, the site of the last debate. Immediately afterwards, Ashley rushed back to Toledo on the Wabash Railroad, to be present at a victory celebration being held in his honor on the night of October 16. The next day he returned to Illinois, where he stayed until the November election. Ashley, like Lincoln and Chase, was dismayed at the plan of some Republicans to aid Douglas in an effort to attract the Little Giant and his followers into the new party. Many radical Republicans opposed this idea, feeling it would undercut the party's antislavery principles. Ashley believed that this scheme, which he called a conspiracy, had defeated Lincoln and that if the Republicans expected any success in the future, they had to rid themselves of temporizers.[52]

It was under the influence of such reasoning that Ashley tried to publish an article exposing the Douglas maneuvers in the Toledo *Blade*, but Williams no longer edited the paper. The more conservative new owner, Clark Waggoner, refused to accept the piece. Disappointed, Ashley stated that he wished a man of "sense and nerve" were running the paper.[53] Though he was disturbed by the Douglas movement, he must have been personally satisfied. Times were anything but dull, and having just turned thirty-four, he was on his way to Congress. He had finally acquired the prestige he so long had wanted.

CHAPTER IV

FRESHMAN CONGRESSMAN

Although Ashley had been elected to the United States House of Representatives in 1858, the first session of the Thirty-sixth Congress was not scheduled to meet until December, 1859. In the meantime he attempted to solidify his political support in the Toledo area, actively participated in Ohio politics, and continued his labors for Chase's bid for the 1860 Republican presidential nomination.

Early in 1859 Ashley made a series of speeches in his congressional district, thanking his constituents for their support in the past election. If some expected him to seek broader support by tempering his opinions, they were wrong. Lashing out at a federal government controlled by a privileged class of slave barons, bent on disunion if unable to get its way, Ashley clearly indicated that he would not deviate from his principles. In his usual forthright manner, he stated, "since the organization of the Republican party, I have contemplated with rapture, not only the triumph, but the inauguration of the day . . . when . . . the people of every race and religion [will] be fully and freely enfranchised."[1] Once again the young radical had publicly advocated black suffrage.

In trying to consolidate his political power Ashley realized that he would have to build up his strength among foreign-born voters if he were to continue to be successful. He expressed his gratitude to "the freedom loving Germans," asked them for their trust, and defended the concept of free labor.[2]

During 1859 many radical Republicans feared that an attempt would be made to water down the principles of the Republican party in an effort to gain broader-based appeal for the upcoming presidential contest. Believing that such a movement was a betrayal, Ashley filled his speeches with ringing denunciations of temporizers. "To preserve inviolate the constitution and the Union, to roll back the dark tide of sectionalism and fanaticism ... under the lead of a privileged class, and bearing the sacred name of Democrat, is the purpose and mission of the Republican party," he said. As far as he was concerned, there could be no compromise with conservative Republicans on the primacy of antislavery as the affirmative principle of the Republican party.[3]

Ashley despised Senator Douglas's conception of popular sovereignty which surrendered "the natural rights of man to the unlicenced will of a majority" to enslave a minority. Ashley did believe in popular sovereignty as expressed in the will of the majority, but only on issues that were proper for human legislation, which slavery clearly was not. To say as Douglas did, that one did not care whether slavery was voted up or down was blatant nonsense, to Ashley's way of thinking. The rights of individuals were sacred and had to be protected, with special favors being granted to none.[4]

For Ohio politics, the most important issue in 1859 was whether the state or federal government had jurisdiction over the enforcement of the 1850 Fugitive Slave Act. The struggle between conservatives and radicals for control of the Ohio Republican party became focused on this issue, with the advantage eventually going to the staunch antislavery elements. Many radicals, including Ashley, had condemned the law and refused to obey it since its passage in 1850. Throughout the 1850s the radicals had adopted a states rights position on this matter, denying that the federal government had any jurisdiction over escaped slaves in the free states. Ashley, who would later become a stalwart defender of national supremacy, spoke in 1859 of the necessity of protecting the rights of the states.[5] The dispute over the Fugitive Slave Law in Ohio revolved around attempted rescue of fugitives who had been seized by federal marshals.

The issue reached fever pitch in 1859, when a group of citizens from Oberlin was arrested for attempting to rescue a fugitive. Two of the rescue leaders were convicted by the United States District Court in Cleveland of violating the law. The Ohio Supreme Court then consented to review the case. During the hearings a series of public meetings protesting the verdict of the federal court was held in the Western Reserve.[6] Ashley, Giddings, Chase, and Wade, among others, took part in the rallies. Giddings spoke of using force to resist tyranny, but Chase urged caution and resorting to legal appeal. Ashley and Wade drew up resolutions which demanded repeal of the Fugitive Slave Law, asked for the elimination of life tenure for federal judges, called for the preservation of the rights of states, and hinted at nullification.[7]

The Ohio Supreme Court handed down its opinion on May 31, 1858, and the radicals were bitterly disappointed. In a three-to-two decision, the court, headed by Chief Justice Joseph R. Swan, upheld the constitutionality of the law. Having failed in the courts, the anti-Fugitive Slave Law forces now directed their attention to the Republican state convention which was to begin on June 2.[8]

The enraged radicals, determined to achieve some form of vindication, refused to endorse Swan's renomination. By working with the conservative delegates from Hamilton County they managed to obtain the nomination for William Y. Gholson of Cincinnati. The radical northern section of Ohio had combined with the conservative southern part, to defeat the candidate of the central and western portions of the state. Chase had decided to seek election to the United States Senate, and thus William Dennison, a successful lawyer and businessman acceptable to the radicals, was nominated for governor. The real fight, however, was over the platform.[9]

The platform was drafted by some of the leading men of the party: John A. Bingham, Lewis D. Campbell, Thomas Corwin, Benjamin Stanton, Ashley, and Giddings. The radicals wanted the Fugitive Slave Act to be declared unconstitutional, but the conservatives, led by Corwin and Campbell, refused to go along with this proposal. The committee worked out a compromise plank demanding that the law be repealed and the federal judiciary be reorganized. Other resolutions called for a homestead law and opposed the reopening of the African slave trade. Though the staunch antislavery men had been forced to back down somewhat, they were pleased; having managed to make the Fugitive Slave Law and states rights the major issues of the upcoming campaign, they had denied renomination to Swan and emerged from the convention as the dominant faction in the party.[10]

The Republicans waged a strong campaign, attacking the Fugitive Slave Law and the proslavery outlook of the Democrats. In conservative southern Ohio, Corwin tempered the rhetoric; in the Western Reserve, Giddings hammered hard at the Fugitive Slave Law. Ashley made twenty speeches during the campaign, appearing with Giddings in Toledo on September 24. The Republicans carried the state, winning the governorship, all state offices, and both houses of the legislature.[11]

Only a small part of Ashley's energies in 1859 were devoted to Ohio politics; the main share went to Chase's effort to get the Republican presidential nomination in 1860. In March, Ashley warned Chase that Seward was making a strong attempt to win the nomination, and he stressed the need for developing a powerful Chase organization in order to stop the New Yorker. Ashley properly foresaw that if Chase did not move soon, all would be lost. He then told the governor that the pro-Chase newspapers must begin to play up the extravagances and frauds of the Buchanan administration, and to insist that a man with a record of economy in government should receive the nomination.[12]

Ashley also worried about the Republican inability to attract more former antislavery Democrats. He blamed this on the false notion that the Republicans were nothing more than the old Whigs in disguise. In an effort to correct that distortion, Ashley suggested that Horace Greeley publish an article in the New York *Tribune*, which would show that the Democratic party had formed a union with the proslavery wing of the Whig party and with proslavery Know-Nothings. At the same time, the article ought to mention the names of the leading radical and Jacksonian Democrats who, Ashley claimed, were the first to organize the Republican party in the West.[13] The Republicans were still a minority party and they needed all the help they could get from solid antislavery men.

During July and August, Ashley traveled to Minnesota, Wisconsin, Illinois, Pennsylvania, New Jersey, and New York. While in Minnesota, he had an accident at the Falls of Minnehaha, and suffered such a severely sprained ankle that he had to hobble around on crutches. Hampered though he was, Ashley continued his political activities, discovering that Seward had considerable strength in Wisconsin, where there were many former New Yorkers, and among the German-born throughout the Middle West. After a friendly conversation with the German editor of the Illinois *State Times*, Ashley determined that the paper would support Chase and that Carl Schurz (the radical antislavery German immigrant) might then rally to the governor's cause. But the newly elected congressman was mistaken, for Schurz had announced in January that he was for Seward. At this time Joseph Medill was working for Chase, and Ashley felt that he had done a good job in St. Paul.[14]

Believing that the time to act had come, Ashley urged Chase to insist that their friends not postpone their activities until the fall or winter. In reaction to protests over some of Ashley's radical speeches, the Toledoan informed Chase that these men were "a nervous timid race of reptiles and must I suppose, be gingerly dealt with [but] . . . these men . . . are neither your friends or mine—I know *them.*"[15] Ashley believed that the time for temporizing on slavery was over, and that the age called for boldness, not caution.

Early in August, Ashley left Toledo on a political sounding trip in the East, stopping first in Philadelphia. One of the major obstacles which confronted prospective Chase supporters was the tariff issue. Pennsylvania wanted protection for the iron industry, and Chase had a reputation as a free trader. Chase quickly realized that if ex-Whigs were to be attracted to him he would have to modify his position in the direction of a revenue tariff with "incidental protection." As practical men, Chase and his fellow ex-Democrats understood that they would have to compromise on economic issues if they hoped to keep antislavery the centerpiece of the Republican party. Ashley explained Chase's views on the tariff to the Philadelphians and the New Jerseyites; and although many of the ultraprotectionists seemed satisfied, they nevertheless wanted him to publish a letter clarifying his position. Ashley was also told that Seward could never obtain the Pennsylvania vote in the convention, but Chase might get a substantial number of delegates. This seemed too good to be true.[16]

Upon arriving in New York, Ashley discovered that most of the radicals opposed the idea of publishing a letter on the tariff. He was becoming disgusted with the whole issue. Even though still incapacitated, Ashley, with the help of James A. Briggs, managed to see most of the leading men in New York City. Ashley believed that William Cullen Bryant, the owners of the *Independent*, and all the local radical Republicans were in Chase's camp. He also spoke to Charles A. Dana, the managing editor of the New York *Tribune*. Dana opposed Seward, and was friendly to Chase, but he was more concerned with party success than that of any particular man. Dana believed Ashley was "a good fellow and no fool," but that he overestimated Chase's strength in the North.[17] Unfortunately for Chase, Dana was correct.

While talking to Dana, Ashley detected a rumored scheme involving Edward Bates of Missouri, which was to have an important effect on the campaign for the presidential nomination. Bates was to be prominently brought forth by chairing an Emancipation Republican State convention, where he would make a speech to satisfy the radical antislavery men. Ashley wondered whether this plan might not be stopped, "by letting our friends in Illinois point Lincoln on the track and have our friends in Kentucky—Delaware and Maryland—call similar conventions to this one in Missouri, *if it is to come off* and put men forward that [*sic*] will go much further than *Bates*, as to throw him into the shade?" Ashley was thus suggesting that Lincoln be brought forth as Chase's stalking horse. The Bates scheme never came off, but Chase's friends in Illinois, Medill and Charles Ray, studied the situation and later ended their private efforts for Chase and came out for Lincoln.[18] Ashley certainly did not plan it this way, but his suggestions helped Lincoln.

Ashley had been concerned for some time with the way delegates were to be chosen for the Republican national convention. Fearing that any fusion with Know-Nothings and conservatives would lead to defeat, he wrote to the editor of the Washington *National Era*, setting forth his views in favor of a proportional system of choosing delegates, which he had first presented in Pittsburgh in February, 1856. Ashley hoped to keep the party as radical as possible, in order to prevent compromise on vital principles such as the repeal of fugitive slave laws. He also wanted the convention to meet west of the Allegheny Mountains. Convinced that his ideas were correct, Ashley tried to round up support for his plan.[19]

As he prepared to leave for the opening session of the Thirty-sixth Congress, Ashley, at the age of thirty-five, had constructed a fairly solid political and economic philosophy. Coming from a Democratic background, he had evolved into a radical Republican. The motivating force of his political philosophy was a belief that slavery was a moral wrong, and like other radical Republicans, he categorically refused to compromise with the South on any issue regarding the peculiar institution. His ultimate goal was emancipation. He saw political parties as mere expediencies, means to reach his goals, and not ends in and of themselves. If the Republican party deviated from a staunch antislavery position, he was prepared to leave it. When it came to the issue of slavery, he believed principles were more important than parties.

In terms of his general political ideology, Ashley maintained a commitment to individualism, believing that each person had a right to make his own choices in life and a right to equal opportunity to gain his objectives. As a true advocate of democracy, he brought a Jeffersonian trust in the wisdom of the common man to his political thinking. This allowed him to espouse direct election of all public officials and the referendum and recall, forty years before those ideas became commonplace in the American political landscape. His belief that all the people should have a voice in government had already enabled him to endorse the radical concept of Negro suffrage and would soon lead him to support women's suffrage.

With respect to the national government, the new congressman was opposed to centralized executive power, excessive use of patronage, and standing armies in peace time. He firmly believed that for the sake of representative democracy, Congress should be the dominant branch of government; he feared that power concentrated in the hands of one man would lead inevitably to despotism and the end of democracy. Like his political idol, Thomas Jefferson, he also distrusted an entrenched federal judiciary removed from the control of the people. The influence of Jeffersonian and Jacksonian beliefs was paramount in Ashley's political thinking and combined with his own forward-looking concepts to make him a genuine mid-nineteenth century political radical.

Favoring a dynamic, expanding economy, within a competitive framework, Ashley's economic thinking was generally consistent with his Democratic beliefs. He maintained that the opportunity for economic mobility existed in the United States and that it was there for those who had the courage to grab it. As a practical liberal capitalist, he also recognized that an expanding American economy, which was necessary for a healthy democracy, required him to compromise on some of his economic positions. Although Ashley continued to advocate hard money, he saw the need for a mixed currency, but one which would be tightly regulated. He opposed a protective tariff, but he did see some merit in a revenue tariff with incidental protection built in for infant industries. Ashley was still against excessive government spending; he believed that the fairest method for raising money was by direct taxation and not by loans which would lead to a large public debt. Like most former Democrats from the Middle West, he had favored federal aid for a transcontinental railroad and internal improvements, and he did not think of these proposals as Whig property. Ashley was not doctrinaire. He would not compromise his principles on popular rights or slavery, but issues like the tariff and specie currency were negotiable.[20]

On November 28, 1859, Ashley left Toledo for Washington, but stopped off in Virginia in order to witness the execution of John Brown, who had been condemned to death for his October raid on Harpers Ferry. Since he was still forced to walk with the aid of a crutch, Ashley was quickly pointed out as the "Black Republican" Congressman from Ohio. Other Northerners had attempted to go to Charleston from Harpers Ferry by train, but had failed to get through the tight security established by General William B. Taliafero, commander of the Virginia militia. To avoid this, Ashley decided to travel by horse and buggy, and managed to sneak into the city without being noticed. After witnessing the execution, which he described as a "horrid sight," he traveled back to Harpers Ferry and spoke to Mrs. Brown, offering as much solace as possible. Ashley asked himself, "Why has there been so much excitement and so much fear expressed by the Southern people at this Harpers Ferry affair?" He supplied his own answer:

> It is inseparable from the system of slavery. A servile insurrection is always to be feared, because it is the most terrible of all evils that can befall a people who claim to own their laborers. Men may talk as they will, but I tell you there is a smoldering volcano burning beneath the crust, ready to burst forth at any moment; and an enemy to the peace of almost every hearth-stone, is lurking in the heart of the apparently submissively lashed slave, and only those who have passed through an outbreak like this or the Southampton insurrection, can comprehend the danger and know for a certainty that it exists.[21]

Like many other radical Republicans, Ashley disapproved of Brown's violent actions, but he admired his heroism and courage. With the unhappy incident concluded, Ashley then proceeded to Washington.

On December 5, the House of Representatives was called to order, and immediately became embroiled in a speakership contest that would leave it

unorganized for eight weeks. On the first ballot Ashley voted for his fellow
Ohio Republican, John Sherman, who fell short of the required votes.
Sherman had endorsed Hinton Helper's *The Impending Crisis*, which at-
tempted to prove that Southern poor whites had suffered because of slavery.
This was anathema to many Southern congressmen, and since neither major
party had a clear majority, the House could not choose a speaker.[22]

The radicals were determined to elect a Republican and stood firmly
behind their candidate. Ashley informed Chase, "we shall stand by Sherman
to the last." But as the weeks rolled by, it became obvious that the Ohioan
could not be elected. On January 30, 1860, Sherman withdrew, and the
Republicans, including Ashley, voted for William Pennington, a conservative Republican from New Jersey. On February 1, with the help of two
Know-Nothings, Henry Winter Davis of Maryland and George Briggs of
New York, Pennington received the 117 votes needed for victory.[23]

The House was soon organized, and Ashley was appointed to the Committee on Territories.[24] Although Ashley, as a freshman congressman, did
not play an important role on the floor of the House, his voice was heard
in the capital, and in his party. Ashley had not come to Washington as a
stranger, but as a politician acquainted with many of the nation's leading
Republicans. His travels on behalf of Chase, and his activities as a founder
of the Republican party, had made him familiar to most antislavery people.
Aggressive and self-reliant, but good-natured, Ashley was blessed with a
radiant smile, which a Washington observer described as "sunshine playing
above a rock." His good looks and jolly humor made him a favorite of
Washington hostesses. Mrs. S.C. Ames captured the essence of the young
congressman, when she described him as a man "who rejoices in the vigorous organism, the full physical life which sends the blood from heart to
brain in bountiful tides, strong, glad, and free."[25] Ashley was well liked by
his colleagues, and he had the confidence and admiration of his public
associates. His easy friendliness and his known political skill quickly made
him a visible presence in the capital, a man many were eager to know. One
of his most lasting new friendships was with Charles Sumner, the radical
senator from Massachusetts.

A giant in the antislavery movement, Sumner's imposing presence
matched his brilliant mind. Ashley greatly admired the senator's extraordinary erudition, his skill as an orator, and the honesty of his convictions.
Sumner in turn respected Ashley's tenacity, his unswerving hatred of human
bondage, and his political skill. Although Ashley's easy-going personality
was not in harmony with Sumner's basically humorless manner, the two
men found each other congenial; general agreement about law and politics
outweighed any differences in temperament. Ashley revered Sumner, and

honored him by naming his third son Charles Sumner Ashley. Sumner was always ready to defend his impetuous younger colleague, and was soon calling him one of the foremost men in the House of Representatives.[26]

During the first congressional session Ashley supported a homestead bill and the Morrill Tariff. But his main concern during this period, as it had been for most of the last four years, was Chase's drive for the presidential nomination. On December 21, Ashley attended a Republican National Committee meeting in New York City, representing Cassius Clay of Kentucky by proxy. Chase did not publicly express any opinions on the place, time, or mode of organization for the national convention, but he did discuss the matter privately, and he informed Thomas Spooner, Ohio's representative on the committee, of his ideas. Supporting most of Ashley's views, Chase wanted the convention to meet west of the Allegheny Mountains and to be held after the Democratic convention. He also favored a proportional system of representation in choosing delegates and wanted all those who opposed the extension of slavery to be invited to the convention. Chase hoped that Spooner and Ashley would act together for the cause. Worried as Ashley was about the effects of a fusion convention, including people not wholly committed to Republican principles, he could not accept Chase's ideas about invitations to the gathering. Ashley's plan for organizing the convention was rejected by the National Committee, but it was considered seriously, for it failed by only one vote. Though Chicago was chosen as the convention city, Ashley and Chase would have preferred Pittsburgh, Wheeling, Cincinnati, or Columbus, since these areas were supposedly friendly territory.[27]

As an opening to the campaign, Chase and his lieutenants had decided that the governor would stand a better chance for the nomination if he were a United States senator. Plans had been laid in the summer of 1859, and with the election of a Republican legislature in the fall success appeared likely. But rumors began circulating that some conservative Republicans might join with the Democrats in an effort to postpone the election to a later session in order to stop Chase. Ashley advised Chase to have their friends fix the time for the senatorial contest for around the first of February. Since all the "knaves and fools" in the Republican party were not dead, Ashley urged his associates to stand firm, yet practice moderation. Following these suggestions the legislature decided to choose a senator during the first session and Chase was easily elected.[28]

With this success in hand Chase now had to try to acquire the united support of the Ohio Republican party behind his presidential bid. Ashley proposed issuing a call for a meeting of Young Republicans on February 22, where Chase would address the gathering, presenting his position on all the issues, "especially the Tariff." Corwin, Stanton, Robert Schenck, Columbus Delano, and other prominent Republicans should be invited to the meeting, and an effort could then be made to obtain their endorsement.[29] Chase chose not to follow this advice, and thus lost a chance to establish a solid presidential campaign organization in Ohio.

Realizing the importance of the German-American vote, Ashley soon began urging Chase supporters in Cincinnati to begin corresponding in German with members of this ethnic group throughout the country, especially in Texas, Wheeling, Baltimore, and Delaware. The correspondence was to encourage the Germans to support Chase and to attend the convention. Ashley firmly believed that the Republican party had some strength in the southwestern and border states. Hence, he was determined to try to persuade people in these areas to participate in the convention, in an effort to create a national party. Because of the importance of New Jersey and Pennsylvania to any strong Chase movement, Ashley suggested that a correspondence must be initiated with prominent Republicans in both states, explaining Chase's views on the tariff. Having received a circular from Chicago touting Simon Cameron, Ashley surmised that Chase's Chicago friends, had switched to the Pennsylvanian.[30] The men in Chicago were indeed about to switch, but to Lincoln, not Cameron.

On March 1, the Ohio state Republican convention met in Columbus. Chase was endorsed by the party as its first choice for the presidential nomination, but he still lacked united support. Each congressional district was to choose two delegates to the national convention, and those who disliked the Cincinnati antislavery leader felt no obligation to adhere to the pledge of the state meeting. Moreover, Supreme Court Justice John McLean still had support in the state, as did Senator Benjamin Wade.[31]

In early April, although feeling somewhat ill and still suffering from a bad leg, Ashley's devotion to Chase drove him out to test the political winds in Baltimore and Philadelphia. Fearing that the work the Seward men were doing in Maryland would swing the state to the New Yorker, Ashley pleaded with Chase to come to Baltimore, but the antislavery leader disagreed and did not make the trip. Although in August, 1859, Ashley had been optimistic about Pennsylvania, he now thought that the state would not back Chase. The American-Whig-conservative element within the so-called People's Organization, was too strong for the regular Republicans. Chase simply could not overcome his background as a low-tariff man, and all Ashley's efforts in the Quaker State accomplished nothing. Ashley was quite depressed and frustrated by Chase's refusal to move forcefully, but the arrival of his wife and children in Washington helped him over his illness and lifted his spirits.[32]

The Republican National Convention was scheduled to start on May 16, and in the preceding days Chicago was a cauldron of political activity. The supporters of the major candidates were everywhere, talking, cajoling, pleading for delegate commitments. The Ohio delegation had its headquarters at the Tremont House. The Chase adherents, led by Ashley, Richard Mott, and Alfred Stone, desperately tried to hold Ohio for Chase. But as was the case in 1856, the delegation was hopelessly divided. The Chase men would not support Wade; the Wade backers led by David Cartter would not help Chase; and McLean was being dismissed because of his advanced age. Unable to reach any decision, the delegation split its vote among Chase, McLean, and Lincoln. On the third ballot Cartter announced the switch of four Ohio votes to Lincoln, and the Illinois lawyer was nominated.[33]

Ashley had labored tirelessly for Chase, but the antislavery leader never had a real chance for the nomination. His self-righteous, rather pompous manner alienated potential supporters; his radical antislavery views frightened many conservative and moderate members of the party. His long-standing low-tariff position gave him little following in New Jersey and Pennsylvania. His cultivation of German-Americans, however half-hearted, made him unacceptable to ex-Know-Nothings. But the major reasons for Chase's defeat were the absence of a strong, nation-wide campaign organization and the lack of one definite campaign manager at Chicago empowered to speak for him. Because of his organizational failures, Chase lost potential strength in Vermont, New Hampshire, Connecticut, New York, Rhode Island, Iowa, Minnesota, Maryland, and Ohio. Ashley had warned Chase in March, 1859, that if he did not organize, all their efforts would be in vain, but the antislavery leader did not follow this sound counsel.[34]

The Republicans drew up a platform which dealt with a number of economic issues and included planks calling for internal improvements, a homestead law, aid to railroads, and a tariff. But as Eric Foner has cogently argued, this was in no sense a Whig platform. Ex-Democrats as well as ex-Whigs favored internal improvements and railroad subsidy, and the word *protection* never appeared in the paragraph on the tariff. After Joshua Giddings attempted a dramatic exit from the hall in protest over the body's refusal to adopt the principles of the Declaration of Independence, the concepts of the document were included in the platform. The declaration that under the due process clause of the Fifth Amendment, slavery could not constitutionally exist in any territory, and that the prohibition could be enforced by law, if necessary, made the platform satisfactory to many radicals. The convention nominated Hannibal Hamlin of Maine as Lincoln's running mate.[35]

After the convention, Ashley diligently prepared for his maiden speech in Congress, which he presented on May 29. The address contained many of the themes which typified radical Republican thought and ideology in the prewar period.

Like many ultras and ex-Democrats, Ashley believed that, during the last twenty years, there had been a conspiracy to establish Southern dominance over the national government. This so-called slave power plot was led by an aristocratic slaveholding class, determined to establish slavery as a national institution. These men had no respect for law. They would obey no judicial decisions which did not sustain their demands of protection for slavery. But worst of all, they were disunionists. "They care nothing for the Union," Ashley said, "except so far as it subserves their purposes of building up, and extending their peculiar institution, and perpetuating their own political power."[36]

The one department of government in which the slave power conspiracy was most strongly entrenched was the judiciary. According to Ashley the Supreme Court had adopted a completely pro-Southern outlook, and he had therefore lost all respect for it. Believing that the judiciary was now a threat to the vital liberties of the nation, he demanded that it be reformed. The Southern judicial circuits, he remarked, had jurisdiction and power far beyond the number of legal proceedings they handled. All the circuits therefore, had to be completely reorganized, so that each had an equal amount of business, without any one area dominating. Indicating a Jeffersonian distrust of judges, Ashley wanted to eliminate life tenure for magistrates. He believed that judges should be immediately accountable to the people, and therefore suggested that they serve limited terms of office. The judicial branch of government should, in other words, be given as little power as possible.[37]

Ashley was also deeply disturbed over the trend set by the Dred Scott decision, which he felt was a part of the general Southern conspiracy. The next step, he said, was:

> To declare that slavery cannot lawfully be excluded from any of the States of the Union; that so long as one State in the Union recognizes and sanctions slaveholding, whether by her Constitution, her laws, or custom, slaveholding shall be legal in all the Territories, and in every State, and neither Congress nor State nor Territorial Legislatures shall have the power to prohibit it.[38]

He was worried about the Lemmon case, which was pending before the Supreme Court. He feared that the court might rule that it was legal to ship slaves through free states, and thus make slavery a national institution.

The radical wing of the Republican party maintained throughout the 1850s that the South contained a potential mass of antislavery feeling.

During his speech Ashley claimed that this latent sentiment could be found among the poor whites, who were terrorized by an aristocratic class of slaveholders. The poor whites, he stated, were dissatisfied with their condition, and the dominant group was petrified lest they unite and then rebel against this vicious class rule.[39]

As for slavery itself, Ashley retained his long-held belief that it was against the teachings of God and condemned it as an immoral and barbarous despotism which not only hurt the victim, but debased the slaveholder and damaged the entire South.[40]

In his oration Ashley called for immediate, uncompensated emancipation, but he also indicated his apprehension about miscegenation. Although strongly believing that blacks should have full political rights, Ashley was not free of racial prejudice. During his speech, in fact, he supported the Blair plan for colonizing blacks on land purchased in Central or South America. The purpose of the Republican party, he asserted, was to end the slave system and "provide a way for the final separation of the two races."[41]

Like Henry Clay, Lincoln, Wade, and Chase, Ashley never fully believed that blacks could successfully merge into the American mainstream.[42] At this stage of his life, Ashley's fear of amalgamation made him doubt the wisdom of an integrated society, yet after this speech he never again publicly discussed colonization. Later he would move closer to accepting most of the tenets of an integrated society, especially in relation to education, but his dread of miscegenation stopped him from ever fully embracing integration.

Ashley's speech went on to tell his listeners that he was deeply troubled by the increasing erosion of basic political liberties in the nation and by secrecy in government.[43] Forthrightly stating his belief in the right of revolution, he said:

> Government is but a means to an end; and whenever it ceases to answer the purposes for which it was created, the people can alter or abolish it.
>
> Sir, neither the executive, nor the judicial, nor law-making power is supreme. The Constitution is above them; and the people, who made the Constitution, and vested temporarily the authority of enacting, executing, and adjudicating the laws, are above and superior to all. . . . If there is an absolute power in any government, above and superior to the people, it is despotism.[44]

To Ashley the essence of democracy was the people, and government was merely their servant.

The future, Ashley concluded, did not look bright: For there were essentially two societies in America, and they could not exist side by side. Citing Seward, he exclaimed that there was an "irrepressible conflict" between freedom and slavery. Correctly predicting that the South would secede if Lincoln were elected in November, Ashley nevertheless firmly believed that in the end right would triumph. "The nation or people," he said, "who do not rule in righteousness 'shall perish from the earth'."[45]

Ashley's address received warm accolades. The *National Anti-Slavery Standard* called it a bold speech "which makes one's blood stir quickly, and which might have been made in an anti-slavery meeting instead of the House of Representatives." Most Republican newspapers praised the oration and the Republican National Executive Committee adopted it as a campaign circular.[46]

On July 12, Ashley returned to Toledo. Within a few days he began traveling around his congressional district campaigning for Lincoln, whose chances of election seemed quite good. The Democratic party had split into a Northern wing, with Stephen A. Douglas as its presidential candidate, and a Southern wing, with Vice President John C. Breckinridge as its standard bearer. A third group, made up of old Whigs and border state Democrats, calling themselves the *Constitutional Union* party, nominated John Bell of Tennessee. In Ohio the real contest was between Lincoln and Douglas, and by early August it appeared that "Honest Abe" would carry the state.[47]

On August 2, Ashley was renominated by acclamation at the Fifth District convention. He thanked the people of the district for their support, and declared that he would stand behind the national platform, especially the homestead plank, and the Maumee City platform of July 1, 1854. Ashley's opponent, his old friend James B. Steedman, was a Douglas Democrat.[48]

Ashley asked leading Republicans for help in the campaign, and his close friend Charles Sumner responded by writing a letter of public support. The main activity of the canvass was a series of four debates, patterned after the Lincoln-Douglas debates of 1858, between Ashley and Steedman. The discussions opened at Defiance on September 14, and ended at Toledo on September 24. The basic positions of both candidates remained the same throughout the meetings. Steedman attacked Ashley's past political career, upheld the concept of popular sovereignty and noninterference in the territories, stressed the need for obedience to Supreme Court decisions, and attempted to prove that the homestead bill was a Democratic party idea. Ashley defended his political record, denounced the Dred Scott decision and Southern dominance of the Supreme Court, insisted that the homestead bill was a Republican measure opposed by the Democrats, blasted Douglas for initiating the Kansas-Nebraska Act, and unequivocally stated that Congress had the power to prohibit slavery in the territories.[49]

During the debates Ashley asked Steedman a series of questions about slavery in the territories, the Dred Scott decision, the Constitution, and the powers of Congress. Steedman's answers were ambiguous as he tried to balance respect for the Dred Scott decision with support for popular sovereignty. Ashley's most effective question was: "Do you recognize the right of a majority in a Territory, by popular vote or legislative enactment, to reduce any class of mankind and their descendants to perpetual slavery?" Steedman committed a major blunder by answering, "I do, emphatically." Ashley noted that this would include Irish and German immigrants, and Steedman admitted that it would. Steedman's reply was published throughout the district. The election was held on October 9, and Ashley won by over 1,200 votes, picking up many Irish and German-American votes in Toledo.[50]

Immediately after his election, Ashley began to campaign for Lincoln, speaking in Toledo and southern Ohio. He was confident that the cause would triumph over any obstacles and that a Republican victory would "inaugurate true democracy in the land of Washington." Ashley's optimism was justified, as Lincoln carried Ohio with 231,610 votes to 187,232 for Douglas, 12,193 for Bell, and 11,405 for Breckinridge.[51] Lincoln received only about 40 per cent of the total nation-wide vote, but he obtained a majority of the electoral college vote. Ashley was elated: the era of Southern dominance of the national government was coming to an end and slavery was to be kept out of the territories. But the cost would be very high.

CHAPTER V

STANDING FIRM

Lincoln's election created an explosive atmosphere across the nation. The Lower South was in a state of turmoil as extremist politicians began clamoring for secession as the only solution to their supposed dilemma. Pleas for compromise and conciliation, in an effort to avert disunion, were heard throughout the land. But the antislavery radicals had fought too hard and too long to negotiate on principle. The time for compromise was over, and in the session crisis Ashley and his fellow radicals were determined to stand firm.

Immediately after the presidential election, Ashley took sick, but he recovered in time for the opening of the second session of the Thirty-sixth Congress on December 3. Under the threat of disunion and civil war the country looked for an omen of hope from President Buchanan. But the weak-willed Buchanan sent Congress a disappointing message. Secession, he clearly pointed out, was illegal, but the federal government did not have the right to stop it. For the current predicament the President blamed Northern antislavery agitators and the radical Republicans. These anti-Northern statements did not satisfy anyone and the crisis grew more dangerous.[1]

On December 4, the House voted 145 to 38 to create a special committee "of one from each state" to consider the present condition of the country. Exhibiting the fierce Unionism of many ex-Democrats, Ashley voted against forming this so-called Committee of Thirty-three.[2] Seeing no cause for the South's actions, he declared that he was unwilling to

> . . . give aid and encouragement to the conspirators in stirring up political animosities, for the sole purpose of precipitating the country into a revolution, unless the North again surrendered as they had uniformly done before under such menaces, and on such terms as it might please the conspirators graciously to dictate. I believe that such a committee would not only do no good . . . but that by creating it we would tacitly admit that there was some necessity for it. It appeared to me like pleading "Guilty" to the indictment of the President, which I could not do, knowing it to be false.[3]

Ashley's constituents, he was happy to learn, approved of his vote on the Committee of Thirty-three.[4]

On December 17, the entire Ohio congressional delegation met in the rooms of Representative Thomas Corwin, in an effort to reach some united stand against the doctrine of secession, but this was impossible. Democratic Senator George E. Pugh and Democratic Representative Clement L. Vallandigham were against enforcing federal law in any state which might secede. Vallandigham informed the gathering that by March 4, 1861, the capital would be under the jurisdiction of a Southern government; Lincoln's inauguration would be resisted, unless some compromise could be made within thirty days. Rumors about Southern representatives leaving the government by February 1, and about efforts to take over and reorganize the national constitution in favor of the South were heard throughout the meeting.[5]

Ashley was appalled that Northern Democrats were still trying to aid the South's treasonable course, and all the talk of compromise and sacrifice of principle disgusted him. Convinced that there was going to be a war, he told Chase that "we ought to have 50,000 men here [Washington, D.C.] well armed and prepared for any emergency before the 4th of March and not only inaugurate Mr. Lincoln but keep possession of the Capital and all the Forts—and Government Property in the States and enforce obedience to the laws of the U.S. at any and every cost." If necessary he was ready to give up his seat in Congress and lead a division.[6]

Ashley was also worried about the make-up of Lincoln's Cabinet. If the party was to stand firm, the administration could not afford to have too many compromisers in its ranks. Along with other ultras, the Ohioan began demanding that Chase be included in the Cabinet. But Ashley later became quite apprehensive over the direction of events, and he advised Chase to decline the honor if it appeared that the administration was to be in favor of compromise. Chase, under the influence of other radicals and with a definite offer from Lincoln, accepted the position of Secretary of the Treasury.[7]

Ashley also wanted to have as many former Democrats as possible in the Cabinet. He thus favored Norman B. Judd of Illinois, who had been Lincoln's campaign manager in 1858, for Secretary of the Interior, and he wrote Lincoln advising the President-elect to appoint Montgomery Blair of Maryland as Postmaster General. Lincoln, who was trying to achieve a balance between ex-Whigs and ex-Democrats in his Cabinet, appointed Caleb B. Smith to head the Department of the Interior, but he did make Blair Postmaster General. At this time Blair was in sympathy with many of the radicals' aims.[8] But the Marylander would soon be a bitter foe of the radical cause.

For Ashley, the most disturbing of Lincoln's appointments was that of William Seward as Secretary of State. Since mid-December it was known that Seward would be in the Cabinet. He was preparing for a major speech on January 12, and Ashley hoped for firmness and guidance. But Seward, by nature a compromiser, tried to appease the South by offering to allow new states into the Union, even if they were slave states. Ashley was shocked at the New Yorker's "foggy," "nebulous" address. Walking away from the Senate with Thaddeus Stevens, Ashley asked the old radical what he thought of the oration. "I have listened to every word," said Stevens, "and by the living God, I have heard nothing." Returning later to the Senate, Ashley spoke to Benjamin F. Wade and the distraught senator told him: "If we follow such leadership we will be in the wilderness longer than the children of Israel under Moses." Ashley would later claim that Seward's action "was like the blind leading the blind."[9]

While Congress debated about compromise, the South was taking the matter out of congressional hands. By mid-January, South Carolina, Mississippi, Alabama, and Florida had withdrawn from the Union; by February, Louisiana, Texas, and Georgia joined them. Appalled by the tragedy that was befalling the nation, Ashley rose to address the House on January 17.

Without wasting words, he directed himself to the crisis. The American Union, as the founders intended it, had to be preserved, Ashley declared, even if force was necessary. The future prosperity of the nation, he said, "demands the maintenance of the National Constitution inviolate, and the faithful execution of all laws passed in pursuance of that constitution, not only in every State but in every Territory ... [and] demands an acquiescence in and support of the legally constituted authorities chosen by the people against any and all combinations of men who may attempt to subvert or destroy the government, because they cannot [any] longer control and dictate its policy." "Is the mere election by the people, of a President who does not favor the cherished policy of a few thousand slaveholders, sufficient cause for destroying the Union, and involving the nation in civil war?" he asked. The answer was self-evident. Stating that the nation had passed through many crises before, Ashley asserted that this time the old Southern tricks would not work, since he was confident that the great mass of freedom-loving people in the North would not back down.[10] Believing that the Union was worth any risk, Ashley was determined to be firm, as concessions had accomplished nothing in the past.

Forcefully pointing out that the Union was perpetual and not merely a compact of states, Ashley said:

The principle of national unity is the very life and soul of our Constitution. Without it, our great national charter is not worth the paper upon which it is written. . . . This modern doctrine of the right of a State to withdraw from the Union at pleasure, is a "heresy" which was denounced by all the leading men of the revolution. . . . there is no such right under the Constitution, and the framers of the Constitution carefully guarded against any such absurd theory.[11]

Accepting the fact that five to ten states would secede, Ashley set forth his views on what the policy of the government should be toward the loyal minority in those states.

Those who remain loyal [he concluded] and refuse to recognize such revolutionary proceedings, may continue to act under the old constitution and laws of the State . . . elect their governor, State officers, and members of the Legislature and Congress. . . . The Governors thus elected could call upon the President . . . for aid to suppress the rebellion, and it would be his duty to grant it. There is no doubt but what Congress would recognize such a government. . . . The Senators and Representatives in Congress thus elected by the loyal citizens of any of the seceding States, would undoubtedly be admitted to seats, each House, by the Constitution, being the sole judge of the qualifications of its own members. In this manner the National Government could fulfill and discharge its constitutional obligations by securing to each State a republican form of government, suppress rebellion, and protect the lives, liberties, and property of the loyal citizens.[12]

These were Ashley's first publicly pronounced ideas on reconstruction, and they were far milder than his later policies. But this program clearly contains three major tenets of his reconstruction ideas: congressional dominance, federal interference in domestic issues of a state, and the constitutional base of reconstruction in Article IV, Section 4, which provides that "the United States shall guarantee every State in this Union a republican form of government."

If civil war broke out Ashley knew what course of action he would follow: declare martial law, proclaim a blockade, confiscate the property of all rebels, and hang or shoot all the leading traitors. Quoting John Quincy Adams, Ashley pointed out that under the war power clause of the Constitution, the commander-in-chief of the armed forces had the power to emancipate slaves in enemy territory. "There is," he exclaimed, "but one course left after all peaceful remedies fail, and that is, to use all the power of the government to crush rebellion and treason, if we would preserve the nation from certain and utter ruin."[13] By thus demanding forceful action if war came, and by connecting the cause of the Union to the fight against slavery, Ashley was one of the earliest advocates of what became radical Republican war policy.

Fiercely disclaiming responsibility for the crisis, Ashley declared "if there is disunion and civil war, it will be no fault of the Northern people." He ended his speech by counseling his colleagues to stand firm against any compromise which would put the nation on the path of making slavery constitutional and perpetual, for it was his opinion that "slavery must die."[14]

Ashley's address received enthusiastic response. William Schouler, the radical Republican Massachusetts journalist, wrote to the Ohioan complimenting him on his oration. The Cleveland *Leader* stated that the speech was one of the most thorough of the session and "worth the most careful reading of every voter in the country."[15]

But schemes for compromise to avoid disunion continued to be brought forth. On January 14, Thomas Corwin, acting on instructions from the Committee of Thirty-three, reported five proposals to the House. The first called for the repeal of state personal liberty laws, as well as for the consistent execution of the Fugitive Slave Act. The second requested a constitutional amendment stipulating that slavery could not be interfered with in the states. The other propositions called for the immediate admission of New Mexico into the Union (New Mexico would have entered as a slave state); guarantee of a jury trial to fugitive slaves in the state from which they had supposedly fled; and a resolution to strengthen extradition procedures in the event of another raid like that on Harpers Ferry.[16]

The debates on the five proposals were long and heated, and when Representative William Kellogg of Illinois supposedly was ready to go over to the side of the compromisers, Ashley became enraged. Believing that such actions were a betrayal of principle, Ashley viciously scolded the Illinois congressman and stated that he "would like to see him kicked by a steam Jackass from Washington to Illinois."[17]

As the proposals of the Committee of Thirty-three came before the House for action, Ashley consistently voted against compromise. The propositions asking for repeal of personal liberty laws, execution of the Fugitive Slave Act, and jury trials for fugitive slaves in the states from which they fled, all passed, and in each instance Ashley voted no. The proposals to admit New Mexico into the Union and to strengthen extradition procedures were voted down, Ashley voting with the majority.[18]

The most important resolution was that for a constitutional amendment guaranteeing noninterference with slavery in the states. On February 28, after days of debate and preliminary voting, the joint resolution passed, 133 to 65. Ashley, who had voted in the negative, immediately rose on a question of privilege. The Constitution, he maintained, required that two-thirds of the House had to approve proposed amendments and not two-

STANDING FIRM 63

thirds of a quorum, which the 133 votes represented. After a short discussion, his appeal was overruled by the Speaker. The amendment was later passed by the Senate, but three-fourths of the states never ratified it.[19]

Ashley was extremely proud of his stand on the proposals of the Committee of Thirty-three. Other radicals had echoed his opinions. A correspondent in the Toledo *Blade* praised him as a man above corruption and as an individual who "preferred principle to mere success." Later in life, when discussing the vote on the proposed constitutional amendment, Ashley claimed that he could not conceive of a more shameful "exhibition on the part of a civilized people."[20] He would not sacrifice the principle of anti-slavery. While others tried to compromise away the ideals of a lifetime, Ashley remained firm.

On March 4, Lincoln was inaugurated as the sixteenth President. The radicals were for the most part satisfied with the tone of his address. Ashley particularly liked Lincoln's statement that "the power confided to me will be used to hold, occupy, and possess the property, and places belonging to the government, and to collect the duties and imposts."[21] Though parts of the speech were conciliatory, for the first time in a decade a Chief Executive seemed willing to stand up to the conspirators, and Ashley, for the most part, was delighted.

Since Chase was to be in the Cabinet, the Ohio legislature would now have to select a new United States senator. The Republicans controlled the legislature, so, in essence, the choice would be made in a party caucus. On the seventy-eighth ballot, after a great deal of political maneuvering, John Sherman was chosen as the party's candidate.[22] In 1861, Ashley considered Sherman a political ally, but future differences over reconstruction and Ohio political matters split the two men apart.

Ashley and the nation now turned their attention to President Lincoln as they awaited action. Would he use force to uphold the Union or would he compromise? The President, as it turned out, had no intention of forcing the South to submit to the federal government. Whether there would be civil war was a question he craftily left up to the rebels.[23] The nation did not have to wait long for an answer. Upon receiving notice that Lincoln had decided to send provisions to Major Robert Anderson at Fort Sumter, the Confederate government ordered a bombardment of the citadel. On April 12, the Civil War broke out.

On April 15, Lincoln issued a proclamation calling for a special session of Congress and for 75,000 volunteers through the states. The North responded with enthusiasm as thousands of men eagerly volunteered to defend the Constitution and the Union. But the reaction in the upper South was hostile. On April 17, Virginia, refusing to bear arms against her sister states of the South, seceded from the Union; within six weeks, Arkansas, Tennessee, and North Carolina followed. Though war had come, Ashley was satisfied with Lincoln's course of action, and like other radicals he was ready to prosecute the conflict forcefully.[24]

During the next few months Ashley traveled through Indiana, Illinois, and Ohio, gauging the mood of the people and attending war rallies. In May, he was highly pleased with the administration's conduct except for its policy of appointing conditional Union men to office in the border states, rather than loyal Republicans. These appointees, he claimed, were "a cursed sight worse than undisguised traitors," and he resented their having the ear of the President. He hoped that in the future he would be able to give Lincoln his unqualified support, but at the moment he did not believe that the administration had kept up with the antislavery feelings of the people. The mad action of the slaveholders, Ashley believed, had made antislavery sentiment grow more in the last thirty days than it had in the last thirty years. "If the administration fully comprehends the true position of affairs," he wrote, "and will seize the golden moment and act up to the expectation and hopes of the entire people all is well. *If not, they will and ought to* fall as well as every man who *now* takes a step backwards." Believing that the nation would demand nothing less, Ashley was determined that the war should bring about complete emancipation. Summing up the position of most radical Republicans, he informed Chase that "slavery cannot by my vote be maintained by federal power, while at the same time I will be called upon to vote men and money without stint to put down the Slave masters at the point of a bayonet."[25] Ashley would support the administration, and at this point was careful not to offend Lincoln, but his support was conditional. The President must continue to oppose slavery.

Desiring to be at the scene of action, Ashley returned to Washington in early May. At first he was concerned that matters were proceeding too slowly, but after visiting General Winfield Scott, he grew confident that there would soon be some movement. (Within a few weeks his assessment of Scott was to change radically.) He was most troubled that soldiers were being used as slave catchers. Such action was an immoral disgrace, he felt; instead of returning runaway slaves, the North should utilize their services. The idea of compromise was still current in Washington, and Ashley, who was still incensed at the Washington Peace Conference, demanded an end to talk of conciliation. Believing that the war should be fought for final victory, he had definite goals in mind: to relieve the Southerners "of the military despotism and mob-rule law with which they were cursed," and "to preserve the Union and our own national existence as a free government." Since he considered slavery the sole cause of the rebellion, he was absolutely certain that the North must fight to end the peculiar institution, and must initiate universal emancipation. Such action would break the back of the rebellion and finally inaugurate true freedom for all. The war had to be fought with vigor and thoroughness, and Ashley was ready to start confiscating property in an effort to achieve victory.[26]

Since little was happening militarily in Washington, Ashley left for Fortress Monroe on May 25, hoping to see some fighting. There he met General Benjamin F. Butler of Massachusetts, who commanded the fort. Butler, like Ashley, believed that a vigorous prosecution of the war was the correct course of action. Ashley admired the general, and the two became close political friends. Faced with the problem of runaway slaves entering his lines, Butler refused to return the fugitives to their Confederate owners; instead he declared them "contraband of war." Ashley heartily approved of the decision and, after some hesitation, Secretary of War Cameron informed Butler that the administration supported his policy. Like other radicals, Ashley admired the flexibility that Lincoln had exhibited. For the moment the Ohioan was satisfied.[27] But he wanted continued forcefulness.

Writing to the Toledo *Blade*, Ashley stated that if he had the power he would direct the army to "sweep before the triumphant march every armed traitor from the Potomac to the Gulf, and hold and occupy the rebellious States as provinces, if necessary until a reconstruction by Union and patriotic men is made possible." Ashley was thus one of the earliest advocates of what became known as the "conquered province" theory of reconstruction.[28]

Clark Waggoner, the conservative Republican editor of the Toledo *Blade*, thoroughly disapproved of Ashley's ideas about prosecuting the war, and he berated the radical congressman in print. Waggoner believed that the war was being fought solely to preserve the Union and to restore it as it had been, and not to abolish slavery. The editor also argued that the government was fighting individual rebels, not states. Concluding that Ashley's reconstruction ideas were inappropriate, Waggoner wrote that he hoped the congressman would moderate his views.[29]

Ashley immediately defended his positions and again stated that there could be no true victory or permanent peace without emancipation. Repeating his assertion of January 17, he maintained that under the war power clause of the Constitution, the government had the right to interfere with slavery in the states and to initiate complete abolition, and that this power should be used against the oligarchic slaveholders. He firmly believed that his views would eventually be accepted by the administration and the American people. Along with other radicals he insisted that neither he nor the people would ever be satisfied with less: anything short of emancipation would be a surrender to and a compromise with the slave power.[30] Ashley was correct in his judgments, but it was too early for action.

Ashley was also still concerned with the administration's policy toward the border states. Suspecting that states like Kentucky would not have voluntarily stayed in the Union, he maintained that the border states were made up of "conditional union men." And as far as he was concerned, a "conditional union man" was a "conditional traitor." Ashley was despondent to hear that Henry Winter Davis of Maryland had lost a bid for reelection. This event only confirmed his assessment of the inappropriateness of Lincoln's border state policy. In line with these opinions, Ashley hoped that John Crittenden would fail in his try for a seat in the House, since he believed the Kentuckian, a conservative compromiser, would cause great harm.[31]

As June came to an end, Ashley realized that when the special session of Congress met in July, the subject of financing the war would certainly come up. Since only a limited amount of money could be raised from the tariff, he preferred direct taxation rather than loans as a way to raise funds.[32] His Democratic background made him cringe at a "borrow now and pay later" policy.

On June 27 or 28, Ashley left Toledo for Washington for the start of the special session of Congress, which was to begin on July 4. In his message to Congress, Lincoln calmly justified his course of action in the Sumter crisis, recounted the emergency measures which he had taken—calling out state militia, proclaiming a naval blockade, calling for three-year volunteers for the army—and asked that his actions be retroactively approved. Sitting within a few miles of the battlefront, with troops marching into and around the capital, and with the streets and hotels jammed with office-seekers, wirepullers, lobbyists, and newspapermen, the Congress approved Lincoln's past actions, granted his requests for men and arms, and passed seventy-six public acts by August 6.[33]

With the Southern Democrats now out of Congress, the Republicans quickly established ascendancy. The radicals secured control of the speakership; Thaddeus Stevens became chairman of the Committee on Ways and Means, and Owen Lovejoy of the Committee on Agriculture. Although he had been in Congress less than two years, Ashley's Republican colleagues showed their confidence in the young radical by appointing him chairman of the important Committee on Territories. This position gave Ashley a prominent role in wartime reconstruction. Maintaining that with secession the states passed back into the condition of territories, he soon became the leading exponent of the territorialization theory of reconstruction. Before leaving home for this session, he had prepared his first reconstruction bill. Immediately after the House was organized, he invited the Republican members of his committee to meet in his rooms for consultation on his measure. The premise of the bill was that under the Constitution, Congress had the power to establish temporary provisional territorial governments in districts in rebellion. But the plan was too radical for his associates. On the advice of his friends, Ashley decided not to present his bill until the regular December session of Congress, and in the ensuing months he attempted to convince the other Republican members on the committee of the soundness of his ideas.[34]

At the opening of the special session the House decided to consider only bills and resolutions dealing with the military, naval, financial, and judicial aspects of the rebellion. Since the radicals looked at the conflict as a war to destroy slavery, they were concerned about the relationship between the army and runaway slaves, and they immediately went on the offensive. Owen Lovejoy, the radical representative from Illinois, introduced a resolution declaring that it was no part of the duty of United States soldiers to capture and return fugitive slaves. The proposition passed 93 to 55, with Ashley voting in the affirmative. The House then passed an army volunteers act, and the first Confiscation Act, which called for the expropriation of property used for insurrectionary purposes, and thus freed slaves employed in the war against the Union. Congress also directed its attention to economic issues: a national loan bill, a higher tariff, and an increased revenue act which included a direct tax and an income tax, were dealt with affirmatively.[35] The financial emergency created by the conflict forced many ex-Democrats to accept economic policies which had previously been closely associated with the Whigs.

Congress was naturally concerned with the problem of war aims, and John Crittenden, on July 22, presented a resolution which limited the war to suppressing insurrection and restoring the Union as it was. The resolution was divided into two parts, the first declared: "That the present deplorable civil war has been forced upon the country by the disunionists of the southern States now in revolt against the constitutional government. . . ." The second part stated that:

> [the war] is not waged upon our part in any spirit of oppression, or from any purpose of conquest or subjugation, or purpose of overthrowing or interfering with the rights or established institutions of those States, but to defend and maintain the supremacy of the Constitution, and to preserve the Union with all the dignity, equality, and rights of the several States unimpaired; and that as soon as these objects were accomplished the war ought to cease.[36]

The destruction of slavery was not a war aim.

Personal and political friends in Washington appealed to Ashley to vote for the resolution and not to separate himself from his party on such an important issue. He voted for the first section, which passed 117 to 2. (Republicans John F. Potter of Wisconsin and Albert G. Riddle of Ohio cast the negative votes.) As his name was called to vote on the second section, Ashley later recalled, he shook his head to abstain with "the blush of shame tingling my face." The resolution passed easily. Ashley had never felt so ashamed in his life, and he emotionally told Thomas Corwin, "Governor, that is the most cowardly act of my life, and no power on earth shall make me repeat it." Surprised at this statement Corwin said that he had voted for the resolution. "Yes, Governor," answered the Ohio radical, "but you do not see things as I do." Similar resolutions presented by Andrew Johnson of Tennessee also passed the Senate.[37]

Among the most disputed items on the House agenda was the additional revenue bill, which called for a direct tax to be levied on the states and territories. Some Midwestern members denounced the basis of assessment, believing that farm lands would be heavily burdened while the banks, corporation stock, and manufacturing plants of the East would escape with a light tax. Ashley, who approved of a direct tax, wanted it to be levied on all property, whether stock or land, according to its worth. The Westerners did not get their way, and the bill passed. Many Midwestern congressmen voted no, but Ashley joined the majority.[38] When the life of the nation was threatened, he was ready to vote for measures which in ordinary times he would oppose.

On July 21, the Union forces under General Irwin McDowell were defeated at Bull Run. The radicals were outraged and demanded that Lincoln take some forceful action. The President responded by appointing General George B. McClellan to command the Union forces in Washington and Virginia. The ultras, who would later regret this move, approved of Lincoln's choice. Ashley, writing to the abolitionist James M. McKim, was now optimistic. He believed that God was on the side of the Union, and that "the end of despotism drowth [sic] near in the United States."[39]

Once the war had started, a Union party movement took root in Ohio. Its purpose was to form a coalition of Republicans and War Democrats to create a party which would insist on victory, but not on the subjugation of the South and its institutions. Ashley was horrified at this proposal since it played down antislavery, and in June, 1861, he tried to stop this so-called "Union for the sake of the Union" movement. During the special session of Congress, he submitted a draft call for a Republican state convention to each Republican member of the Ohio congressional delegation and to the state central committee. All the Republican congressmen but one signed a copy of the call, and Ashley sent it to the Republican committee in Columbus. But the pressure for a Union party was too strong, and leading men in both political parties called for a unity convention to meet at Columbus on September 5.[40]

By declaring that the war was being waged solely "to defend and maintain the supremacy of the Constitution, and to preserve the Union," the convention adopted as its platform the essential aspects of the Crittenden resolution. Governor Dennison, whose blundering at the outset of the war alienated many people, was not considered for renomination. Anxious to show that the Union party would not be dominated by antislavery radicals, and to attract Union Democrats, the convention nominated Democrat David Tod for governor. Tod, who had presided over the Democratic National Convention in Baltimore, had favored compromise during the Sumter crisis, but when the fighting started, he backed the government.[41]

Ashley, who attended the convention, was enraged. Considering the Union party plain "humbug," he wrote to Chase that he had "never before met so many *doughfaces* and *cowards* in any convention. The Democratic element was rather better . . . than our own. It seemed as if an extraordinary effort was made to select the doughiest [*sic*] material in the *late* Republican party, to represent us in this convention." As the Republicans had abandoned their antislavery principles, Ashley informed Chase that if he was ready to support the platform of the Union party, their political friendship would be over. Ashley was ill all during the convention, and Tod's nomination he said, "well nigh killed me."[42]

In a rather lackluster campaign, Tod was easily elected, and the Union party secured a majority in both houses of the legislature. Disgusted with the course of events Ashley did not take part in the campaign. In the beginning of November, after the election was over, he started to speak at war meetings throughout the state. Refusing to adopt the Union party platform, he reiterated his conviction that the aim of the war was to destroy slavery. The speaking tour culminated at a huge rally in Toledo on November 26. Relating to the audience the events leading up to the Civil War, Ashley blamed the conflict on slavery and the conspiratorial activities of the slave barons. Obviously still disturbed by Lincoln's September 11, 1861, order overturning Frémont's proclamation freeing the slaves in the area under his command, Ashley pointedly said, "The overthrow of slavery will not only end the war, but beyond all doubt, save the Union and preserve constitutional liberty by making us what we ought to be, a homogeneous people." He would stand by the President, but he would not be silent if he felt Lincoln made mistakes and adopted policies "which . . . would be fatal to the success of that cause which all true patriots have first at heart." But above all else, there could be no compromise as long as slavery existed.[43] Others might sacrifice the principles of emancipation, but not Ashley. Like his friends Chase and Sumner, on this point he was adamant.

CHAPTER VI

WARTIME CONGRESSMAN

Dissatisfied though he was with the manner in which the war was being conducted, and frustrated at Lincoln's refusal to implement emancipation, Ashley returned to Washington in December, 1861, convinced that in the end his views would triumph. He was determined to keep up the pressure on the administration, and he was so confident that the Union would eventually emerge victorious that his thoughts centered on the problem of reconstruction.

On December 11, along with Benjamin Wade, the chairman of the Senate Committee on Territories, Ashley visited Treasury Secretary Chase's office. The three men discussed the relationship of the rebellious states to the national government. Chase contended that "no State nor any portion of the people could withdraw from the Union . . . but that when the attempt was made, and the State government was placed in hostility to the Federal government, the State organization was forfeited and it lapsed into the condition of a Territory with which we could do what we pleased." Provisional and then territorial governments and courts could be established in the rebellious states and eventually Congress could provide for their readmittance into the Union. The two territorial committee chairmen fully agreed with Chase.[1] Ashley was fortunate to have Wade as his Senate counterpart. Although the two men were at times rivals in Ohio politics, the similarity of their views on the need for a forceful prosecution of the war, on the use of Negro troops, on emancipation, and on reconstruction enabled them to work together harmoniously. Ashley respected Wade's wisdom and courage, and Wade admired Ashley's energy and forthrightness.

Before Ashley could act on the ideas expressed in Chase's office, he was called back to Washington County, Ohio, for the funeral of his beloved mother. Overcome with grief, and knowing that Congress would soon adjourn for the Christmas holidays, he decided to go home before returning to Washington.[2] In Toledo James was surrounded by close friends and his loving wife and family, and with their help he managed to break free of the depression which had gripped him upon receiving the news of his mother's death. Mary Ann Ashley had given her son love and guidance and had instilled in him a desire to succeed. He would miss her greatly. But the crisis of the Union was so great that there was little time to dwell on his personal sorrow.

On December 23, William Vandever, an Iowa Republican acting in Ashley's behalf, introduced a resolution instructing the House Committee on Territories "to inquire into the legality and expediency of establishing territorial governments within the limits of the disloyal States and districts, and to report by bill or otherwise." The resolution was adopted by voice vote.[3]

In January, Ashley again introduced his old bill in the territorial committee, but no immediate action was taken. With the Union victories at Fort Henry and Fort Donelson, Tennessee, however, interest in the process and procedures of reconstruction gained momentum. On February 24, the territorial committee voted 4 to 3 in favor of Ashley's bill, and he was instructed to report it to the House. When, on February 27, Ashley attempted to bring up the bill, Clement Vallandigham, the Ohio Peace Democrat, objected. "I give notice that I shall raise a question on that bill whenever it is brought in," he said. Only after another unsuccessful attempt at introduction, and heated debate with fellow committee member, Democrat Aaron Harding of Kentucky, on whether Ashley had released a copy of the measure to the press, was the bill finally reported out of committee on March 12.[4]

Realizing that the bill would meet vigorous opposition, Ashley decided to request that it be printed and then recommitted. The minority members of the territorial committee immediately attacked the measure in two harsh reports. George Pendleton, an Ohio Democrat, stated that the legislation "ought to be entitled a bill to dissolve the Union and abolish the Constitution of the United States," and moved to lay it on the table. This was agreed to by a vote of 65 to 56. Usually a bill is ordered to be printed before action is taken, but because of the strong feeling against this measure, such was not the case. Not only did the Democrats and border state Unionists vote against the bill, but so did twenty-two Republicans.[5]

Ashley's measure set the tone for much of the future congressional debate on reconstruction. (On February 11, Sumner had introduced eight resolutions in the Senate, expressing the theory that the seceded states had committed suicide, thus forfeiting all rights and were therefore now territories.) The bill was the first to deal systematically with the territorialization concept of reconstruction. The Ohioan's initial premise was that the rebels in the seceded states had overthrown and destroyed the official state governments, terminating their legal existence, and thus had reduced them to territories over which Congress had jurisdiction. The insurgent state governments had, in other words, forfeited the rights and obligations which they were no longer discharging, and reverted to the condition of territories. According to this theory the constitutional power for congressional control over districts in rebellion, came from the sovereign power of the federal government to promote justice, to administer laws fairly, to see to the general welfare, and to insure domestic tranquility in all national territory.

Working from these assumptions, Ashley wished to set up temporary governments over conquered insurgent areas. The President would be authorized and required to establish a temporary civil administration in organized rebel territory. The Chief Executive also had the power to set boundaries for the territories. According to the bill, the civil government thus established was to be "maintained and continued . . . until such time as the loyal people residing therein shall form new State governments, republican in form, as prescribed by the Constitution of the United States, and apply for and obtain admission into the Union as States."[6] Since the President could set boundaries, there was no assurance that when the rebellious areas were back in the Union, they would again comprise eleven states. It should be mentioned that no definite percentage of loyal citizens was required for completing the process of readmittance. In his later reconstruction proposals Ashley was more specific on this point.

The temporary governments would have an executive, a legislative, and a judicial branch, consisting of a governor, a legislative council of between seven and thirteen members, the size being determined by the President, and a supreme court and such inferior courts as the council might establish. The grant of legislative power included "all rightful subjects of legislation, not inconsistent with the Constitution and laws of the United States and the provisions of this act." This implied interference with slavery. Since state governments were destroyed, it was reasoned that former state laws were no longer in effect, and this naturally included the slave laws. But not to leave any doubt on this matter, Ashley's measure stated that the council could not pass any law "establishing, protecting, or recognizing the existence of slavery, nor shall said temporary government . . . give, sanction, or declare the right of one man to property in another." Commentators at the time, and years later Ashley himself, pointed out that one of the main purposes of the bill was the emancipation of all the slaves in conquered territory.[7]

Ashley's bill also included radical sections on confiscation. All public land was to be seized and held for the use of members of the armed services as well as to compensate loyal citizens. Leases to public lands and confiscated estates, not to exceed 160 acres, were to go to "actual occupants who are loyal." Ashley did not specify any racial qualifications for loyalty, and thus former slaves were entitled to land. This interpretation was recognized by the minority members of the Committee on Territories, and was condemned in their reports. There was, in fact, no clear statement of transfer of land title in the measure, although Ashley did believe that, under the war powers of the Constitution, the federal government had a right to take title to enemy property and to distribute it in any way it wished. Ashley's intention was that eventually ex-slaves and poor whites would get permanent possession of some land, and thus obtain economic and political power.[8]

Other parts of the legislation instructed the provisional governor and legislative council to establish public schools, and limited the work day of laborers and field hands to twelve hours. Since there was no racial requirement for school admittance, the schools were to be open to black children. Ashley excluded from political privileges not only former United States civil and military officers, as well as lawyers and ministers, but also any person who had taken an oath to support the Constitution and who had joined the Confederacy. All loyal persons were to be admitted as electors and were entitled to sit on grand and petit juries. As there was no racial qualification for loyal persons, Ashley was granting blacks the right to vote and to serve as jurymen. Finally, the Senate had to consent to all presidential appointments, and Congress was given the power to remove territorial appointees from office, and the right to veto any law passed by the district legislature.[9] It was evident that Ashley viewed Congress as the dominant force in reconstruction.

For a variety of reasons, Ashley's bill had no real chance to pass in March, 1862. Historian Herman Belz has pointed out that Lincoln, who was against the territorialization concept of reconstruction, undercut the bill when he established a military government in Tennessee, headed by Senator Andrew Johnson. Many congressmen who previously supported territorialization now saw no need for it, and the military government served as an alternative for conservative Republicans who hated Ashley's advanced ideas. Lincoln also made concessions to antislavery opinion by his March 6 message asking Congress to pass a resolution embodying the principle of federal aid to states which adopted a system of gradual compensated emancipation. The resolution passed on March 10. Though this idea was not acceptable to advanced radical Republicans, it was admissible for a certain number of moderates who now felt free to back away from Ashley's bill.[10]

Democrats and border state Unionists, believing that the bill stood for subjugation of the white race and black emancipation, and that it was virtually an ordinance of secession, were extraordinarily hostile to the proposal. Some Republicans opposed territorialization because the idea seemed to validate the secession ordinances of the rebellious states, which were at variance with the notion of a perpetual Union. Finally, any bill which spoke of emancipation, confiscation, Negro land grants, and Negro suffrage simply frightened too many people, was too radical for many Republicans, and broke too many precedents. Many years later, Ashley recalled how a few days after his bill was tabled, Senator Jacob Collamer, a conservative Republican from Vermont, approached him and asked where he found the precedents for his reconstruction ideas. Ashley's answer was, "Sir, we make precedents here," and "before we get through with this rebellion we will compel all loyal men in Congress to vote for measures far more radical than my bill."[11] Ashley's prognostications were correct, but in March 1862, his ideas were too advanced for most of the nation.

Although Ashley's reconstruction proposals came to naught, he and his associates never ceased the pressure for emancipation, and one of the first places to which they directed their attack during the long session of the Thirty-seventh Congress was the District of Columbia. Ashley was one of the main protagonists in the battle for freedom in the capital. On December 16, 1861, Republican Senator Henry Wilson of Massachusetts introduced a bill "for the release of certain persons held to service or labor in the District of Columbia." Republican John Hutchins of Ohio introduced similar resolutions into the House and these were referred to the Committee for the District. Ashley was a member of the committee, and he prepared a bill which simply stated:

> That from and after the passage of this act, neither slavery nor involuntary servitude, except as punishment for crime, whereof the party shall have been duly convicted, shall exist in the District of Columbia; and thereafter it shall not be lawful for any person in said district to own or to hold a human being as a slave.[12]

Such a bill was clearly too radical to pass at this time. The Ohioan discussed the proposal with Chase, Lincoln, Senator Lot Morrill of Maine, who had charge of the Senate bill, and with other members of the District Committee. The outcome of the deliberations was a bill which provided for compensated emancipation. The amount to be paid for each freed slave was not to exceed three hundred dollars. On March 12, Ashley, reporting the bill, asked that it be printed and recommitted so its consideration could be delayed until the Senate had acted.[13]

The Senate bill also contained a proposal for compensation and like the House version called for the creation of a three-man commission to pass on claims. Amendments making re-enslavement a crime and limiting compensation to loyal slaveholders were added. Voluntary colonization proposals were put into the bill and it passed on April 3. Seven days later, the House began discussing the measure.[14] On April 11, Ashley gave a short speech in defense of the proposal.

Though he was not entirely happy with the Senate bill, he planned to support it, since it was the best that could be obtained at the moment. He had always been opposed to the idea of compensated emancipation because it admitted the right to property in man, but he said: "If I must tax the loyal people of the nation $1,000,000 before the slaves at the national capital can be ransomed, I will do it. I would make a bridge of gold over which they might pass to freedom ... if it could not be more justly accomplished." Citing the achievements of freed blacks, Ashley belittled the charges that passage of the bill could lead to a race war, and that prejudice against Negroes was so implacable that the white and black races could not live in peace. "I have," he said, "no such apprehensions. Experience teaches me that such fears are groundless." On this occasion, he was sure that blacks could successfully assimilate into American society, but as mentioned earlier, the congressman at other times questioned the likelihood of racial harmony. Concluding, he asserted in the rhetoric of the time, "the golden morn, so long and so anxiously looked for by the friends of freedom in the United States, has dawned." The bill easily passed the House, and on April 16 Lincoln signed it into law.[15] Implementation of this long-cherished abolitionist and radical Republican goal was a great victory for freedom, and Ashley was a major contributor to the achievement. The Toledoan would have preferred a more direct act, without compensation, but as a practical man he realized that he would have to accept bills which moved the nation in the right direction even if the pace was slower than he desired.

Since he was chairman of the Committee on Territories, Ashley directed a great deal of his attention during the session to the problem of slavery in the territories. Along with other radicals, he believed that the time to prohibit slavery in the territories was at hand. On March 24, Representative Isaac Arnold of Illinois introduced "a bill to render freedom national and slavery sectional," which was referred to the Committee on Territories. The Arnold measure died in committee. On May 1, Owen Lovejoy reported out a bill which prohibited slavery in the territories, in areas occupied by the government, on vessels on high seas, and also "in all places whatsoever where the National government is supreme, or has exclusive power." Herman Belz maintains that if territorialization had been accepted, the seceded states would have come under the provisions of the act.[16] Ashley more than likely endorsed the bill as it was, but the House would not accept such a broad proposal. Lovejoy then agreed to limit the act to the statement, "There shall be neither slavery nor involuntary servitude in any of the territories of the United States." With this change the House accepted the bill. On June 17, the House approved a slightly different Senate version of the prohibition which Lincoln signed two days later.[17] A dream which antislavery men had entertained for decades was now fulfilled. Ashley, for one, was deeply gratified.

During this session Ashley also gave much attention to a bill providing a temporary government for the Territory of Arizona. He first reported a proposal for a temporary government to his committee on February 13, but it was not until March 10 that the committee instructed him to introduce it in the House. Ashley complied with this directive on March 12. The first two sections of the legislation were routine, but the third section which contained the Wilmot Proviso generated excitement. This part of the bill stated that there would be no slavery in the territory and that "after the passage of this act, slavery or involuntary servitude is hereby forever prohibited in all Territories now organized; and all acts and parts of acts, either of Congress or of any organized Territory, establishing, regulating or in any way recognizing the relation of master and slave in any of said Territories, is hereby repealed." The Democrats were extremely disturbed by this provision of the bill and tried to have the measure laid on the table, but the attempt failed. It was not until May 8 that the Arizona measure was again discussed, and since Lovejoy's bill prohibiting slavery in the territories had already been introduced, Ashley agreed to limit the Wilmot Proviso section of his measure to Arizona.[18]

Ashley then spoke in favor of the bill, demanding that Congress pass it with its prohibition of slavery. After using some of his time to denounce supposed traitors in the army and the navy, he concluded his presentation by reminding his Republican colleagues that if they did not pass the measure they would be breaking with the cause for which they had pledged to fight. Ashley was thus a major force (along with Senator Wade) in the passage of an act which the New York *Independent* called "a triumph for the causes of human freedom."[19]

During the session Ashley also voted for a bill which made it a crime for military officers to return fugitive slaves, and for a measure authorizing the President to appoint diplomats to the black governments of Haiti and

Liberia. In addition he endorsed Lincoln's resolution on gradual compensated emancipation and worked for a proposal which sanctioned the enlistment of Negro soldiers.[20] But the measure which created the most controversy was the second Confiscation Act.

A confiscation bill was introduced into the Senate in early December, 1861, by Lyman Trumbull, and in the House by Lovejoy. Various other propositions were also put forward, and the issue was debated for months.[21] The ultras favored a far-reaching bill which included unconditional confiscation and emancipation, and on May 23, 1862, Ashley rose to defend this position.

Beginning with a plea that an enduring peace could only be obtained by defeating the rebels, confiscating their property, and emancipating the slaves, he pointed out that the people demanded the rebellion be crushed, not compromised, and thus favored forceful action. The soldiers, he argued, went to war for a principle worth dying for, and not for compromises worked out by politicians which would exempt rebels from punishment for their crimes and "leave them in undisputed possession of all their property and thus offer a premium to rebellion and treason." After blasting the weak policy of the administration which did "more to encourage treason than to terrify traitors," he returned to his theme. "If this question of the confiscation of the property and the liberation of the slaves of rebels could be submitted to a vote of our Army . . . ," he said, "there would be no doubt about its passage."[22]

Ashley based his defense of the constitutionality of confiscation on the war power clause of the Constitution, buttressing his arguments with quotations from John Quincy Adams. It was only justice to make the rebels pay, for the North demanded no less. After a digression in favor of his reconstruction ideas, he concluded by saying:

> More than a year ago, I proclaimed to the constituency which I have the honor to represent, my purpose to destroy the institution of slavery if it became necessary to save the country—as I believed then and still believe it is—in every State which had rebelled, or which should rebel, and make war upon the Government. I then demanded, as I now demand, "that not a single slave claimed by a rebel slavemaster shall be delivered up if he escapes or be left in the wake of our advancing and victorious armies." I then declared, as I now declare, that "justice, no less than our own self-preservation as a nation, required that we should confiscate and emancipate, and thus secure indemnity for the past and security for the future."[23]

On May 26, the House passed a confiscation measure, but the companion emancipation bill was defeated by four votes, as sixteen conservative Republicans voted against it. The Senate passed a weaker confiscation bill on June

28, which was referred to a conference committee, and the compromise finally passed the House on July 11.[24] Though the act was not as encompassing as Ashley had desired, he supported it, since it provided for the confiscation of rebel property, emancipated slaves belonging to disloyal persons, and authorized the President to employ Negroes to suppress the rebellion. In response to Lincoln's view that the act violated constitutional proscriptions against forfeiture of property beyond an individual's life and the prohibition against ex post facto legislation, Congress passed an explanatory resolution. With this done, Lincoln signed the bill, though he angered Ashley and the radicals by sending Congress the veto message he would have used had they not heeded his request.[25] But all in all, great progress had been made and although Ashley would continue to pressure Lincoln to issue an emancipation proclamation, for the moment he seemed if not satisfied, at least appeased.

From the onset of the war, Ashley had made it clear that he would vote for all the men and measures needed to crush the insurrection, and he acted accordingly in this session. He cast affirmative votes for a higher tariff, an internal revenue measure, legal tender bills, and for the National Banking Act. He voted no on an amendment to the legal tender bill, which authorized the Treasury to sell bonds at market value for coin. It appears that Ashley would have preferred the sale to be made at par value, since as a hard money proponent, he was philosophically opposed to speculation.[26]

During the long session of the Thirty-seventh Congress, the Republicans attained many of their goals and thus greatly aided the future growth of the nation. A transcontinental railroad bill, a homestead measure, and a land-grant college act all passed. Ashley supported all three proposals.[27]

The war did not go well for the North during the seven months that Congress was in session, and the radicals, led by Wade and Senator Zachariah Chandler of Michigan, placed most of the blame for this situation on General McClellan. Believing that McClellan's indecisiveness and conservative opinions on slavery were causing the army's lack of success, the radicals vociferously demanded his removal. Ashley agreed with this position. One day the Ohio radical called on the President to discuss the laggard commander. When Lincoln started to tell a humorous story, Ashley rose to his feet and said: "Mr. President, I did not come here this morning to hear stories; it is too serious a time." With a sad face, Lincoln replied, "Ashley, sit down! I respect you as an earnest sincere man. You cannot be more anxious than I have been constantly since the beginning of the war; and I say to you that were it not for the occasional *vent*, I should die." Ashley apologized, and the two men then rationally discussed McClellan.[28] The radicals eventually had their way, but only when Lincoln felt the time was right.

The second session of the Thirty-seventh Congress finally adjourned on July 17, and Ashley returned home to begin his reelection campaign. The Union party movement had gained strength in his district, and the "Union for the sake of Union" men did not share his views on confiscation and emancipation. Quickly realizing that he faced a tough renomination fight, Ashley called on his friends George Julian and Charles Sumner for help. The Democratic adherents of the Union party movement joined with a group of conservative Republicans (mainly ex-Whigs) led by Clark Waggoner to nominate former Whig Morrison R. Waite (the future Chief Justice of the United States) as their congressional candidate. Ashley's supporters held a separate convention and renominated the Toledoan.[29]

The campaign started immediately and soon degenerated into a mud-slinging contest. Ashley and Waggoner accused each other of lying about who first brought up the idea of a federal job for the newspaperman in 1860, and what it was supposed to cost. The *Blade* charged Ashley with discouraging enlistments in the army, of not supporting Lincoln, of being in favor of disunion, and of not upholding the Crittenden resolution. Except for the last statement, which Ashley never denied, all the other charges were inflated campaign rhetoric, misinterpretations, and outright lies. But the most vicious attack on Ashley came when the *Blade* published five letters that he had written in 1861 to Frank Case, then of Ohio, but in 1862, surveyor general of Colorado. The newspaper tried to imply that in these letters, Ashley had set prior conditions—his brothers William and Eli were to receive positions in Colorado—for working on behalf of Case's appointment. The *Blade* also accused Ashley of being part of an illegal land speculation deal with Case. Even before the story broke, A. S. Latty had written to Chase condemning Ashley's actions in the Case letters and claiming that the congressman really did not believe in the antislavery cause. Waggoner wrote to Sumner, accusing Ashley of corruption. Neither Chase nor Sumner was persuaded to withdraw his support for Ashley. Chase thought that Ashley may have been in error in the Case matter, but that he was not corrupt and should be reelected. "General Ashley," he wrote to Waggoner, "has been too faithful a representative in Congress of the great cause to which I have devoted my life, and too true a friend to myself, to allow me, without dishonor, to do anything which could be interpreted into distrust or disregard of him."[30]

Ashley waged an aggressive campaign, and if his critics expected him to soften his tone they were mistaken. In a passionate speech at Bowling Green, he denounced slavery and disunion, and appealed to workingmen to crush the rebellion. And then, as if to defy his conservative opponents he asked his constituents to support "a free ballot for all, black as well as white, and equitable representation in Congress and in all legislative assemblies, . . ." At first Ashley refused to answer the corruption charges, but in one public letter, he defended his actions on Case's appointment, believing that he had not acted improperly and had not pressured Case.[31]

Even before the Case letters controversy arose, Ashley had realized that he could win the election only if a Democrat entered the contest and thus split the conservative vote. The Democrats, hoping to gain from the division in the Union party, obliged by putting up Edward L. Phelps as a candidate. Ashley claimed that he had nothing to do with bringing Phelps into the race, but if he and his supporters did not actually initiate the idea, they at least nudged the Democrats in the right direction.[32]

When Lincoln issued the Preliminary Emancipation Proclamation on September 22, another factor was added to an already confused situation. Ashley immediately claimed credit for having repeatedly called upon the President to follow such a course of action. Since he had always maintained that emancipation and confiscation of rebel property were essential for victory, Ashley was able to put his opponent on the defensive. Waite could no longer oppose these measures and claim to support the President at the same time. Antislavery newspapers throughout the country rallied to Ashley's defense during the campaign. The New York *Independent* stated that the nation could not afford to lose the services of such a "brave, bold man, who always fights on the side of humanity and justice," and that "the President is desirous of Mr. Ashley's re-election." The Boston *Commonwealth* condemned the scandalous charges of his Hunker opponents and hoped he would win.[33]

By October 7, Ashley's supporters were confident of victory, as they expected him to win big majorities outside of Toledo. The results proved their forecasts to have been correct. Waite beat Ashley by a three-to-one margin in Toledo, but the congressman's vote in the surrounding areas was large enough to offset this. Phelps polled over 5,000 votes, many of which would have gone to Waite and thus would have elected him. Though Ashley was victorious, the election was a disaster for the Union party in Ohio, as the Democrats won fourteen of the nineteen congressional seats.[34]

Many observers believed that the cause for this strong Democratic comeback was the Preliminary Emancipation Proclamation. But Ashley, who considered his victory a personal vindication of his antislavery views, disagreed with this assessment. He maintained that the defeat was due to the weak-willed stance of the Union party, halfway antislavery measures, and the administration's lackadaisical prosecution of the war. In fact, he warned Lincoln that the slightest rescinding of the administration's antislavery positions would evoke a counterrevolution in the North.[35] Determined to have the final Emancipation Proclamation issued as scheduled, he returned to Washington in December for the opening of the last session of the Thirty-seventh Congress.

Ashley was still troubled by the accusations made against him in the recent campaign, and on December 4, he rose on a question of personal privilege. Maintaining that he had been slandered by the publication of the Case letters, he asked that a committee of five be appointed to investigate the truth of the allegations. His request was granted, and a committee of two Republicans, two Democrats, and one Union party man, was charged to investigate.[36]

The committee collected evidence, questioned witnesses, and ran a very thorough investigation. Case and others in Colorado sent sworn depositions stating their positions. Case denied that Ashley had exacted any conditions from him concerning the appointment. Waggoner appeared before the committee on January 22, but refused to be sworn in as a witness. Ashley testified on February 14. At first he seemed reluctant to answer questions, but then he quickly consented to do so. He introduced some new papers and letters into evidence in an attempt to prove that he had recommended Case for the position before proposing a partnership in land deals. Ashley said that he "neither made nor intended to make any of the requests for appointments or other favors contained in my letters to Mr. Case *conditions precedent*, and a consideration for, the use of my influence in obtaining his appointment." He pointed out that he had never intimated that if Case declined his requests he "would cease to labor for his appointment."[37]

On February 28 the committee issued a report completely exonerating Ashley of any misconduct. The report said that the only real charge the Toledo *Blade* had made against Ashley was *"that he corruptly procured the appointment of F. M. Case as surveyor general of Colorado Territory, for a consideration previously agreed upon."* But the investigators concluded that it was not until March 12, 1861, that Ashley first told Case that he had promised some sub-appointments to members of the Indiana congressional delegation in return for their aid, and that it was not until this date that he first mentioned the land deal to Case. This letter was written ten days after Ashley, along with twenty-five other congressmen, made a formal request for Case's appointment. This proved "that at that date no bargain or agreement had been made either with reference to subordinate appointments or with reference to speculations in Colorado." As for the land deals the report stated, "the speculations have no reference whatever to any *official* transactions, but . . . relate to the purchase of such valuable lands as a man residing at the place would have an opportunity to purchase as a private citizen." The committee concluded that it was not "aware of any rule that excludes members of Congress from buying and selling as other men, or from availing themselves of such means of information in relation to such purchases as may be accessible to them as to all the world." Finding that the evidence had conclusively shown that Ashley had committed no illegal or corrupt acts, the committee asked to be discharged from further consideration of the matter.[38] Although Ashley had not committed a technically illegal act, his statements in the Case letters about land deals, could easily be interpreted as improper or unethical. But since he and Case never did engage in any land deals, there was no specific illegality to investigate.

Waggoner was naturally disappointed at the outcome of the investigation and refused to accept the conclusions. But many of the leading newspapers in the country found that justice had been done and that Ashley had been completely vindicated.[39] Yet his political opponents would never let the matter die, and at every future election they dragged out the Case letters. But they always neglected to mention two important facts: first, that Ashley and Case never shared any land deal, and second, that no new evidence disproving the findings of the report was ever found.

While the investigation was proceeding, Ashley concerned himself with other matters, such as statehood for West Virginia and emancipation. At the onset of the Civil War, the strongly Unionist inhabitants of northwestern Virginia refused to go along with the secession ordinance and set up a restored government at Wheeling. Under the leadership of Governor Francis Pierpont, the Unionists requested admittance into the Union as a separate state. A referendum on the subject was approved by the residents of the area in October, 1861. On July 14, 1862, the Senate passed a statehood bill, with a provision for gradual emancipation. The House voted to delay consideration of the bill until December, 1862, when the measure passed. Ashley and Stevens, following Sumner's action in the Senate, voted against the proposal. Like his friends, the Ohioan simply refused to vote for the admission of any state which still practiced slavery. Lincoln signed the bill on December 31.[40]

Although Lincoln and the radicals were often at odds, it is not true that they were at "war." The President and Republicans like Ashley more often than not had similar purposes. It was on the pace of movement toward their goals that they most often differed.[41] Ashley, for example, was dissatisfied with Lincoln's December, 1862, message to Congress, since it called for a constitutional amendment which would provide for compensation for loyal slaveholders who freed their slaves by 1900. This was far too slow for Ashley, who wanted immediate, uncompensated emancipation. What the radicals were most concerned about in December was to keep

Lincoln from backing away from promulgating the final Emancipation Proclamation. Ashley pressured the President on this matter, but it is wrong to assume that Lincoln was pushed into following a course he did not wish to pursue. This is clearly indicated in a letter which Ashley wrote to his friend, the abolitionist George Cheever, in late December:

> The Proclamation . . . will be issued: the President assured me of that today. So far so good. After the Proclamation, if the President would only infuse vigor and life into the army and all the Departments to act as if they were in earnest (as I have no doubt the President is.) [sic] it would add greatly to our hopes of success.
>
> I was greatly disappointed when I first read the message: but after I saw and talked with the President I felt confident that *in heart*—he was *far in advance of the message*. Let us all unite in demanding a faithful execution of the Proclamation, and forgive the folly and political stupidity of those who have opposed it; if they will now heartily cooperate with us in sustaining it.
>
> I will chearfully [sic] cooperate with all who unite with the President in sustaining his Proclamation of freedom.[42]

Ashley's goal was the abolition of slavery, and he was willing to work with anyone who shared this aim, including and especially Lincoln. The President often used Ashley and the radicals as the cutting edge, enabling him to move in directions which might otherwise have been closed off.

When Lincoln issued the Emancipation Proclamation on January 1, 1863, Ashley was ecstatic. "Today," he joyously exclaimed, "the Rubicon was crossed and the nation, thanks to the persistent demands of her earnest sons, is at last irrevocably committed to the policy of universal emancipation. . . . I may be ever sanguine in my hopes of the future, but it seems to me as if the hour has struck when the Union contemplated by our fathers is about to be realized."[43]

Ashley had now completely triumphed over his conservative opponents, who had tried to ridicule his emancipation commitments. It was due to men like him that the Proclamation had been issued, said the Perrysberg *Journal*. For his efforts he had been called a "radical . . . a howling abolitionist. . . . But his triumph over his adversaries has been complete. He has the satisfaction of knowing that he retains the confidence of the administration—the confidence of his co-laborers in the welfare of our country—the confidence of his constituency."[44] The hour of final victory over the "peculiar institution" was close, but because the Proclamation applied only to areas which the Union did not control, a constitutional amendment would be needed to free all the slaves. This became Ashley's next goal.

During the final session of the Thirty-seventh Congress, Ashley devoted much of his energy to territorial matters. He introduced statehood bills for Nevada, Nebraska, Utah, and Colorado, and a bill to establish a territorial government for Montana. All the bills were recommitted to the Committee on Territories. The Montana measure contained a provision prohibiting slavery, and it passed the House on February 12. In the Senate the name for the territory was changed to Idaho, and the boundaries of the area were adjusted somewhat. Ashley opposed these minor changes, but the bill passed the House on March 3.[45]

Reconstruction was still a matter of concern to the Ohioan, and on January 5, 1863, he tried to introduce a new reconstruction measure. The proposal prohibited slavery and was quite similar to his March, 1862, bill. But Vallandigham and Holman objected to its introduction since no notice had been given, and the Speaker refused to receive it.[46]

Reconstruction had also been on Lincoln's mind. In October, 1862, he had issued instructions to the military governor of Louisiana to hold elections for members of Congress. (New Orleans had been captured on April 25, 1862, and a military governor appointed on June 27, 1862.) Two representatives, Michael Hahn and Benjamin Flanders, were elected. Lincoln wanted them to be seated in order to set a pattern and a precedent for future reconstruction. The House voted to admit the two men. Ashley and radicals such as Stevens, Julian, Kelley, and Bingham all voted no. They objected to the use of presidential power to authorize an election, but more importantly, they did not want to agree to a reconstruction policy established by the executive branch of government. Ashley and his allies looked at reconstruction as a legislative, not an executive, right.[47]

On other issues Ashley gave the President full support and did not break with the majority views of the Republican party. He voted for the Confiscation Act, for a bill which indemnified Lincoln for suspending the writ of habeas corpus, for the National Banking Act, and for a resolution of thanks to General Benjamin Butler. He also worked diligently for passage of a bill authorizing the enlistment of Negroes in the armed services, but it was never approved by the Senate.[48]

Deeply worried about the inroads made by the Democratic party in Ohio in the 1862 election, and troubled by the rise in power and influence of the peace, or Copperhead, faction of that party, Ashley immersed himself in state politics, even before Congress adjourned. He regarded Clement Vallandigham as a great threat to the safety of the nation and he badgered the Copperhead leader on the floor of the House. As for the battered Ohio Union party, Ashley was determined to change its philosophy and make-up. Having blamed the defeats of 1862 on the conservative "Union for the sake of Union" men and their support of the Crittenden resolutions, he wanted to transform the organization into an unconditional Union party, an organization which would not compromise with the rebels or temporize issues or principles, which would work for the election of antislavery men, be loyal to the national government, and support the President's policy of emancipation. After returning to Toledo in early March, he constantly re-iterated these basic criteria in speeches before Union League rallies and war meetings. The one new requirement that Ashley demanded of a reconstructed Union party was opposition to any attempt "at intervention or mediation in our affairs by foreign governments."[49] Only this type of Union party, in Ashley's view, could possibly negate the growing strength of the peace Democrats.

By protesting against federal violation of state and individual rights, arbitrary arrests, the Confiscation Act, and the Emancipation Proclamation, and by indicating that they were ready to accept a compromise solution to the war, the Copperheads, led by Vallandigham, George Pendleton of Cincinnati, and newspaperman Samuel Medary, had become the dominant force within the Ohio Democratic party. By the spring of 1863, the efforts of the peace movement had created tension, which at times slipped into violence. Vallandigham evoked excitement wherever he went in the state. On May 1, in a speech at Mt. Vernon, he was highly critical of the war, accusing the Republicans of needlessly prolonging it. It was, he said, "a war for the freedom of blacks and the enslavement of the whites."

On April 19, 1863, General Ambrose Burnside, head of the Department of Ohio, had issued General Order No. 38, declaring that statements of sympathy for the enemy would no longer be tolerated and that treason, expressed or implied, would not be allowed. Enraged at what he thought was a violation of his order, Burnside had Vallandigham arrested. He was tried by a military court, found guilty, and ordered imprisoned for the duration of the war. The trial was a *fait accompli* before the President learned about it. Lincoln was in an embarrassing situation: upholding the conviction would evoke a bitter reaction from the conservatives, yet overruling Burnside would weaken his position. Since part of General Order No. 38 said, concerning punishment, "or be sent behind our lines into the lines of their friends," Lincoln decided to hand Vallandigham over to the Confederacy.[50]

The whole episode had made Vallandigham into a martyr, and a movement developed for his nomination as the Democratic gubernatorial candidate. At the Democratic convention he easily obtained the prize. The Confederacy allowed Vallandigham to escape, and in July he turned up in Canada. On July 15, he accepted the nomination in exile and his friends waged an active campaign.[51]

Because of the rise of the Union Leagues in Ohio, and because of the efforts of men like Ashley and Benjamin Wade, the radical elements gained increased influence in the Union party. The party convention held on June 17 nominated John Brough for governor. Ashley attended the gathering and voted for Brough. Though the platform did not mention emancipation, Ashley felt he could live with it, for it was much stronger than the previous documents.[52]

By June 23, Ashley had become disturbed over the manner in which the administration was handling sedition cases and arbitrary arrests. On June 1, Burnside had suspended the Chicago *Times* for making disloyal statements, but Lincoln had rescinded the order. A committee of Ohio Democrats was also on its way to Washington to ask Lincoln's permission for Vallandigham to return to Ohio. "We must have *uniformity* & *certainty* in military *'orders,'* " Ashley wrote to Chase. "Order 38 is defied by George E. Pugh & others and it ought to be *revoked* or *enforced*."[53]

Ashley wrote to Lincoln, asking him to clarify his position. He informed the President that if Vallandigham was returned to Ohio, it "would be a terrible blow for the Union cause in the State." Concerning the suppression of newspapers, the Ohioan indicated that it could be justified, and that there might be a need for such action. But the important thing was uniformity. As for General Order No. 38, he wrote Lincoln saying:

> I do not think I should have issued such an "order" as No. 38 had I been in command and I do not know that I would have advised the arrest of Vallandigham, or interfered with the Chicago Times, but after the arrest and the order for suppression they should have been enforced without fear or favor.
>
> *Certainty* and *uniformity* is [sic] what the people want. They would chearfully [sic] sustain No. 38 or one more stringent if approved by the government.[54]

Lincoln followed Ashley's advice, refusing to allow Vallandigham to return to Ohio and attempting to establish uniformity in orders.

The Northern victories at Vicksburg and Gettysburg in early July helped the Union ticket. Ashley campaigned extensively for Brough in his congressional district and constantly defended the administration's policies. He also campaigned in the Western Reserve with George Julian and John Bingham, and by September 28 he was confident of victory. But on September 30, his mood turned somber.

> Some military *ass* [he wrote Chase] had ordered all paroled Solders [sic] in the State to start for their Reg. on the 9th of Oct.—*only 4 days before the election* . . . . If the man who made this order is a *friend* he is an infernally *stupid ass*. If a friend of Vallandigham, I can admire his devilish imprudence . . . . If this order is not revoked we shall lose 8 or 10,000 votes in Ohio—on the *home vote*. . . . Damn the man who issued the order & damn the man who having the power to revoke, permits it to stand.[55]

But Ashley's pessimism was unwarranted. Brough defeated Vallandigham by over 100,000 votes. The Copperheads were completely shattered, and a revitalized Union party was now firmly in control. Ashley interpreted the victory as a command to stamp out treason and rebellion, and as a full endorsement of the Emancipation Proclamation.[56] With this mandate from the people, the Ohio radical was now prepared to carry the fight for emancipation to its logical conclusion. To accomplish this he was ready to cooperate with Lincoln, but if the President moved too slowly, Ashley would not hesitate to protest.

CHAPTER VII

ACHIEVING A DREAM

When he arrived in Washington in December, 1863, for the start of the Thirty-eighth Congress, Ashley had reason to feel proud. He had won a national reputation as an unswerving foe of slavery, a defender of the oppressed, and a man of intelligence, enthusiasm, and conviction. Ashley was a practical politician who knew when to compromise and how much he could achieve at any given moment, but he also had an impatient and impulsive side which could "inflame the coolness of judgment."[1] Although he was a radical, far from doing him any damage, his radicalism had brought him fame. His quick mind and comprehensive approach to problems had won him the respect and admiration of his peers. Fond of a good time, he had a genial nature, and made friends easily. Hardworking, progressive, and generous, the Ohio radical had achieved power and prominence in the House of Representatives. He was now determined to see that before this Congress passed into history, slavery would be dead and a definite plan of reconstruction would be implemented. He was to realize the first desire; the second would be frustrated.

Congress held its first session on December 7, and the House galleries were overflowing. The floor was alive with a sense of urgency. Emerson Etheridge, the southern Unionist from Tennessee, who had served as Clerk of the previous House, was conspiring to give control of the body to a coalition of Democrats and conservative border state Unionists, by excluding several duly elected Republican congressmen from the roll, while placing on it the names of three conservative representatives from Louisiana. Ashley was partly responsible for this predicament. The Democrats' gain of strength in the 1862 elections had given him cause to worry about the future ability of the Republicans to organize the House. Hence he had introduced a bill, instructing the clerk on the proper procedure for composing the roll, which specifically excluded congressmen-elect from occupied rebel states. Ashley's bill did not get out of committee, but a similar proposal by John W. Menzies of Kentucky passed on March 3. Only the names of those members whose credentials indicated that they had been elected in accordance with the laws of their states, or United States law, would be entered on the roll.[2] With this act as legal backing, Etheridge decided to try his coup. But Lincoln and the Republicans were well aware of the plot and were prepared to meet it.

After the House was called to order, Etheridge read the roll of the members-elect, excluding sixteen representatives from Maryland, Missouri, Kansas, Oregon, and West Virginia (on the basis of improper credentials), and added the names of three Louisiana representatives. Thaddeus Stevens immediately protested this action but Etheridge defended it on the basis of the March 3 law. Henry L. Dawes of Massachusetts then introduced a resolution asking that the names of the Maryland members be included in the roll. A move to table this resolution came from the Democratic side. John Stiles, a Democrat from Pennsylvania, asked whether the Dawes motion was in order. Etheridge ruled that the resolution was in order and should be acted on. The acting clerk was gambling that the Democrats and border state Unionists would have enough votes to defeat Dawes's proposal and thus establish hegemony. The gamble failed; the vote went against the conspirators. The House then approved the credentials of the excluded members, refused to dismiss the Louisiana representatives, and elected Schuyler Colfax as Speaker. Edward McPherson of Pennsylvania was eventually elected Clerk. The Republicans, with Lincoln's full support, had turned back their Democratic opponents. The President had even informed Colfax that, if it seemed necessary, force should be used against Etheridge.[3]

During the early part of the session, the Union League of America held a meeting in Washington. The League instructed John Covode, former Pennsylvania congressman, Ashley, and George Boutwell of Massachusetts to urge Lincoln, for the safety of the nation, to remove four conservatives from office: Postmaster-General Montgomery Blair, Attorney-General Edward Bates, General-in-Chief Henry Halleck, and the commanding General in Missouri, John Schofield. The three-man committee met with the President on December 13 and had a very serious discussion. After this meeting Lincoln talked with the Missouri radical B. Gratz Brown, who agreed with the committee's position.[4]

Brown was a leader of the Charcoal, or radical, faction in Missouri politics. The Charcoals despised the conservatism of the Blair family and hated Schofield whom they believed to be an ally of their enemies. The Missouri radicals constantly demanded that Lincoln take some sort of action, and by the middle of 1863 he seemed sympathetic to their cause, telling John

Hay that they were closer to him than the conservatives. The New York *Tribune* speculated that the Union League committee had suggested to the President that he replace Schofield with General Burnside.[5]

Ashley had discussed the Schofield matter with Lincoln on other occasions. The Ohioan wanted General Robert Schenck, who had acted in behalf of the Republicans in the recent elections in Maryland, to be the new commander in Missouri. Schenck had just been elected to Congress from Ohio, and it appears that Ashley had an ulterior motive in promoting him: desire to eliminate a potential political rival from the scene. Lincoln did not dismiss Blair, Bates, or Halleck, but to appease the radicals, he did replace Schofield with the more acceptable William Rosecrans.[6]

On December 14, Ashley introduced a number of bills and resolutions in the House, presenting measures to admit Colorado and Nebraska to statehood, and a bill for a new territory to be called Montana, which were referred to the Committee on Territories. He presented a joint resolution authorizing Negroes in the rebellious districts to be enlisted into the army at equal pay and rations with other soldiers. Their enlistments were to be counted in the quotas of the states that did the recruiting. He also offered a bill, "to repeal the fugitive slave act of eighteen hundred and fifty, and all acts and parts of acts for the rendition of fugitive slaves." Another proposal was to amend the Confiscation Act, so as to eliminate the explanatory resolution which Lincoln had requested in July, 1862. Both bills were sent to the Committee on the Judiciary, where they died.[7]

The most important measure Ashley introduced was a proposition calling for a constitutional amendment prohibiting slavery or involuntary servitude. This was the first such proposal offered in the House. The amendment read as follows:

> Article. Slavery or involuntary servitude, except in punishment of crime, whereof the party shall have been duly convicted, is hereby forever prohibited in all the States of this Union, and in all Territories now owned or which may hereafter be acquired by the United States.[8]

The measure was referred to the Committee on the Judiciary, along with a similar proposal, by Representative James Wilson of Iowa. Resolutions relating to constitutional amendments prohibiting slavery were also presented in the Senate in January, 1864, by John Henderson of Missouri and Charles Sumner.[9]

While the judiciary committees were considering the various proposals, Ashley devoted his time to other legislative matters, particularly to reconstruction. On December 8, 1863, Lincoln issued his Proclamation of Amnesty and Reconstruction. The President set forth guidelines by which loyal governments might be recognized in the rebellious states. Offering a full pardon to all except high Confederate officials and their accomplices, he proposed to reestablish state governments as soon as 10 per cent of those qualified to vote in 1860 had taken the required oath of allegiance. The new states would have to comply with the Confiscation Acts and recognize emancipation. But he allowed the states to make their own laws about former slaves as long as they recognized their personal freedom and provided for their education. Other laws which might "be consistent, as a temporary arrangement, with their present condition as a laboring, landless, and homeless class" were also possible. This last statement rather weakened the commitment to emancipation by implying sanction for a temporary peonage. In an effort to appease Congress, Lincoln pointed out that the legislative body had the ultimate say on who would be admitted to seats, and that other modes of reconstruction were also acceptable.[10]

The reaction to Lincoln's proposals was mixed. Since the proclamation insisted on acceptance of the Emancipation Proclamation and required a loyalty oath it was acceptable to many Republicans. But Chase was unhappy with it, as was the increasingly radical Maryland Unionist Henry Winter Davis, who felt that the President was too lenient with the insurgents. Ashley, who had been cooperating with the President since emancipation, approved of the general outline of the new proposal and immediately began preparing a new reconstruction bill in line with the President's ideas.[11]

A week after Lincoln's message concerning amnesty and reconstruction had been issued, the House began moving to establish a select committee to deal with those parts of the statement which dealt with the rebellious states. The House passed such a proposal and a nine-man select committee was established. Winter Davis was chairman, and Ashley was a member of the committee.[12]

On December 21, Ashley introduced a bill to establish provisional military governments "over the districts of [the] country declared by the President's Proclamation to be in rebellion against the Government of the United States, and to authorize the loyal citizens thereof to organize State governments, republican in form, and for other purposes." Ashley's present bill was completely different from his March, 1862, measure. The territorialization concept was discarded and replaced by his January, 1861, idea: the constitutional guarantee of a republican form of government for each state as the basis for reconstruction. The essence of his 1862 bill had been that in levying war and seeding, the rebellious states had terminated their legal existence as states, but his new proposal maintained that the states were still in existence. This was also Lincoln's view. The rebellious states had simply "renounced their allegiance to the Constitution of the

United States, and abrogated the Republican form of Government therein established." The state suicide, or conquered province idea was no longer part of the bill, though those who maintained that the states had left the Union could interpret Ashley's terminology as upholding their view.[13] Upon examination it will be seen that Ashley's bill followed Lincoln's guidelines in the proclamation, even though the Ohioan did expand on them in certain areas. Lincoln's commitment to emancipation as a condition for reconstruction appears to have been the motivating force behind Ashley's willingness to yield to the President.

In the preamble Ashley stated that it was the duty of Congress, "After the rebellious States have been reduced to obedience, and the citizens thereof are willing to establish State governments under the Constitution, to provide by law for eliciting the will of the loyal people of said States." Until such loyal governments, republican in form, were established, Congress had the obligation "to provide by law for the internal government of such States." For only in this way could the rights of the states and the liberties of the people be secured. Since slavery was incompatible with the concept of a republican form of government, emancipation was to be required, along with a constitutional guarantee for perpetual freedom.[14]

The President was authorized to take possession and occupy insurrectionary districts, and to establish temporary military governments, until the loyal people residing there, in compliance with the act, organized a state government republican in form. Ashley thus followed Lincoln's idea of appointing military governors to administer the districts until the state governments were organized. The governors were also required to see that the laws of the United States, the Constitution, and the President's proclamation were maintained, enforced, and obeyed.[15]

The actual process of reconstruction was to begin when the people of a district indicated to the military governor that they wished to return to obedience to the Constitution. The governor would then authorize the enrollment of all loyal male citizens twenty-one and older, and when this number equaled 10 per cent of the aggregate vote of 1860, he was to call for an election of a constitutional convention. Only those male citizens who had reached the age of twenty-one and had not voluntarily borne arms against the United States or held military or civil office in the Confederacy or in any rebellious state might vote. Before voting, each person, whether previously loyal or disloyal, had to take the loyalty oath prescribed by Lincoln in his Amnesty Proclamation.[16]

Ashley thus followed Lincoln's lead by using the 10 per cent formula and by requiring a loyalty oath. What separated the two men, as Herman Belz has demonstrated, was that Lincoln's plan specified as voters those qualified under the old state laws, meaning white men. Ashley, by simply enfranchising "all loyal male citizens of the age of twenty-one" (with certain exceptions), was calling for Negro suffrage.[17] This was still a highly radical idea, toward which Lincoln was moving only slowly and in limited fashion. Ashley was also much harsher than the President in his exclusion of rebels from political life.

The new state constitutions had to be republican in form "and not repugnant to the Constitution of the United States" or the Emancipation Proclamation. Certain specific criteria had to be met by the new constitutions. No person who had held civil or military office in a rebellious state or in the Confederate government would be allowed to vote for governor, or members of the legislature, or to hold any office until pardoned by the state legislature. There could also be no recognition of Confederate debt. The freedom of slaves who had been emancipated by acts of Congress or by presidential proclamation, had to be "recognized and guaranteed by the new Constitution." Finally, after the adoption of the constitution, slavery was "forever prohibited in said state."[18]

If the state constitution met the foregoing stipulations, it was to be presented to the people for ratification. If a majority of the voters approved it, the President would then issue a proclamation "declaring the government formed by such Constitution, and none other, to be the constituted government of said state." Congressmen elected under this constitution would be "entitled to appear in the Senate and House of Representatives." Unless the new constitution met the specific requirements, the state would remain subject to the provisional government and such laws as Congress might prescribe. When the people were ready to draw up a new constitution in conformity with the act, the President might initiate another election for a constitutional convention.

Ashley's bill was thus much more detailed than Lincoln's proclamation and spelled out the specific steps to be followed for reconstruction to take place. Lincoln always tried to avoid any set pattern; Ashley did not. Some people criticized the 10 per cent feature and the use of military governors in both plans. The procedure for acceptance of the new constitutions outlined in Ashley's bill worried some legal scholars, since they believed that after adoption the state could fall quickly into the hands of pardoned ex-rebels.[19]

As for the judiciary, Ashley's bill stipulated that federal district courts were to have jurisdiction in the rebellious states. Existing law was to remain in force. But all existing state laws and codes on slavery were null and void. All those qualified to vote could serve on juries; this included Negroes. All remaining slaves were to be freed and any person attempting to re-enslave them could be fined between fifteen hundred and five thousand dollars and be imprisoned for not less than five or more than twenty years.[20]

Reaction to Ashley's bill was quite favorable and for the moment it appeared that Lincoln and the Congress agreed about reconstruction. But the President's actions on Louisiana quickly ended this short honeymoon. On December 24, he ordered General Nathaniel P. Banks, Commander of the Department of the Gulf, to set up "a free-state" organization in Louisiana. Banks acted accordingly and prepared to hold elections for state officers under the old constitution. The radicals were appalled. Ashley, especially angry because Banks had acted without congressional authorization, said: "I hold that neither General Banks nor any other general, in command of a district, has authority to order an election for State offices in any of the rebel States, under any fundamental law, whether it be martial law or civil law." It was an unauthorized intrusion of military power which Ashley could not sanction. Winter Davis and Stevens also objected to Lincoln's action. The House was rapidly growing weary of presidential reconstruction.[21]

Ashley's December 21 reconstruction bill had been sent to the Committee on the Rebellious States. With the harmony which seemed to have been established between Lincoln and the Congress now dissolving, Ashley's measure underwent changes. On February 15, Winter Davis introduced a new reconstruction bill from the committee. Though similar to Ashley's bill, the Davis measure was a direct challenge to presidential policy. Ashley, angry over Lincoln's and Banks's methods, fully supported the new proposal.[22]

Like Ashley's measure, the Davis bill based reconstruction on the concept of guaranteeing to each state a republican form of government. But it receded from Ashley's proposal for black suffrage, by calling for the enrollment of all white male citizens living in a state, each of whom would be required to take an oath supporting the Constitution. The bill did retain the 10 per cent idea, but added an extra or "ironclad oath." Those who wanted to vote for delegates to a constitutional convention had to swear that they had neither held Confederate nor state office nor voluntarily borne arms against the federal government. This then entailed an oath of past as well as future loyalty. As in Ashley's bill, the new constitution had to prohibit slavery and did not require confiscation of property.[23]

Debate on the Davis bill began on March 22, and Ashley expected to speak that day or the next, but delays prevented him from talking on reconstruction until March 30. When he did speak, he stated that Congress had put off dealing with the problem of reconstruction too long; it must act now. Indicating that the Davis bill contained no set theory for reconstruction, he said:

> Whether the rebel usurpation has destroyed the constitutional governments of the seceded States, or whether those State governments are simply suspended or in abeyance by reason of the abdication of their officers, or whether by the acts of treason and rebellion on the part of their citizens and constituted authorities, the States thus in rebellion have committed State suicide, the committee [on the Rebellious States] have thought best to leave to the determination of each member for himself.

He himself still leaned toward the territorialization theory, believing that no state governments existed in the South. The rebellious states had forfeited their rights as states, and the notion "a State once a State is always a State" was false. But as a practical man he wanted a reconstruction bill which would assure the peace and stability of the nation, and to accomplish this there was no theory to which he would not adhere, as long as the new states had governments republican in form and constitutions prohibiting slavery.[24]

One major point in his presentation was that the Constitution gave Congress the right to legislate on, or set the conditions for, reconstruction. Thus neither the President nor any general had the right to carry out reconstruction without congressional authority. No power in the Constitution granted the executive department such rights. "I believe," Ashley said, "this entire power is vested by the Constitution in Congress, and not in the President." Lincoln's actions were usurpations of legislative power, and Congress had to act to stop this dangerous precedent. Ashley was always concerned about the growth of executive power at the expense of Congress. But he was not seeking a fight with Lincoln. He wanted to work in harmony with the President, and Ashley spoke authoritatively when he said that Lincoln did not intend to recognize governments formed under his proclamation, "without the concurrence of Congress."[25]

The 10 per cent provision did not satisfy Ashley. He had incorporated this provision into his own measure, he said, in an attempt to make it harmonize with Lincoln's proclamation. If an amendment to the present bill increasing the percentage of loyal voters required to form a state government was offered, he would vote for it. Summing up his position, he said: "I believe the democratic idea the better one, that the MAJORITY and not the MINORITY ought to be invested with the organization and government of a State. Certainly it is safer to entrust a State government to the maintenance of a MAJORITY than to ONE-TENTH claiming to be loyal, while NINE-TENTHS are openly disloyal." But if Congress deemed 10 per cent safe, "so be it."[26]

He then went on to attack Banks's whole course of action in Louisiana, calling it "a most wanton and defenseless assumption of military power." "Let us see to it," he said, "that there is no repetition of those acts by any general. . . . Enact this bill as a law, and you insure the liberation, regeneration and restoration of the South. Refuse to pass it, and the loyal men of the South are left to the mercy and caprice of military rulers."[27] Ashley was indeed a radical, but he was anything but a single-minded fanatic.

The Davis bill was later amended. The 10 per cent plan was dropped and replaced by a clause requiring a 50 per cent participation to initiate the process of forming new state governments. Thus amended the measure passed the House on May 4, and then went to the Senate, where Wade took charge. The Senate did not act on the bill until July 1. Wade, realizing that an amendment calling for black suffrage might jeopardize the bill, agreed to drop the idea, though he personally favored such a provision. A substitute motion by B. Gratz Brown, which proposed that Congress declare its intention not to count the presidential votes of any seceded states until the rebellion was suppressed, passed over Wade's bitter objection. The House refused to consent to the change. On July 2, Wade pushed through the original proposal without amendments and the Wade-Davis bill was born.[28]

Now the question was whether Lincoln would sign the measure. The answer was no. Unwilling to be committed to a definite plan of reconstruction and not wanting to interrupt the process of restoration which he had already started, Lincoln could not accept the Wade-Davis bill. Furthermore, he disliked the "ironclad oath" with its demand for past loyalty. Thus, as Congress was adjourning, and to the utter dismay of the radicals, he pocket vetoed the bill.[29]

While the debate over the Davis bill had been going on in the House, the Senate had turned its attention to the Thirteenth Amendment. The Senate Judiciary Committee, after considering the various proposals, reported the following joint resolution to amend the Constitution:

> Neither slavery nor involuntary servitude except as punishment for crime, whereof the party shall have been duly convicted, shall exist within the United States, or any place subject to their jurisdiction.[30]

The wording was slightly different from the form Ashley had originally used in his resolution in December, but the meaning was the same. In this sense he was one of the originators of the Thirteenth Amendment. After debating the resolution for months, the Senate approved it on April 8, 1864. But on June 15, the House vote fell short of the two-thirds needed for passage. Ashley, who was in charge of the parliamentary maneuvers for the amendment, then changed his vote to the negative, in order to be able to move for a reconsideration at a future date.[31]

As the days passed Ashley made no move toward a motion to reconsider and on June 28, Holman of Indiana asked him whether he intended to call up the defeated resolution during this session. Not believing the amendment could carry, the Ohioan answered: "The record is made up, and we must go to the country on the issue thus presented. When the verdict of the people is rendered next November I trust this Congress will return determined to ingraft that verdict into the National Constitution." He then gave notice that he would call up the resolution in December.[32]

Ashley also concerned himself with other legislative matters during this session. He led to passage in the House bills to admit Colorado and Nebraska to statehood, and he also helped to carry a Senate measure for Nevada statehood. Each bill had a section stating that the constitutions in the new states had to contain a prohibition against slavery. An Ashley bill establishing a territory of Montana out of the northeastern portion of Idaho passed, although an attempt to include black suffrage in the proposal failed. A substitute measure resembling his proposal to repeal fugitive slave laws passed on June 13. He also, at considerable political risk, voted in favor of eliminating the $300 substitute clause from the enrollment bill, though this amendment failed. Finally, along with other radicals like Davis, Julian, Boutwell, Garfield, Kelley, and Stevens, he voted against a bill which would have promoted Grant to Lieutenant-General.[33] The radicals doubted Grant's antislavery leanings.

At the same time that Ashley was concerning himself with congressional affairs, he was also involved in the transcending issue of 1864—the presidential election. Although, in December, 1863, Ashley had been satisfied with Lincoln, he still privately nursed presidential hopes for his friend, Treasury Secretary Chase. With the breakdown of relations over reconstruction, Ashley began actively to oppose Lincoln's renomination. Chase's friends were now determined to put him forward. Led by Senator Samuel Pomeroy of Kansas, head of the Republican National Executive Committee, Chase adherents distributed a pamphlet and a circular praising Chase and attacking Lincoln's record, stating that he could not be reelected. Ashley was one of the congressmen who allowed this material to be mailed under his franking privileges. The publication of these documents proved to be an embarrassment to Chase, and when the Ohio legislature endorsed Lincoln's renomination, the secretary withdrew from contention. In an effort to make sure that the secretary of the treasury did not again attempt a run for the presidency, political opponents, such as Fernando Wood of New York and Frank and Montgomery Blair, attacked him at every opportunity.[34]

For those who opposed Lincoln time was rapidly running out. The Republican convention was scheduled to begin on June 7, and a movement to postpone the opening failed. A group of dissidents then turned their energies toward nominating General John C. Frémont on a separate ticket. Ashley was asked to support a call for this event, but he refused. Since Ashley believed that Frémont was politically naive, he felt the movement for him was ruinous folly. Ashley denounced the general as "an ass." To replace Lincoln with a man of Chase's brilliance was a risk worth taking; to replace him with a discredited general was not. John Hay, Lincoln's secretary, believed that Ashley was now inclined to support the regular ticket. On May 31, a convention in Cleveland nominated Frémont for the presidency. Faced with the choice of Lincoln or Frémont, Ashley at this point was willing to stick with the President.[35]

Thus when the Republican convention convened in Baltimore, the disenchanted antislavery men had no one to turn to. Popular with the rank and file, Lincoln was easily renominated. The Tennessee War Democrat, Andrew Johnson, was nominated for Vice President. The platform incorporated the only real concession made to the radicals, the plank demanding adoption of a constitutional amendment abolishing slavery. Many disgruntled Republicans disliked the results of the meeting, but for the moment, were ready to accept Lincoln as the best available choice. When one of Ashley's constituents protested about Lincoln's not having crushed the rebellion in four years, the Ohioan replied, "this was unreasonable, as the Lord has not crushed the devil in a longer time."[36]

But the veto of the Wade-Davis bill soured Ashley's support for Lincoln. The radicals were furious about the veto. Sumner told Chase that there was "intense indignation" against the President because of the veto. Davis's rage against Lincoln was boundless, and along with other radicals, he began a movement to displace Lincoln as the Republican nominee.[37]

The radicals' answer to the veto was the Wade-Davis Manifesto of August 5. Berating Lincoln, it declared that he had defied the judgment of Congress and that "a more studied outrage on the legislative authority of the people has never been perpetrated . . . ." Many Republicans reacted negatively to the manifesto. It was condemned by *Harper's Weekly*, the Chicago *Tribune*, and the *New York Times*. Although Ashley refused to sign the document, he was sympathetic to the Wade-Davis position.[38]

The course of the war also caused Ashley to become weary of Lincoln. In March, 1864, the Ohioan had visited General Grant's headquarters at the President's request. Impressed by what he had seen and heard, Ashley returned to Washington feeling confident. But the war had not gone well during May and June; the ordeal of Cold Harbor in particular had shocked the North. A visit to the Army of the Potomac in mid-July only increased

Ashley's disenchantment. Talking to Major T. T. Eckert, he reported that "he found a good deal of discontent and mutinous spirit among staff officers . . . . A good deal of McClellanism . . . was manifested, especially by officers of very high rank."[39] Extremely distressed by these events, Ashley now firmly believed that Lincoln could not be reelected.

After the President's veto of the Wade-Davis bill, Ashley began plotting to force Lincoln from the ticket. He was trying to make common cause with the War Democrats in behalf of his good friend Benjamin Butler. After talking to Thurlow Weed of New York, Thomas Corwin, newspaper editor John Forney, and John Hickman of Pennsylvania, Ashley wrote Butler that "they all agree with singular unanimity that such a movement as we talked of ought to be. . . . All did not say that they would support it, but I *know* that a majority with whom I exchanged opinions will support it. . . . The trouble will be to get the preliminary steps taken to successfully start it." Enclosed in the letter was a proposed draft call for a Union and War Democracy meeting to be held at Cooper Institute in New York City, on August 17: "For the purpose of the consultation and *organization* preparatory to the Presidential canvass." The radical document invited all those who favored a vigorous war policy, enlistment of Negro troops, abolition of slavery, the single-term principle, the enforcement of the Monroe Doctrine, the election of a president who consulted and took the advice of his cabinet and who opposed arbitrary arrests by executive decree, to attend the meeting.[40] But as Ashley had accurately pointed out, it would be hard to get such a movement started.

Ashley sent the call to friends in the East and urged them to obtain support for it. He said that they could change the call if they found it unsatisfactory. The Ohioan believed that the War Democrats were ready to join such a movement, but it was obvious that his call was too radical for them. But as usual, the congressman was planning for the future as well as the present. He told Chase that he was pledged by the convention that renominated him to vote for Lincoln, but he was "free to act with loyal Democrats in advising the permanent organization of the War Democrats into a National party, which properly managed could take possession of the . . . Government in 1868—even if *they fail now*." He expected to be a member of such a movement within two years and hoped that the government could be placed "in the hands of radical men in 1868."[41] But Ashley was fooling himself.

The disorganization of the stop-Lincoln forces, and the radical nature of his call brought Ashley's plans to naught. Yet along with New Yorkers like David Dudley Field, George Opdyke, Theodore Tilton, and J. K. Hubert; and people like George Wilkes, editor of *Wilkes Spirit of the Times*; abolitionist George Cheever, radical Winter Davis, and Butler's chief aid, John Shaffer, Ashley continued trying to force Lincoln to withdraw. Numerous meetings were held. Various proposals were put forth. The result of these efforts was a call for a meeting at Cincinnati on September 28. The meeting never took place. When on September 3 the North heard that Atlanta had fallen to General William T. Sherman, the mood of the country changed in Lincoln's favor. Republican detractors, who hated the Democratic nominee George McClellan more than they disliked Lincoln, were soon stumping for the President.[42]

The one remaining stumbling block in Lincoln's path was Frémont. Senator Zachariah Chandler of Michigan had been quietly working on this problem. He sought a compromise, trading off Frémont's withdrawal for Montgomery Blair's dismissal from the Cabinet. Early in September, Chandler won Lincoln's approval for the project. Then he went to New York to try to persuade Frémont. The Pathfinder refused to commit himself before consulting with his advisors. Then, Frémont decided to withdraw unconditionally. Disturbed, Chandler dashed back to Washington and told Lincoln that Frémont had met the conditions for Blair's removal. After some doubt about the next step, Lincoln finally agreed to dismiss Blair. With their hated conservative enemy removed from power, Ashley, Chase, and other radicals gave Lincoln their full support.[43]

Ashley was also concerned about his own reelection campaign. With the help of his friends and the support of local newspapers he had easily secured renomination on May 24. His Democratic opponent was a one-legged war hero, Colonel A. V. Rice, of Putnam County. During the canvass the old charges of corruption in Colorado were flung at Ashley by a group of Republican conservatives led by Clark Waggoner, who sided with Rice.[44]

Taking credit for the general authorship of the Thirteenth Amendment, and voicing strong support for the national ticket, Ashley waged his usual fast-moving, aggressive campaign. John Sherman, George Julian, and John A. Bingham all spoke in his support. Colonel Rice refused to endorse McClellan and backed Lincoln. An old Ashley political antagonist, General James B. Steedman, came to Rice's assistance. The election was held on October 11, and the home vote gave Rice a clear lead. But the soldier vote went overwhelmingly for Ashley; and he was elected by over 800 votes.[45]

Immediately after the election Ashley went to New York and Michigan to campaign for the President. On November 8, Lincoln, with the help of the soldier vote, was reelected. Ashley wrote to the President congratulating him on his great victory. He also had a request. Chase had resigned as Secretary of the Treasury on June 30, and the subsequent death of Chief Justice Roger B. Taney had created an opening on the Supreme Court.

Realizing that the Supreme Court might soon be required to pass on issues relating to reconstruction, Ashley urged that Chase be appointed the new Chief Justice. "I know," Ashley said, "the appointment of Mr. Chase would give great satisfaction to the earnest men of the country." Lincoln had previously promised Charles Sumner that he would make Chase Chief Justice, and he kept his word despite strong conservative opposition. The President, anxious to continue the better relationship which he had developed with the radicals during the campaign, recommended Chase's appointment on December 6.[46]

On November 29 a banquet honoring Ashley was held at the Oliver House in Toledo. Letters of praise for the Toledoan were received from all over the country. Chase called him a true and faithful friend, and said: "To him as Chairman of the important Committee on Territories, more than to any other man, do we owe the consecration of all new States to Liberty by irrepealable provisions of fundamental law." His dear friend Sumner praised Ashley as a statesman of practical wisdom. As far as the Thirteenth Amendment was concerned, Sumner declared, "Nobody has done more for it, practically, than your Representative." Deeply moved, Ashley responded to these accolades by calling the most recent election "a victory which proclaims with trumpet tongue *'Liberty throughout all the land unto all the inhabitants thereof.'*"[47]

The second session of the Thirty-eighth Congress convened on December 5, and Ashley's main concerns continued to be passage of the constitutional amendment prohibiting slavery and passage of a reconstruction bill. Ever since the resolution for the amendment had been defeated on June 15, Ashley had been working for its triumph. He had drawn up a list of thirty-six Democrats and border-state Unionists who had voted against the resolution, and worked tirelessly to persuade some of them to change their votes. At this time political opinion did not agree on the joint resolution's chances in the House. Sumner was confident of success. The Boston *Commonwealth*, the New York *Independent*, and the *National Anti-Slavery Standard* were doubtful.[48] But with characteristic tenacity Ashley was determined that the resolution should pass.

In his annual message to Congress on December 6, Lincoln specifically recommended the adoption of the Thirteenth Amendment, reminding the House that the recent election made it certain that the next Congress would pass it. Lincoln had been quietly working for passage of the amendment. He had used his patronage to facilitate the admission of Nevada into the Union, in case an additional state was needed for ratification. If the House did not act, he was also quite ready to call a special session of Congress.[49]

On December 15, Ashley gave notice that he planned to call up the joint resolution on the constitutional amendment for reconsideration on January 6. Believing that he would call for a vote on the measure on January 9, Ashley sent out a printed circular to every Republican member of the House on December 25, asking for his help. At this moment he felt that he still lacked nine votes of the necessary two-thirds needed for passage. He hoped that eight to ten members of the opposition might still change their votes, but he was certain that there were fifty-six votes against the resolution. In a handwritten note at the bottom of the circular he said, "*You must help us* [with] *one vote*. Don't you know of a Sinner in the opposition who is on praying ground?"[50]

On January 6, Ashley brought the joint resolution before the House and made a strong plea for its passage. He opened his speech by quoting Lincoln. "If slavery is not wrong, nothing is wrong." Slavery, he declared emphatically, was the cause of the war, and the nation must rid itself of this evil. The fathers of the Constitution did not intend it to be used to defend injustice. Basing his arguments on the fifth article of the Constitution, Ashley then pointed out that the Constitution could be amended if three-fourths of the states now represented in Congress ratified the proposition. He also denied that the rebel state governments still existed, reiterated his territorialization theory, and told the House:

> The duty of the true statesman is to provide that the enemy, once vanquished, shall never again be permitted for the same cause to reorganize and make war upon the nation. Pass this joint resolution . . . and I am sure the nation will adopt it with shouts of acclamation, and when once adopted, you know . . . and I know, and the enemies of the government know, that we shall have peace, and that no such rebellion will ever be possible again.

> Pass this amendment, and the gloomy shadow of slavery will never again darken the fair fame of our country or tarnish the glory of democratic institutions in the land of Washington. . . . I implore gentlemen to forget party, and remember that we are making a record, not only for ourselves individually, but for the nation and the cause of free government throughout the world.[51]

A partisan debate on the joint resolution now consumed the energies of the House. On January 7, believing that he still did not have the necessary votes, Ashley announced that he would not press for a decision on the ninth. By January 12, he still hoped for success, but Speaker Colfax who was also counting heads, believed the radicals would fail. Being practical, Ashley moved on January 13 to postpone further consideration of the resolution for a few weeks.[52]

With Lincoln's help, Ashley had been making an all-out effort to round up needed votes. In mid-January, the President himself persuaded Congressman James Rollins of Missouri to vote yes and implored the young legislator to try to convert his fellow Missourians in the House. At the same time Ashley was arranging that a number of Democrats should either absent themselves from the House when the vote was taken, or vote yes. Congressman Albert Riddle of Ohio was told that Anson Herrick, a Democrat from New York, had been informed that his brother's chances for a federal job would be enhanced if he voted in favor of the joint resolution. Alexander H. Coffroth of Pennsylvania was promised support when the next House considered the results of his recently contested election. On January 18, John Nicolay, one of Lincoln's secretaries, went to see the President on Ashley's request: Officers of the Camden and Amboy Railroad had let Ashley know that if he arranged the postponement of the Rantin railroad bill which was against their interests, they would try to influence the votes of certain New Jersey Democrats. Ashley went to speak to his friend Sumner, who was in charge of the measure in the Senate, but the senator was reluctant to put off considering the bill. Lincoln, when informed of this situation, told Nicolay, "I can do nothing with Mr. Sumner in these matters."

No direct evidence indicates that Sumner became involved in the behind-the-scenes manipulations, but on the day of the vote on the joint resolution, Democratic Congressman Andrew Rogers of New Jersey was absent; he was too ill to attend. Apparently, Samuel S. ("Sunset") Cox, the Ohio Democrat, helped keep Rogers at home. Secretary of State Seward and the highly organized lobby that worked at his direction should be credited with six votes for the resolution. As Thaddeus Stevens later commented, "The greatest measure of the nineteenth century was passed by corruption, aided and abetted by the purest man [Lincoln] in America."[53] Lincoln and Seward had always been pragmatists, and when necessary, so was Ashley.

On January 24, Ashley sent out another printed circular, informing all Republican congressmen that their presence in the House on the thirty-first of January was absolutely essential. The climactic vote was to be taken on that date. "It is now believed," he said, *"that if every administration member is present*, a sufficient number of the opposition will either absent themselves or vote with us to secure its passage." Until the very day of the vote no one was certain of the final outcome. The Toledo *Commercial* was doubtful of passage, but Ashley was confident that he had done his job well.[54]

On the morning of January 31, a new obstacle appeared. Rumors were circulating in Washington that peace commissioners from the South were on their way to the city. If this were true, the joint resolution would be defeated. Ashley quickly wrote Lincoln asking him whether there was any truth to the story. The President answered immediately: "So far as I know, there are no peace commissioners in the city or likely to be in it."[55] Armed with this assurance, Ashley prepared for his proudest moment.

On January 31, the House galleries were crowded with eager, anxious spectators. Vice President Hannibal Hamlin, Chief Justice Chase, Postmaster-General William Dennison, Treasury Secretary William Fessenden, foreign diplomats, and various other dignitaries were present. As the mover of the motion to reconsider, Ashley was given the floor, but he gave up his time to members of the opposition who wished to explain themselves. First, old Archibald McAllister of Pennsylvania had a note about his yes vote read to the House. Then Anson Herrick and Alexander Coffroth told why they were changing their votes to yes. Other Democrats used the occasion to attack the joint resolution. As time passed, Republicans gathered around Ashley's desk and complained of the delay. Thaddeus Stevens berated Ashley for allowing the debate to drag on. But the Ohioan remained calm: he was confident of victory.[56]

Finally a roll call vote was taken on a motion to table the motion to reconsider. It failed, 111 nays to 57 yeas. The House now voted 112 to 57 to reconsider the action of June 15, 1864. A shudder passed over the galleries as the vote was announced: it was less than the two-thirds needed to pass the joint resolution.

Ashley now refused to yield to a motion to postpone, and amid great tension a roll call on the resolution began. Anxious spectators fidgeted as, one by one, representatives rose to cast their votes. When the balloting was completed, an intense hush came over the House. Finally the Clerk announced the results—119 yes, 56 no, 8 not voting. The measure had carried by three votes.

Pandemonium broke loose. Members on the floor jumped up and down and threw their hats into the air. Some cried with joy. Women in the galleries waved handkerchiefs. Shouts of "Hurrah for Freedom!" and "Glory enough for one day!" filled the hall. No one could recall witnessing such a scene in the House before.

An overjoyed Ashley rushed away from the tumult, jumped into a carriage, and drove over to the War Department to inform his ally Stanton of the result. He then sent the following telegram to the Toledo *Commercial*: "Glory to God in the highest! Our country is free!"[57] The hope of a lifetime was now reality.

Ashley deserves full credit for guiding the Thirteenth Amendment to passage in the House, and contemporaries were well aware of his achievement. The *National Anti-Slavery Standard* wrote: "The credit belongs principally to Mr. Ashley of Ohio. He has been at work the whole session, and it is his management that secured the passage of the Joint Resolution." The *Independent*, the New York *Tribune*, the Toledo *Commercial*, all lavished praise on the Ohio congressman. Years later, James G. Blaine of Maine and Henry Dawes of Massachusetts concurred with this assessment. Dawes wrote that Ashley had been the first to move the amendment, and "to him more by far than to any one else, is due its reserection [sic] after its enemies had supposed they had laid it in its grave."[58]

At the very time that he was seeking votes for the Thirteenth Amendment, Ashley was also absorbed in his second major concern—reconstruction. Since Lincoln's victory, a number of Republicans were prepared for a compromise solution to the problem of reconstruction. On December 15, Ashley reported such a measure from the select Committee on the Rebellious States. The proposal was like the original Wade-Davis bill, but with two major changes. One called for the recognition of Louisiana under Lincoln's 10 per cent plan, which meant accepting Banks's actions. The other provided that Negroes should be voters and jurors.

This compromise bill, it was said, was agreed to by the reconstruction committee of both houses and the seventh section (dealing with Louisiana) had been framed after consultation with Lincoln. Many thought that the measure would pass quickly and be signed by the President. It seems likely that Ashley agreed to the compromise reconstruction proposals because the Banks faction in Louisiana had recently promised to vote for the emancipation amendment in Congress, if the state was again admitted into the Union.[59]

Lincoln, however, was dissatisfied with two parts of the bill. Meeting with General Banks and Mongomery Blair on December 18, the President indicated that some people might find it objectionable to have blacks made jurors and voters. The second reservation concerned the section dealing with emancipation. Lincoln believed that the clause though "not objectionable" was beyond the scope of his proclamation. Hay reported that except for these qualifications, Lincoln was satisfied with the measure, and that he and Banks saw no reason to fight against it, since Congress wanted no more than a hand in reconstruction.[60]

Two days later Ashley reported H. R. 602 back from committee with amendments, in line with Lincoln's criticism. The section on emancipation now stated "that all persons held to involuntary servitude or labor in the States or parts of States in which such persons have been declared free by any proclamation of the President, are hereby emancipated." This recognized Lincoln's proclamation as the source of authority, and limited emancipation to areas covered by the 1863 edict. Suffrage and jury duty were now limited to loyal white citizens and Negroes who had served in the army or navy. Ashley had hoped to pass the bill on December 20, but final consideration of the measure was postponed until after the Christmas holidays. Since at that time it appeared likely that the House would approve the bill, Ashley did not object to the delay.[61]

But many of the nation's leading antislavery men were unhappy with the compromise proposal. Abolitionist Wendell Phillips feared that if Louisiana were readmitted, a dangerous precedent would be established. The Boston *Commonwealth* was disturbed by the seventh section of the bill. If Congress authorized the return of Louisiana to the Union, it asked, "What resistance can it make when he [Lincoln] brings Florida and Alabama along?" Upon returning from the recess, the radicals seemed more inclined to press for a stronger bill.[62] Criticism of the compromise appears to have influenced Ashley to strengthen his proposals for reconstruction.

On January 7, he introduced two additional amendments to his measure. The first change was a guarantee not only for freedom but for "equality of civil rights before the law . . . to all persons in said states." If this proposal was not radical enough, the second amendment completely destroyed any chance for a compromise. Ashley and the members of the Committee on the Rebellious States now stipulated that Congress would recognize the state governments of Louisiana and Arkansas only if they submitted to the 50 per cent enrollment process and incorporated into their constitutions articles required of all Confederate states—prohibition of slavery, repudiation of all Confederate debt, and exclusion of certain civilian and military officeholders from political privilege. Thus the Louisiana and Arkansas governments set up under Lincoln's 10 per cent plan would be invalid.

Conservative and moderate Republicans immediately grasped the significance of the changes and withdrew their support from Ashley's measure. They thus effectively killed any real chance for passage which the bill might have had. Moderate Republicans James Wilson of Pennsylvania and Thomas Eliot of Massachusetts introduced substitute proposals which undercut the new Ashley amendments.[63] If they really intended the measure to pass, Ashley and his allies simply misread the mood of the country and of their more moderate colleagues.

The reconstruction bill finally reached the floor of the House on January 16. Ashley, on instructions from the Committee on Rebellious States, presented the January 7 substitute for the original bill. The measure was immediately attacked. Radical Republican William D. Kelley of Pennsylvania

tried to broaden the suffrage sections to include all male citizens who were
able to read the Constitution, and made a stirring plea for Negro suffrage.
Moderates like Eliot objected to legislating a rigid plan for reconstruction.
On January 17, Wilson moved to postpone consideration of the bill for
two weeks. The radicals protested, but to no avail; the motion to delay
passed 103 to 34.[64]

At this point chances for the passage of any reconstruction measure
seemed rather meager. Ashley and his fellow committee members saw their
programs opposed from all directions. Abolitionist Gerrit Smith condemned Ashley for not including black suffrage in the January 16 measure; it
would be morally wrong, said Smith, to leave the Negroes unprotected
from their enemies. On the other hand the moderates believed the bill
went too far; moreover, they did not want a set plan of reconstruction.[65]
But Ashley and the select committee were not ready to quit.

On February 18, Ashley brought forward another version of the bill.
This measure, an attempt to please all factions, was a hodge-podge which
pleased no one. There were to be no racial qualifications for the enrollment process and for voting for delegates to a state constitutional convention. The procedural features of the bill remained the same, and the guarantee of civil equality was also maintained. But Tennessee, Louisiana, and
Arkansas were given provisional recognition. Tennessee was required to
include in its constitution prohibition of slavery, repudiation of Confederate debts, and exclusion of rebel officeholders from political rights.
Louisiana and Arkansas had to meet the same stipulations, but they did
not have to adopt the 50 per cent enrollment process. The last section of
the measure included the remarkable proposal to recognize the rebel state
governments as the loyal governments, if they would surrender, and if
their governors and legislatures would swear allegiance to the Constitution
and ratify the Thirteenth Amendment. Ashley later explained that he did
not think this section really important. He had included it only "to strength-
en the hands of Union men in rebel States, to stop the mouths of northern
rebels and approve by act of Congress the outstanding Proclamation of
the President." Henry Dawes voiced the opinions of most conservative and
moderate Republicans against the bill, and again killed any chance for
passage.[66]

Ashley, on February 21, withdrew the bill and offered a final substitute.
This measure did not recognize Tennessee, Louisiana, or Arkansas and
restored the "white only" qualification for loyal citizens, with an exception made for Negro soldiers. In a rather bitter speech defending the bill,
Ashley explained how, at the beginning of the session, he had introduced a
proposal in an effort to reach an accommodation with all sides. The measure had included, against his better judgment, a recognition of Tennessee,

Louisiana, and Arkansas, in an effort to acquire acceptance of Negro suffrage which he concluded was of "paramount importance." But his efforts had been fruitless, and he ruefully admitted "that no bill providing for the reorganization of loyal State governments in the rebel States can pass the Congress." His ally Henry Winter Davis also defended the bill, but it was a futile exercise, as the House voted 91 to 64 to table the whole matter.[67]

The day after, Ashley tried to amend James Wilson's reconstruction bill, by substituting his February 21 measure. Kelley then moved to strike out the word *white* but was not allowed to do so. Ashley did not expect the bill to pass, but he wanted a vote on the Negro suffrage issue. He hoped for more forceful action by the Thirty-ninth Congress and clearly stated his position on the subject: "If there is to be any limitation of the right of suffrage in the reorganization of the rebel governments, for one I am determined," he declared, "that it shall not be one of caste, of color, of nationality. If there is to be any restriction let it be one of intelligence, and let no man vote unless he can read in the English language the Constitution of the United States." A motion to table the bill and the various amendments passed 80 to 65.[68]

Thus Ashley's desire to have Congress establish a set policy of reconstruction was frustrated. Most Republicans were not ready for his advanced ideas on reconstruction. Yet, throughout the session abolitionists had criticized him for reporting out bills which did not include black suffrage. Ashley felt that he was being attacked unjustly. He had been against the "white only" clause, but his committee had overruled him. In a letter to New York abolitionist Theodore Tilton, Ashley defended his position and indicated that he fully endorsed the concept of Negro suffrage. As for the term *white* in his last reconstruction bill, he said: "You know enough about our rules to understand that without the consent of the House, after the previous question is called I could not get my amendment in, and so consented to 'write' the word *White* in the printed bill—with the understanding that Judge Kelley of Pa.—should move to strike out the word 'White' and thus give us a fair vote."[69] But Kelley, as has been shown, was not allowed to make his motion.

Ashley's other activities during this session were of minor significance. Congress adjourned on March 2; two days later, Lincoln was inaugurated for a second term. On April 9, the North heard that Lee had surrendered at Appomattox Court House. The war was almost over, and the people in the North began preparing for a glorious celebration.

CHAPTER VIII

IMPARTIAL SUFFRAGE

On the evening of April 14, while attending a play in Ford's Theater, President Lincoln was shot; he died on the following day. Ashley was in Toledo when he heard the news. His initial response was shock, sorrow, and uncertainty. Writing to Sumner, he said, "the nation is shrouded in gloom and every loyal heart is stricken with anguish. What shall we do? What do our friends propose? Had I better come to Washington or not?" The Ohio radical then sent a note of encouragement to President Johnson. "The prayer of every loyal heart in the nation is that God will bless, preserve and keep you from all harm. I hope all is for the best. You have been called by a most solemn event and in a perilous hour to discharge the most difficult and most responsible office on Earth."[1] Ashley was trying to establish a harmonious relationship with the new President, but this would prove to be impossible.

The crime at Ford's Theater stunned the country, but it had a peculiar effect on the radicals. The change in chief executives seemed to solve many problems. Julian reported that "The universal feeling among radical men here is that his [Lincoln's] death is a god-send." Johnson had impressed the radicals in the past as a firm Union man who would be more in tune with their reconstruction ideas than Lincoln had been. On Easter Sunday the members of the Committee on the Conduct of the War met with Johnson. The chairman, Ben Wade, satisfied with what he had heard, told the President, "Johnson, we have faith in you. By the gods, there will be no trouble now in running the government." Once recovered from his first shock, Ashley agreed with his allies. "The decease of Mr. Lincoln," he wrote, "is a great national bereavement, but I am not so sure it is much of a national loss."[2] Unfortunately, he could not have been more wrong.

Publicly, Ashley was still mournful. At funeral solemnities in Toledo, on April 20, Ashley eulogized the martyred Lincoln, saying that he would miss the Emancipator. Lincoln, he said, "was truly a great man," but "under Providence, that sad event will be turned to the good of the nation." When Lincoln's coffin moved through Cleveland, Ashley was one of the pallbearers.[3] But while the nation was mourning, Ashley's thoughts had already turned to politics and the fight to obtain impartial suffrage.

During the next few weeks Ashley's faith in Johnson seemed justified. A couple of days after the President's accession, General William T. Sherman had negotiated lenient surrender terms with General Joseph E. Johnston. The radicals were infuriated, but the President put them at ease by overruling Sherman. Sumner was among the many who called on Johnson in his first days in office, and the Massachusetts radical was convinced that the President would favor black suffrage.[4]

By mid-May, Ashley began to have vague doubts about the President. On May 9, Johnson extended recognition to Governor Francis H. Pierpont's conservative Unionist regime in Virginia. It seemed that Johnson was trying to hurry the insurgent states back into the Union. The conservatives, Seward and Welles, still remained in the Cabinet, and it did not appear that Johnson planned any changes in the executive branch.[5]

In the latter part of May, Ashley was in Washington, conferring with an informal gathering of congressmen about the nation's future course in regard to reconstruction. The Boston *Advertiser* reported that the legislators had been invited to the capital by Ashley and three other congressmen. Ashley met with the President, alone and with the group. On one occasion he asked Johnson to rescind Lincoln's Amnesty Proclamation, pointing out, "that the Rebels who had committed Treason since its issue should not have the benefit of its promises or provisions." To act otherwise would be like "issuing a pardon in advance of the crime." The group differed with the President over the issue of Negro suffrage. Ashley felt that Johnson had shown his conservatism by indicating that the states which rebelled were still states, that their governments had not been destroyed, but were merely in abeyance; and that neither the President nor the Congress had the authority to prescribe qualifications for voters. Impetuously, Ashley told Johnson that the radicals "intended under God to crush any party or any man who stood by against the universal enfranchisement of the country." Johnson angrily responded, "Good day gentlemen."[6]

Ashley then went to Virginia to investigate matters first hand, and he quickly became convinced that under Johnson's policy, the state would soon be grasped by former rebels. This is exactly what happened. On June 7, he told friends that this pattern would be repeated in every Southern state if Johnson had his way. The insurgent states would, Ashley feared, assume the Confederate debt and adopt laws which could lead to enslavement. As to the correct course to follow, he counseled "forbearance, and kindness, but earnestness; and then with the press of the country taking up this matter, we may bring the administration of President Johnson to the right point, as the anti-slavery men brought President Lincoln, after a contest of two years."[7] But the humble, stubborn, strict-constructionist tailor from Tennessee was not Lincoln.

On May 29, Johnson issued two proclamations. The first provided amnesty to all ex-rebels willing to take an oath of allegiance to support the laws of the United States, including those pertaining to emancipation, except civil and military leaders of the Confederacy, and persons whose taxable property was valued at $20,000. The second proclamation appointed William W. Holden provisional governor of North Carolina. This measure also called for the restitution of the state government by a constitutional convention elected by loyal citizens who had the franchise in 1860. Thus, there would be no Negro suffrage, nor any provisions to insure the safety and freedom of the black man. Through the next few weeks Johnson followed similar reconstruction policies in the other insurgent Southern states.[8]

Ashley approved of the amnesty proclamation, but he was troubled by the lack of a commitment for black suffrage in the second one. Though doubts about Johnson had crept in, Ashley still had confidence in the Executive. "The President," he said, "desires earnestly to carry out the wishes of the Union men of the country." But they would need to put pressure on Johnson.[9] Many of Ashley's radical friends were uneasy; others continued to hope they could work out an accord with Johnson before Congress met in December. Ashley, in the meantime, was leaving for a trip to the western territories and California.

Accompanied by Colonel John B. Frothingham, formerly of Toledo, and by Mr. W. A. Havemayer of New York City, Ashley visited Kansas, Colorado, Oregon, and the territories of Idaho, Montana, and Washington. Everywhere he stopped, Ashley was honored at dances, banquets, and receptions, and did a great deal of sightseeing. In Oregon, the Toledoan spoke out in favor of Negro suffrage; the Oregon *Statesman* commented that such a radical view was not endorsed by the Union party on the Pacific Coast.[10]

On September 17, Ashley made a speech on reconstruction in San Francisco. The effort was basically a restatement of his long-held beliefs on the subject. The Confederacy, he said, had been a *de facto* hostile government. The constitutional governments of the insurgent states had ceased to exist when they broke with the Union. Maintaining that a state could alter or dissolve its government if it wished, he pointed out that, nevertheless, "the sovereignty of the United States over the territory and people within such

State or States remains unimpaired." He was again speaking about territorialization.

The main thrust of his address was a plea for Negro suffrage. He proposed that all loyal men, white and black, be permitted to vote for delegates to a constitutional convention, and to vote for acceptance or rejec-
tion of the document it drafted. If, after a loyal government had been reorganized, whites and blacks wanted to limit the franchise to Negroes who
had served in the armed forces, or who could read and write in the English
language, Ashley could agree to such a limitation. In other words, at this
time, he was willing to settle for impartial as opposed to universal
suffrage.[11]

Ashley fervently hoped that the President would support these objectives. As for his relationship with Johnson, the congressman maintained
that it was still cordial. "At all events," he said, "until Mr. Johnson proves
false to the party which elected him, I shall support his administration."
Ashley's speech was well received and enthusiastically endorsed.[12]

In Sacramento, at the end of his stay in California, Ashley again spoke
on reconstruction. His thesis was essentially what it had been in San Francisco, except for a few points. This time he was slightly more critical of
the way Johnson was dealing with the rebellious states. He also forcefully
stated that, next to obtaining impartial suffrage, the most important feature of any reconstruction settlement was guarding against assumption of
the rebel debt by any new state government. He approved of paying the
prewar debt, but he did not want loyal people subjected to taxation for
the rebel debt.[13]

During his journey back from the West (going North first), Ashley
heard more about Johnson's reconstruction policy, and he became increasingly disturbed. In a speech at Olympia, he asked whether if abolitionists,
such as William Lloyd Garrison, Wendell Phillips, or Gerrit Smith, had led
a Northern revolt, the South after victory would have allowed these individuals to be provisional governors of the reconstructed states? The answer
was obvious! So, asked Ashley, why should Americans make Southern
traitors the heads of the new state governments? On November 14, Ashley
arrived home in Toledo. He soon learned that Colonel James, Collector of
the Port of San Francisco, who had introduced him at a rally in September,
had been dismissed by Johnson.[14] Whether Johnson did this because
James was friendly to Ashley, or because of patronage, is impossible to
determine. On the surface it seems that the respect-craving President had
not forgiven Ashley for his haughty manner when the two met in May.
Ashley was not at all pleased by this development, and his distrust and
dislike for Johnson were growing every day.

As they gathered in Washington in late November for the start of the opening session of the Thirty-ninth Congress, Ashley and his colleagues were faced with a *fait accompli* with respect to reconstruction. Without the approval of Congress, Johnson had initiated and carried out a policy of restoration, which enabled ex-Confederate leaders to return to power. The basic rights and liberties of Negroes were being bypassed by Black Codes which established a quasi serfdom for the freedmen. Finally, delegates from the former insurgent states, including the Confederate Vice President Alexander Stephens, were waiting to be seated in Congress. The President's reconstruction policy had turned out to be, as Kenneth Stampp has indicated, one of "disenfranchisement, discrimination and segregation."[15] Many people, including Ashley, began to feel that the war had been fought for nothing.

The Ohio congressional delegation caucused in the rooms of Columbus Delano, on December 1, to discuss the situation. In a harmonious atmosphere, the group decided to support Schuyler Colfax for speaker and Edward McPherson for clerk. The congressmen also agreed to oppose the admission to Congress of any representative from the rebellious states. General Robert Schenck then indicated that he planned to introduce a constitutional amendment basing representation on suffrage. A state if it wished could limit the franchise to whites, but it would pay for the privilege by forfeiting representation. There was no dissent from this proposal. Rutherford B. Hayes of Fremont then suggested that an educational test or condition (each voter had to be able to read and write) be added to the amendment. This idea was adopted, with only Ashley and Samuel Shellabarger voting no.[16] Ashley apparently thought that if a literacy test were included in a suffrage amendment, it would have immediately disenfranchised the great mass of black men in the South, who had generally been forbidden to learn to read and write. Thus, Ashley was leaning toward universal suffrage.

Even before Congress met, McPherson had indicated that he did not plan to place the names of the Southern representatives on the roll. On December 4, the clerk simply omitted the names of the representatives from the Johnson governments from his call, and when Horace Maynard of Tennessee rose to protest, he was not recognized. Just before Congress went into session a Union caucus, on a motion by Thaddeus Stevens, agreed to establish a committee to inquire into the condition of the insurgent states, and report whether any of them were entitled to representation. On December 12, the radicals carried a resolution calling for the establishment of a Joint Committee of Fifteen on Reconstruction (nine from the House and six from the Senate) to which all matters concerning reconstruction would be referred.[17]

Ashley was in the forefront of the ensuing battle between Johnson and Congress, and because of this he has often been portrayed as a depraved, vindictive fanatic, determined to force his ideas on Negro suffrage and equality upon an unwilling nation. This view is still partially accepted, even by the revisionists. Hans L. Trefousse places Ashley in the category of "impractical radicals," whose intransigence and inflexibility on immediate racial equality, whatever the political consequences, embarrassed their allies, the "practical radicals."[18] Ashley's reputation as a fanatic stems from his role in the impeachment. He genuinely believed that Johnson was guilty of usurping power and of violating his oath of office. Ashley did on occasion allow his zeal for impeachment to get the better of his discretion, and this passion caused him to speak in an impractical manner, but on other issues he was not impractical at all. No one can deny his leadership in the fight for Negro suffrage and equality, but he fought for humanitarian, not vindictive reasons, and this attitude had been clear since 1856 when he first courageously spoke up for black enfranchisement.

As far as the charge of instransigence is concerned, although stubborn when he felt he was right, Ashley was often willing to accept less than his stated goal, rather than obtain nothing. At various times, he showed himself quite ready to compromise with Johnson on reconstruction (he would, for example, have taken the rebellious states back into the Union in 1866 if they had ratified the Fourteenth Amendment). He did not break with the President until just before the 1866 elections. Ashley's readiness to reach an amicable accord with the Chief Executive was indicated in the rather mild reconstruction bill which he offered on December 18, 1865.

The measure was based primarily on the theory of guaranteeing a republican form of government, and partially on the concept of territorialization. The bill spoke of states "whose constitutional governments were usurped or overthrown by the recent rebellion," but did not specifically mention that the states reverted back into territories, as had his reconstruction proposal of March 12, 1862. In many respects, the measure was like the various bills Ashley had presented in the second session of the Thirty-eighth Congress. It provided for the appointment of provisional governors charged with running the civil administration, until new state governments were formed, and it required that Negroes have the same rights as whites to fair trial and jury service. All male citizens of the age of twenty-one, regardless of race, were to be enrolled, and each was to be required to take an oath to support the Constitution. When a majority did so, the governor would invite the loyal men to elect delegates to a convention to reestablish a state government. Those who took an additional oath of allegiance, the "ironclad oath"—that they had never voluntarily borne arms against the United States, or held any office, military or civil under the Confederacy, as provided for in the Test Act of July 2, 1862—could vote for, and serve as, delegates.[19]

One of the new ideas in the measure was the requirement that a state had to draw up "a perpetual covenant between the people of the State ratifying it and the United States, which covenant when ratified shall be forever irrevocable without the consent of the United States." The covenant had to stipulate that involuntary servitude was forever prohibited, that "the freedom and equality, both civil and political, of all persons before the laws thereof is hereby guaranteed," and that no rebel debt would be recognized or paid. These were basically the same requirements as those in Ashley's bills of the previous session. But now there was the added provision that no person could hold state office without first taking an oath to maintain the Constitution of the United States, and "an oath to maintain the perpetual union of these States." Finally, perfect toleration of religion had to be secured and no person could "be molested in person or property on account of his or her mode of religious worship." The convention also had to draw up a new state constitution republican in form "and not repugnant to the Constitution of the United States and the principles of the Declaration of Independence."[20] By requiring adherence to the Declaration of Independence, Ashley was stipulating equality before the law and government by the consent of the governed.

Both the covenant and the new constitution had to be approved by the eligible voters. If they accepted the documents, the President, after obtaining the assent of Congress, could recognize the government as the constitutionally established ruling body of the state.[21] Congressional approval before presidential recognition was a new idea and appears to have been included to lessen Johnson's power in reconstruction.

In an effort to appease Johnson, the last section of the bill granted congressional recognition to the government of Tennessee inaugurated under the convention assembled on January 1, 1865, provided that the state legislature adopted the conditions of the covenant and the people approved it at the polls. At such an election, those who were already authorized by law as electors would vote. In other words, there was no demand for Negro suffrage for this referendum, yet approval of the covenant implied future black enfranchisement. But the act would not constitute "a recognition of a State government in the State of Tennessee" until all the foregoing conditions were met.[22] The bill was referred to the Joint Committee of Fifteen, where it was discussed along with many other ideas.

Ashley sent a copy of the bill to William H. Seward, specifically calling his attention to the sections dealing with the covenant and the recognition of Tennessee. Ashley told Seward that he was doing "this in order that I may have the benefit of any suggestions you may have to make when I see you."[23] Since Ashley had distrusted Seward for years, such a statement could be nothing less than a direct offer to attempt a compromise with the executive department on reconstruction. Unfortunately, neither Johnson nor his secretary of state was in a conciliatory mood.

The radicals, including Ashley, realized that if reconstruction was to be successful, there had to be minimal safeguards for Negro rights. Ashley's reconstruction bill, with its clear call for black civil and political rights, was an example of this recognition, and his proposal was not impractical. Ashley genuinely hoped that some adjustment between Johnson and the Congress could be worked out. In January, 1866, he wrote his friend, Governor A. C. Gibbs of Oregon, that most Union men in Congress did not want a rupture with Johnson, and that there would be none, unless the President caused it by conspiring with rebels and their Northern sympathizers. "Every loyal man in Congress," he wrote, "desires harmony, union & honest cooperation with the Executive. We can have this unless he *wills it otherwise.*"[24]

Ashley realized that the President was opposed to Negro suffrage. In order to avoid a total split on reconstruction, and still give Negroes some political protection, the Ohioan was willing to compromise on a bill granting suffrage to blacks in the District of Columbia. Instead of demanding universal suffrage, he recommended impartial suffrage. The franchise would be limited to whites and blacks who could either read the English language, or who had served in the military, and to all those who paid taxes, while excluding those who had served in civil or military positions under the Confederacy.[25] He believed that such a bill would pass and that Johnson would sign it.

This bill, along with the Freedmen's Bureau bill, he told Gibbs, "& the bill to guarantee to the Emancipated their civil rights will, if the President approves save us from *division.* If he should not approve them, you can see where we will go."[26] At this point Ashley was quite willing to settle for moderate civil rights measures, which men like Lyman Trumbull and John Bingham were seeking. The Toledoan was prepared to go part way toward the President to prevent discord, but Johnson was not prepared to take the few steps which would have assured harmony. When the final break did occur, Ashley was secure in the knowledge that he had tried to avoid it.

In February, Congress passed a bill extending the life and increasing the powers of the Freedmen's Bureau, an agency which had been established toward the end of the war to give assistance to the freed blacks. The next month, Congress passed a civil rights bill, designed to guarantee the freedmen the basic privileges of citizenship. Both measures had been drawn up by Trumbull. Refusing to heed warnings from the moderates that these proposals were their minimum terms for continued support, Johnson vetoed both measures on narrow constitutional grounds. On February 22, the Tennessean had sown further discontent by making a tactless Washington's Birthday speech, in which he publicly branded Sumner, Stevens, and Phillips as traitors. On April 9, Congress overrode the civil rights veto. The Senate refused to reenact the Freedmen's Bureau bill after the veto, but a revised measure was later passed, vetoed, and on July 16 repassed.[27] The break between Johnson and the Congress was now almost complete. The rupture, as Ashley had predicted, was caused not by the radicals, but by the President.

While relations between the Executive and Congress were deteriorating, the Joint Committee had been working on a constitutional amendment, in an effort to prepare a definite program for reconstruction. In mid-March, Ashley suggested the following amendment to the committee:

> Representatives shall be appropriated among the several States which may be included within this Union according to their respective numbers, which shall be determined by taking the whole number of persons and excluding Indians not taxed: *Provided*. That whenever male citizens of the United States over the age of twenty-one years shall be excluded from the elective franchise in any State, except for particpation in rebellion, the basis of representation therein shall be reduced in the proportion which the number thus excluded bears to the whole number of male citizens of the United States over the age of twenty-one years in such State.[28]

This amendment would have allowed Southern states to exclude rebels, without losing representation, and also held out an inducement to those states to enfranchise Negroes.

After months of discussion, the Joint Committee presented a five-part constitutional amendment on April 30. It guaranteed civil rights and citizenship to Negroes. It reduced representation for denial of the right to vote of any male citizen over twenty-one, but did not specifically call for black suffrage. It also called for the repudiation of the rebel debt and for the disenfranchisement until July 4, 1870, of all those who voluntarily aided the rebellion. The second section dealing with representation was not too different from Ashley's March 13 resolution.[29] Ashley was disappointed by the report of the Joint Committee, since he believed that its proposals left too much power in the hands of ex-rebels and did not do enough for the loyal men in the South. He was also distressed that the question of black suffrage was left ultimately to a decision by the Southern states. But he said, "I intend to go for it, however, because I believe it is the best proposition we can get, and because it reflects the aggregate sentiment of the country."

On May 10, the amendment was initially approved by the House. The Senate changed the disqualifying clause to a provision giving Congress the power to remove the disability by a two-thirds vote, and added a guarantee for the federal debt. The amendment in its final form passed on June 13.[30]

On May 29, Ashley made a speech in favor of a reconstruction bill reported by the Joint Committee. At the outset, he declared that he approached the subject not with malice, but with a forgiving spirit. What he desired was "to see the States recently in rebellion restored to all rights, privileges and dignities of States of the American Union at the earliest day consistent with national safety, and upon such terms as shall secure the power, unity, and glory of the Republic."[31] These were hardly the words of a vindictive fanatic bent on destroying the South.

He did not entirely approve of the bill to implement reconstruction, as presented by the Joint Committee on April 30. But if he could get nothing better, he intended to vote for it as he had already voted for the Fourteenth Amendment. The measure (H.R. 543) stipulated that the Fourteenth Amendment had to be ratified by three-fourths of the states before any of the insurgent states could be readmitted to the Union. Ashley believed the Southern states should be admitted as soon as they ratified the amendment, without waiting until it became part of the Constitution. All that the states had to do after ratification was amend their constitutions in conformity with the amendment, and elect new senators and congressmen and a new governor. He wanted new elections because he did not believe that the persons elected under the Johnson governments were loyal. Arkansas and Tennessee, which he felt had already elected loyal men, would only have to ratify the constitutional amendment to be entitled to readmission. The idea of admitting the rebel states into the Union, as soon as they ratified the amendment, was also suggested by Bingham, Trumbull, and Colfax.[32]

In his oration, Ashley presented the following amendment, which he intended to offer at a later date:

No State shall deny the elective franchise to any of its inhabitants, being citizens of the United States, above the age of twenty-one years because of race or color; but suffrage shall be impartial. And on the 4th day of July, A.D. 1876, all citizens of the United States above the age of twenty-one years, not convicted of crime or excluded from the right of the ballot by act of Congress or by the law of any State because of insurrection or rebellion against the United States, shall be electors in each State and Territory of the United States; and on or after the 4th of July, A.D. 1876, all naturalized citizens of the United States thereafter becoming twenty-one years of age, and all aliens who may thereafter be naturalized and are above the age of twenty-one years and can read and write the English language, shall be qualified to vote for electors of President and Vice President of the United States, for members of the Congress of the United States, and for Governors and members of the State legislatures.[33]

He noted that this proposal embraced women's suffrage, as he was "unwilling to prevent any state from enfranchising its women if they desired to do so." Emma Ashley was active in the women's suffrage movement, and she appears to have influenced her husband's support of the concept.[34]

The presentation of this radical amendment would prove politically costly for Ashley. Foreign-born electors resented the language qualification. But Ashley, as we shall later see, was not trying to limit the naturalized citizens' right to vote. He was trying to encourage the growth of public education, since he believed an educated population was essential to the preservation of democracy.

Believing that if reconstruction was to work, Congress had to secure the rights of the loyal men in the South, he stated that he desired to strengthen these men by giving suffrage to the Negroes. Firmly convinced that all citizens had a natural right to vote, he made an impassioned plea for black suffrage, pointing out that it was the only sure weapon for the protection of the freedmen. All he asked was justice for all, black and white; and justice demanded liberty and equality before the law.[35]

Congress had a golden opportunity before it. If action was not taken, he said, "I warn you that agitation will follow your refusal to enact justice, and that there shall be no repose until every citizen of the republic is enfranchised and stands equal before the law."[36] But for the moment he would settle for less. Like other radicals he was ready to accept ratification of the Fourteenth Amendment as a final solution to reconstruction.

Ashley held some extremely radical views concerning reconstruction during this session of Congress, but he was exceedingly practical about their implementation. When Tennessee quickly ratified the Fourteenth Amendment, and asked for readmission, the extreme radicals tried to block it, until the state adopted impartial suffrage. In the House, Julian, Kelley, and George Boutwell all voted against admission, but Ashley, as a man of his word, voted for it.[37]

The more inflexible radicals, seemingly unconcerned about the political importance (increasing the strength of the Republican party in Congress) of having Colorado and Nebraska admitted as states, delayed passage of admission bills by demanding the removal of "white only" suffrage requirements from their constitutions. Although he did not like the "white only" qualification, as chairman of the Committee on Territories Ashley guided the admission measure through the House. He voted against an amendment to the bill requiring the removal of the word *white* from the constitution, and in favor of admission with the qualification left intact. He realized that that was the only way the bill could pass. A bill to admit Nebraska also passed Congress, but Johnson vetoed both measures.[38]

Congress adjourned on July 28, with the President and the Republican-controlled Congress in a state of open hostility.[39] Johnson had refused to accept the Fourteenth Amendment as a final solution to reconstruction. He actively worked against the amendment by encouraging the Southern states to reject it, which all except Tennessee did. If the radicals would later impose harsher terms for reconstruction, Johnson was the cause. The scene was now set for the bitter 1866 elections.

Fully aware of the importance of the elections, the radicals were well prepared. Ashley informed Gibbs that their strategy was to go to the country with the Fourteenth Amendment as the basis of reconstruction. Negro suffrage would not be made a direct issue. "The question of representation and suffrage," he said, "will be discussed in the abstract." He believed that the public's mind would be so educated on the subject that, if the South rejected the terms offered, the next Congress would demand universal suffrage as a condition for reconstruction. As for Johnson, Ashley felt he had passed "the Rubicon and, no doubt . . . will eventually cooperate with the opposition."[40]

On August 22, Ashley was renominated at the Tenth District congressional convention. In his acceptance speech, he repeated most of the ideas and arguments about reconstruction which he had offered in his speech of May 29. Ashley told his audience that he had tried to have Negro enfranchisement included in the reconstruction proposals, but he had failed. He still felt that suffrage was the only true solution to reconstruction, but as a practical man he would take what he could get. The congressman then publicly announced that he favored ratification of the constitutional amendment, and that on this basis he was ready to proceed with reconstruction. The Toledo *Blade*, now controlled by Ashley's friend David Ross Locke—the creator of "Petroleum V. Nasby"—enthusiastically endorsed the congressman. His Democratic opponent was a Civil War general, Henry Steele Commager.[41]

Quickly gauging the political forces in the opposition, Ashley realized that he had a tough campaign ahead. It was rumored that Johnson had singled him out for defeat, and would use all means to accomplish this end. On September 11, the Toledo *Commercial* was bought by Ashley's persistent political enemy Clark Waggoner. The newspaper immediately began to attack him. Waggoner's opposition took the form of personal malice, and soon some newspapers wanted to know how much of a rumored $25,000 sent into the district to elect Commager went to the *Commercial*. In an effort to obtain as much outside help as he could, Ashley asked James Garfield, Charles Sumner, Carl Schurz, Benjamin Wade, Nathaniel Banks, and Benjamin Butler to speak in his behalf.[42] Only Sumner and Banks were unable to accept the plea for aid.

Johnson was so determined to defeat the radicals that he went out to campaign. In his "swing-around-the-circle" to Illinois, he made undignified speeches and allowed himself to be drawn into vulgar debates with hecklers. The radicals quickly took advantage of his indiscretions. Ashley was disturbed by Johnson's behavior, and by General Grant's accompanying him on the trip. Fearing "danger ahead," Ashley asked Secretary of War Stanton: "What are we coming to? What is in store for us?" Stanton was not sure, but he had forebodings of new troubles.[43]

As the campaign developed and rumors of Johnson's determination to defeat Ashley grew, the congressman's dislike for the President increased. In a speech in Toledo on September 24, he called Johnson a "usurper and a tyrant," and spoke of a possible attempt at impeachment in the next congressional session. Ashley's intense campaign efforts paid off; he was easily reelected. After his victory, he went to New York, where he campaigned in Brooklyn and Albany for other Republicans. The radicals emerged from the election in a commanding position, for two-thirds of the new members of Congress were in opposition to the President.[44] Ashley, having done his best to reach a compromise with the President without weakening his basic commitment to the cause of human freedom, would now endeavor to stiffen the terms for the reconstruction of the South, but more importantly he was preparing a course of action to remove Johnson from office.

CHAPTER IX

LOYALTY BETRAYED

The galleries of the House of Representatives were crowded on Monday morning, January 7, 1867. People had come hoping to witness a historic event, but two impeachment resolutions against President Johnson, one by Benjamin F. Loan of Missouri, the other by John R. Kelso of Missouri, had failed. When the morning hour for offering resolutions had expired, many spectators began to leave. Then Ashley suddenly rose from his seat to announce a high question of privilege. The spectators rushed back to their seats. Friends and opponents crowded around Ashley's desk. He explained that he had hoped not to have to perform this painful duty, but since older and more experienced members of the House had declined, he had no other choice. Then, his hands trembling, he said, in a voice quivering with nervous excitement: "On my responsibility as a Representative and in the presence of the House, and before the American people, I charge Andrew Johnson, Vice President and acting President of the United States, with the commission of acts which, in contemplation of the Constitution, are high crimes and misdemeanors, for which in my judgment, he ought to be impeached."[1]

Excitement filled the hall. Members who had been in the lobby scurried back onto the floor. All eyes were riveted on the Ohio radical as he charged Johnson with usurping power and violating law; with misusing the presidential power of appointment, pardon, and veto; with illegally disposing of public property; and with corruptly interfering in elections. He then presented a resolution calling on the Committee on the Judiciary to inquire into Johnson's official conduct and to report whether he had "been guilty of acts designed or calculated to overthrow, subvert, or corrupt the Government of the United States . . . or has conspired with others to do acts, which, in contemplation of the Constitution, are high crimes and misdemeanors, requiring the interposition of the constitutional power of this House."[2]

When Ashley concluded his remarks, the House was galvanized into frenzied action. The gold speculators raced back and forth between the reporters' gallery and the telegraph key. Republican Rufus Spalding of Ohio (a moderate) moved to lay the resolution on the table, but the motion failed. Other parliamentary maneuvers designed to kill the resolution were quickly disposed of, and the proposal passed by a vote of 108 to 38, with only four Republicans having voted in the negative.[3] For the moment, the Republican party seemed united on the issue of impeachment.

Why did Ashley initiate an impeachment investigation against the President? Why did he spend months attempting to find evidence to support his charges? Historians have never presented a realistic appraisal of either his motivations or his actions. Ashley has been accused of having started the process for $50,000, and of having been the tool of others. Some of his critics have claimed that he suborned witnesses, tried to manufacture evidence against Johnson, and declared that Johnson was directly involved in Lincoln's assassination.

A recent *New York Times Magazine* article by C. Vann Woodward summed up the case against Ashley: Woodward characterized the Toledoan as a "nut with an *idée fixe*," who believed that Presidents William Henry Harrison and Zachary Taylor had been assassinated by their Vice Presidents, and that Johnson conspired with John Wilkes Booth to kill Abraham Lincoln, and thus was guilty of "murder most foul." According to Woodward, the Judiciary Committee soon tired of Ashley's ideas and voted 5 to 4 against bringing out a resolution of impeachment.[4] Most of the accusations against Ashley have been one historian's repeating the statements of earlier scholars with no real investigation of the charges. In the course of explaining Ashley's actions, we shall see that the incriminations against him are inaccurate, and that he had specific legal, political, and constitutional reasons for starting the movement to impeach Andrew Johnson.

True, on one occasion Ashley did voice the bizarre theory that Presidents Harrison and Taylor had been killed for the express purpose of putting their Vice Presidents into office. But one should point out that Ashley made this statement on November 23, 1867, more than ten months after he had formally moved for an impeachment investigation. Moreover, during his testimony before the House Judiciary Committee, the Ohio radical readily admitted that his theory did not amount to legal evidence, which accounts for his not bringing the matter before the committee nor presenting any evidence to it until he was asked about his hypothesis.[5] Nowhere in Ashley's formal charges of January 7, 1867, is there any mention of his theory. For historians to make it appear that the Toledoan's assassination thesis was his only reason for moving impeachment is to misstate the facts.

Furthermore, Ashley never directly accused Johnson of complicity in Lincoln's murder, and he never said that the President was guilty of "murder most foul." The contention that the Judiciary Committee did not vote to recommend impeachment in June, 1867, because it found Ashley's ideas wearisome is contrary to the facts. The committee did not even learn about his theory until five months later. Further, after hearing Ashley's admittedly foolish theory, the committee did vote in favor of recommending impeachment in November, 1867. It was only in July, 1867, Woodward claims, that the impeachers advanced the real issues, charging Johnson with abusing his pardoning power and his appointing power, and with failing to execute the laws. Yet, these were the specific charges Ashley raised on January 7, 1867, and again on March 7.[6] Historians are correct in asserting that the House voted against a resolution of impeachment on December 7, 1867, because many representatives believed that the President had not committed an indictable crime and thus was not impeachable. But the defeat of a number of Republican congressmen in the 1867 elections and the unstable financial conditions of the country had as much, if not more, influence on the decision of many representatives to vote no.[7]

Throughout 1867, Ashley devoted much time and effort trying to prove his charges of usurpation against Johnson. During that attempt, he did on occasion imply that he had suspicions about Johnson's involvement in Lincoln's assassination. He did seek for evidence which would tie the President to Lincoln's death. And he did talk to some unsavory characters. But any objective analysis of the Toledoan's behavior must keep the following points in mind: first, he never directly charged Johnson with conspiracy in Lincoln's demise. Second, he never presented any false or perjured evidence against the President. Third, although the after-the-fact presentation of his theory was absurd, it was not Ashley's prime motive in favoring impeachment. Fourth, he did have specific legal, constitutional, and political reasons for initiating the impeachment.

One factor motivating Ashley was his feeling that Johnson had betrayed him politically. Ashley had been optimistic when the Tennessean became President, but in the year and a half since, relations between the two had deteriorated dramatically. Their first official meeting in June, 1865, when they discussed reconstruction and Negro suffrage had been stormy. When Colonel James was removed as the Collector of Customs in San Francisco, Ashley believed the action was politically motivated. In guiding the Thirteenth Amendment through the House, Ashley had made various arrangements to acquire votes. Lincoln had been aware of these maneuvers and had given his approval. But when the Ohioan mentioned this to Johnson, the President refused to honor the commitments of his predecessor and reneged on the prior agreements.

Although Ashley was enraged over this breach of political trust, he continued to try to compromise and work with Johnson on postwar problems until the election of 1866.[8] But during the campaign Johnson channeled funds to Ashley's political opponents, removed his allies from patronage positions in Toledo, and appointed his political enemies. Ashley was extremely upset by these actions. His disenchantment with Johnson only increased when the Chief Executive rejected the reconstruction ideas of the Republican Congress.[9]

Nevertheless, to suggest that Ashley endeavored to impeach Johnson solely for political differences is to imply that he was both unprincipled and cynical. He was neither. Although political factors were undoubtedly a consideration in his efforts, his constitutional and legal reasoning had greater influence on his decision to start the impeachment investigation. Ashley firmly believed that Johnson's policy of trying to implement his own reconstruction program in 1865 was a blatant usurpation of the constitutional powers and prerogatives of Congress. Johnson, Ashley thought, was arrogating to himself powers which belonged to the legislative branch of government; this was a dangerous accretion of power by the President. In addition, Ashley strongly believed that, to preserve democracy, the legislative branch of government had to be dominant over the executive branch. Furthermore, Johnson's refusal to administer properly the Confiscation Act, the Civil Rights Act, and other laws, gave Ashley a clear indication that the President could not be trusted to carry out his constitutional duty to see that the laws were properly executed. Johnson's course of action, according to Ashley, patently denied the separation of powers. From Ashley's perspective, Johnson was guilty of maladministration and nonfeasance in office. Finally, the Toledoan, like other radical Republicans, was coming to believe that there could be no real, effective reconstruction program so long as Johnson was President. In other words, the Civil War had been fought for nothing; unless Johnson was removed from office, Ashley reasoned, the results of the war might well be reversed.[10]

Ashley's desire to impeach Johnson became a consuming passion. At times his zeal caused him to speak and act intemperately, and in this respect, he committed a major political blunder, which hurt his career. Ashley proceeded in a rash, and at times a foolish manner, but he acted for what he perceived to be the best interests of the country.

The movement toward impeachment had been gaining momentum for some time. As early as December 11, 1865, Secretary of the Navy Gideon Welles's diary refers to the impeachment. By late winter, 1866, Stevens had received a memorial requesting impeachment, and Edward Bates and Welles both speculated about the possibility in their diaries. In the fall of

1866, during the excitement of the election, talk of removing the President increased. The Chicago *Tribune* reported that in August, a secret meeting in St. Louis, attended by Governor Thomas Fletcher of Missouri, Governor Richard Oglesby and Senator Richard Yates of Illinois, and General John Logan, had been called to discuss plans for impeachment. Johnson also began receiving letters of warning from loyal supporters.[11]

By September and October, 1866, Butler and Ashley were publicly calling for impeachment. Ashley impetuously attacked the President on September 24, calling him "an usurper and a tyrant . . . a base-born wretch, who had no concept of truth, fidelity and honesty," and October 1 he spoke directly of impeachment. Campaigning in Ohio and Illinois, Butler stated that it was the duty of Congress to remove Johnson, and during his speeches he indicated one of the radicals' objectives in pursuing this course. From the moment that Johnson was impeached, Butler claimed, the President would cease to perform his duties, and the president *pro tem* of the Senate would serve as Chief Executive. This view was also put forth by Wendell Phillips. The *New York Times* would later report that the radicals felt that unless Johnson could be suspended from office, his impeachment and trial would be of little value.[12] If this theory was legally valid, Johnson would then be eliminated from dealing with reconstruction.

On October 17, Ashley spoke in Brooklyn, New York. He waved the bloody shirt, demanded imprisonment and hangings for some ex-rebels, and indicated that he favored a stronger reconstruction policy. But he would still settle for less if the Fourteenth Amendment was ratified by the rebellious states. As for the election returns in Ohio, to him they showed that the people desired impeachment. He lashed out at Johnson, calling him an "ignorant, vicious, unscrupulous man" and referred to him as "his accidency." If the President had made "the rebels take a back seat," Ashley said, "we would have no trouble now." The Ohioan then rashly implied that many men had had suspicions about Johnson when Lincoln was murdered. "If Hannibal Hamlin had been Vice President instead of Johnson," Ashley asserted, "Abraham Lincoln would never have been assassinated."[13]

As the opening of the second session of the Thirty-ninth Congress drew near, the cries for impeachment grew louder. But the Republicans were by no means united on the desirability of the project. Congressmen George Boutwell of Massachusetts and Thomas Williams of Pennsylvania, along with Stevens, Chandler, and several abolitionists, favored the step, as did the Toledo *Blade* and the New York *Independent*. On the other hand, radicals like John W. Shaffer and Horace Greeley, and such Republican journals as *The Nation* and the Cleveland *Leader*, were opposed to, or unsure about, impeachment. It was a complicated and risky business. No one was certain what effect such a move would have on the economy of the nation, or whether the people in general would respond favorably if it appeared that the action had been taken for partisan purposes. But Ashley was not to be dissuaded. He was convinced that Johnson was acting in defiance of his oath of office by refusing to execute reconstruction laws; he believed that the Tennessean meant to resurrect the "lost cause," "and establish the late rebels in power; thus rendering valueless the victories of the Union Armies."[14]

On December 17, the Ohio radical presented a resolution providing for a select committee of seven to inquire whether any officer of the government had attempted to subvert it by high crimes and misdemeanors. The motion was vague, but it clearly looked to the impeachment of the President. Ashley felt that by making the resolution less specific, he gave it a better chance of passing. Since it was introduced out of order, a two-thirds vote suspending the rules was required to get the proposal before the House, but it failed by four votes. The closeness by which the motion lost indicates that support for a movement looking toward impeachment was stronger at this time than generally believed. Because of the vagueness of the resolution, Ashley was later accused of wanting to include General Grant in the investigation. The project was alleged to have been a conspiracy that he, Butler, and Stevens had concocted. Ashley vigorously denied these allegations. He admitted that he had discussed the resolution with several men, including his friends Stevens and Elihu Washburne. But, he said, there was nothing unusual or conspiratorial in this fact. Had he intended to include Grant in the resolution, he would not have shown it to Washburne, who was a close personal friend of the general. Moreover, Washburne approved of the proposal and had voted for it. Stevens also denied the validity of the accusations, and the reporter who broke the story was later forced to retract.[15]

During the Christmas recess, Ashley remained in Washington, attending to territorial committee business, preparing a new reconstruction bill, and working on the impeachment project. On January 5, a caucus of about sixty House Republicans met to discuss impeachment. Rufus Spalding of Ohio, who was opposed, presented a resolution that no measure looking toward the impeachment of the President should be offered in the House unless previously agreed upon in caucus. Ashley moved to amend this resolution to the effect that "no Article" of impeachment of the President should be presented without first being considered by the caucus. This was agreed to. Ashley then stated that he was in favor of immediate action, but that he wanted every member to act "fairly and openly and help dispose of this matter." Pointing out that it would be impossible to reconstruct the South as long as Johnson was President, Stevens said that while the latter was in office "the laws of Congress would be inoperative. . . . Either the door must be opened and the rebels admitted to their seats, or the President removed." A discussion then arose whether articles of impeachment drawn up in the Thirty-ninth Congress could be utilized in the Fortieth Congress. John A. Bingham said no, since one-third of the Senate would change with the new Congress; Stevens insisted that the Senate was a perpetual body, and thus capable of trying the President on charges made by a previous session. Washburne then moved to amend further Spalding's resolution, so that all propositions looking toward impeachment of Johnson would be referred to the Judiciary Committee. After some further discussion, Washburne's amendment carried.[16]

Thus a compromise was reached: No articles of impeachment would be offered at this time, but Ashley was free to present his resolution asking for an investigation of Johnson's official behavior (which he did so dramatically on January 7). The resolution would now be sent to the Committee on the Judiciary, rather than to a select committee, which Ashley would have chaired as mover of the motion. Some of those in favor of impeachment seemed to feel that Ashley was too partisan to head such an investigation. But Ashley had accomplished his main objective: the beginning of an inquiry into Johnson's conduct.

Reaction to Ashley's motion of January 7 was mixed. The Toledo *Blade* believed that an investigation was called for, and the editors were glad that preliminary steps had been approved. Believing that "right reconstruction" was impossible as long as Johnson was in office, the *National Anti-Slavery Standard* approved of the action. The Worcester *Daily Spy* generally concurred with these opinions. But other journals were less than enthusiastic. The New York *Tribune* felt that nothing was to be gained by the inquiry since the 1866 elections had left Johnson politically dead. Moreover, if articles of impeachment were brought against the President, the paper doubted the legality of the position that he was suspended from duty until the trial was over. Also such a movement could lead to uncertainty, which might seriously aggravate an already unstable financial situation. The *Nation*, the Toledo *Commercial*, the Boston *Journal*, the *New York Times*, and the Chicago *Tribune* presented similar arguments.[17]

Those who supported Johnson vilified Ashley. Writing in his diary, Gideon Welles called the Ohioan "a calculating fanatic." The Baltimore *Gazette* tried to portray him in the worst possible light. He was soon accused of having been paid $50,000 by gold speculators to initiate the inquiry against Johnson. But as with so many of the charges leveled against Ashley, there was no truth in it. The congressman was trying to raise money for a business venture with his Ohio friend Robert K. Scott, and Ashley was astonished to learn that the monied men of New York were frightened by impeachment, and thus would not lend him money. The financial community believed that conditions were too unstable to risk any new enterprises.[18] If Ashley had recently been paid a large sum to initiate the impeachment movement, would he at the same time be desperately trying to raise money? It seems most unlikely.

Throughout January, the Judiciary Committee prepared for an inquiry into Johnson's actions. The committee decided not to make public what took place at its meetings, and each member was sworn to secrecy. On January 9, Ashley appeared before the committee to give statements in support of his charges. It was rumored that one of the items that Ashley mentioned was the possibility that the President had illegally sold United State railway property to former rebels. But by January 17, *The Nation* reported that the investigation had been suspended for the moment. The committee, according to various newspaper reports, was awaiting Ashley's movements, as he was directing much of his energies attempting to collect and catalogue evidence. In the beginning of February, speculation abounded that Ashley had discovered some new facts, and that formal questioning of witnesses would soon begin.[19]

On February 6, the Judiciary Committee began its formal investigation. The first witness called was General Lafayette C. Baker, former Chief of the Detective Bureau. Though Ashley was not a member of the committee, he was permitted to question the witness. Baker, who had a reputation for general unreliability, related a strange story: toward the end of the war, Johnson had written a letter to Jefferson Davis indicating that he was ready to go over to the rebel side. The letter was supposedly stolen from Johnson's desk and eventually came into the possession of John W. Adamson of Nashville, who allowed Baker to keep the document for a short time. The general checked the authenticity of the letter, supposedly found it to be genuine, and returned it to Adamson. Claiming that he could produce this letter, Baker was dispatched to find Adamson and the evidence. But Baker and investigators for the committee never were able to find Adamson, the letter, or a Mrs. Harris who also reputedly knew about the affair.[20]

The following day, John H. James of Nashville testified (once again Ashley was permitted to ask questions) that Johnson had turned over a railroad built at government expense in Tennessee to a corporation run by ex-rebels, and that the President had made a financial profit on the deal. Johnson's archenemy, Secretary of War Stanton, later proved that this was not true and exonerated the Chief Executive of any wrongdoing in this affair.[21]

For the next month, the committee continued to take evidence about supposed customs house frauds in New York City, campaign irregularities, removals from office for political reasons, and the New Orleans race riot. On March 2, the Judiciary Committee reported to the House. The majority thought that although nothing definite had as yet been established, the testimony given did warrant continued investigation by the next Congress. A.J. Rogers, a Democrat, submitted a minority report stating that the evidence did not justify further investigation. Both reports were laid on the table and ordered to be printed.[22] The Thirty-ninth Congress ended on March 4, 1867, but, lest Johnson have a clear field, Congress had previously provided that the Fortieth session begin on the same day.

On March 4, Butler and John Covode called a private caucus of approximately twenty radical Republicans, including Stevens, Ashley, and Boutwell. Impatient with the slow progress of the impeachment investigation, Butler wanted to discuss a proposal to take the matter out of the hands of the Judiciary Committee and place it with a Select Committee of Thirteen (seven members from the Judiciary Committee, plus six others). No decision was reached, but the congressmen seemed to be in favor of a select committee. According to newspaper reports, Ashley announced that he did not want a position on any committee charged with the investigation. A regular Republican caucus was held in the evening of March 6. Ashley immediately offered a resolution directing the Committee on the Judiciary to continue its investigation of the charges preferred against Johnson, to sit during the session, and during any recess. Covode moved to amend the resolution by calling for a select committee of thirteen to deal with impeachment. Butler and Logan spoke in favor of Covode's motion; Bingham and Blaine indicated that they preferred to have the matter remain with the Judiciary Committee. When a vote was taken, the amendment failed, and Ashley's motion carried easily. The investigation could now continue.[23]

The next day the Ohio radical introduced his resolution into the House, and then spoke impetuously, at times bitterly. Once again he accused Johnson of usurping legislative power, which imperiled the life of the Republic. The nation, he argued, would not allow any man, "certainly no man who came into the Presidency through the door of assassination," to act in defiance of Congress and the people. Further, he said:

> Sir, a man of Mr. Johnson's antecedents, of his mental and moral caliber, coming into the Presidency as he came into it—and I say nothing now of the dark suspicion which crept over the minds of men as to his complicity in the assassination plot, nor of the fact that I cannot banish from my mind, the mysterious connection between death and treachery which this case presents—I say such a man, in view of all that has happened, coming into the presidential office as he came into it, ought to have walked with uncovered head and very humbly before the loyal men of this nation and their Representatives in the American Congress.[24]

During his speech, Ashley accused Johnson of dealing with thieves and pardon-brokers; being drunk at Lincoln's second inaugural; having used seditious language; having shamed the country by his drunken and boisterous election tour in 1866; and having grossly misused patronage. As far as reconstruction was concerned, the Ohio radical believed that as long as Johnson was President, there would be no real protection for loyal men in the South, and thus no real restoration.

Like many Republicans, Ashley felt that Johnson should be impeached because he had violated his oath of office to see that the laws were faithfully executed. The President's obstructionism in carrying out the confiscation laws, the Freedmen's Bureau Act, and various reconstruction measures, clearly nullified the purpose of legislation which had been passed over his veto. As Ashley pointed out, "the duty of the President is to execute, not make law. His oath requires him to see that the laws are faithfully executed. That the President has neglected or refused to execute many of the laws of Congress no man questions. That he has failed to execute the civil rights bill, nay, that he has not even attempted to execute it, the whole country knows. . . . In his failure to execute this just and most necessary law the crime of the President becomes colossal." Ashley contended that Johnson could not arbitrarily choose which laws he would execute. The Ohio radical most certainly agreed with Massachusetts conservative Nathaniel Banks, who stated that when Congress decided on a course of action and the President refused to execute it, "it is our duty to lay aside the question of reconstruction for a time and proceed to a consideration of the position and purposes of the President himself."[25] What Ashley and other Republicans were suggesting was that in failing to administer the laws properly, Johnson was guilty of nonfeasance in office.

During his passionately delivered oration, Ashley said that he was worried that if Congress did not take some action against this expansion of executive power, a dangerous precedent would be established for future presidents. Fear that presidential power was growing at the expense of congressional authority, and belief that if Johnson's abuses of power were not curtailed no president would ever be impeached, only increased Ashley's desire to have Johnson removed from office. As he continued, he became nervous and excited. His sense of betrayal eroded cool judgment. He exclaimed emotionally: "The nation cries out in its agony and calls upon the Congress of the United States to deliver them from the shame and the disgrace which the acting President has brought upon them. They demand that the loathing incubus which has blotted our country's history with its foulest blot shall be removed. In the name of loyalty betrayed, of law violated, of the Constitution trampled upon, the nation demands the impeachment and removal of Andrew Johnson."[26]

At this point, Speaker Colfax was forced to remind Ashley that he was exceeding the license allowed in debate. He must abstain from using language which was personally offensive.

The Ohioan then resumed his discourse, urging his colleagues not to be timid when boldness was called for. He also pointed out that he realized it would be technically hard to prove Johnson guilty, but that if Johnson was not impeached, the provision of the Constitution providing for impeachment would be useless. With deep emotion Ashley concluded by noting that anyone with evidence against the President had a duty to bring it to the attention of the Committee on the Judiciary. Any person failing to produce evidence in his possession would be an accessory to the crime. After some further comments from both sides of the House, the resolution was agreed to without division.[27]

For the next few months the Committee on the Judiciary proceeded to investigate, question witnesses, and gather evidence, and Ashley continued to work on the inquiry. On June 3, the committee voted on the question of asking for articles of impeachment. Four members (Boutwell, Lawrence, Williams, and Thomas) were in favor of impeachment; five others (Wilson, Woodbridge, Churchill, Eldridge, and Marshall) were opposed. The seven Republicans nevertheless seemed to be in favor of a motion of censure against Johnson. It was reported that Ashley was troubled by this result, but still determined to bring the question of impeachment up for a direct vote by the House, whether the committee reported it out or not. On June 27, the committee decided to continue the investigation and to take more evidence. During the July meeting of the first session of the Fortieth Congress, Wilson announced that the committee could not report before October, at the earliest.[28] A final report was not forthcoming until late November.

During this period Ashley and his ally Butler began investigating rumors about Johnson's possible involvement in Lincoln's assassination.[29] Ashley—obsessed by his feeling of political betrayal, convinced that workable reconstruction was becoming ever more difficult as Johnson continued to veto legislation, and worried about the unchecked growth of presidential power—was willing to listen to anyone who claimed to have evidence against the President.

One such person was Sanford Conover, who was being held in the Old Capital Prison in Washington. Conover, whose real name was Charles A. Dunham, but who used *Sanford Conover* and *James W. Wallace* as aliases, was a lawyer by profession, a former rebel, and at the end of the Civil War was the Canadian correspondent for the New York *Tribune*. Dunham had recently been convicted for perjury before the Judiciary Committee of the House. He had furnished the Bureau of Military Justice and the Committee on the Judiciary with evidence about Jefferson Davis's alleged involvement in Lincoln's assassination. His statements were corroborated by two men who called themselves *Campbell* and *Snevel*. In May, 1866, however, Campbell and Snevel admitted that their real names were *A.J. Hoare* and *William H. Roberts*, and that they had been paid to give false testimony fabricated by Dunham. Dunham claimed that this was not so and that he could prove his innocence. In the custody of an officer he was allowed to return to New York City to find witnesses in his support. But on his arrival he escaped and temporarily vanished.[30]

In November, Dunham was apprehended and, while being transported back to Washington, confessed to his guard that he had committed perjury. Not wanting to go to jail, he soon attempted to make it appear that he was an innocent victim of others. He sought to show that he had merely acted on the orders of Judge Advocate General Joseph Holt. Some letters and documents between Holt and Dunham (alias Conover), published in the New York *Herald* in the fall of 1866, supposedly proved that Dunham was simply doing what Holt wanted. This ruse did not work, however, and Dunham was convicted of perjury on February 11, 1867. The New York *Herald* was later shown to have been duped by Dunham. In August, the *New York Times* published a series of affidavits which proved that Dunham had tried to fabricate evidence against Holt and the Bureau of Military Justice.[31]

The convicted perjurer then somehow convinced a group of Democratic congressmen, led by William Radford, F.C. Le Blond, and Andrew J. Rogers, that if he were freed he could make important disclosures against prominent radicals. The congressmen formally wrote to Johnson asking for a pardon for Dunham, but the President did not act upon their recommendation.[32] Desperate to get out of prison, the perjurer now turned to the radicals.

Using his wife as a go-between, Dunham spread a rumor that he could furnish evidence which would implicate Johnson in the assassination plot. Mrs. Dunham quickly made contact with Ashley who, anxious to obtain information, was quite willing to hear what her husband had to say. Sometime in mid-March, Ashley went to see Dunham in jail.[33]

The two men were allowed to meet in a private room, and Dunham told the congressman that he could obtain letters supposedly written by Johnson to John Wilkes Booth and Booth to Johnson, documents which would clearly incriminate the President. For his part, Dunham wanted Ashley to help him get out of prison. Ashley asked the convict to write a statement explaining the contents of the alleged letters, and stating who now had possession of them. If Dunham could furnish "actual letters," Ashley would try to obtain his release. After the first meeting, Dunham was permitted to use a special room, and was supplied with writing paper, pens, envelopes, and law books. His wife was also allowed to visit him from early morning to six in the evening.[34]

Ashley himself visited Dunham several more times during the next few weeks; on other occasions he sent the Reverend William B. Matchett with instructions to the effect that if Dunham managed to get the letters to Ashley, the congressman promised he would not allow them to be used without his consent. (Matchett claimed to be a former army chaplain, and later was clerk of Butler's Assassination Committee. His vocation at the time seemed to have been procuring government positions for people, for a price.) But by mid-April, Ashley had still not received a statement from Dunham. It seems that the convict wanted to be freed before he would produce his alleged evidence.[35]

On April 25, Judge George P. Fisher sentenced Dunham to ten years in the Albany Penitentiary for perjury before the Committee on the Judiciary. Obviously worried that he was going to be taken away immediately, although Matchett assured him otherwise, Dunham quickly sent Ashley, who was then in Toledo, a statement of facts. Upon returning from Ohio, Ashley went to see Dunham to discuss the affidavit, which he believed was of no value, since it was too vague and indefinite. Consequently, the congressman never showed it to the Committee on the Judiciary. But he was still convinced that Dunham really did have some important information about Johnson; hence, Ashley asked Judge Fisher and Judge David Cartter to delay the transfer to Albany until all leads could be checked. He also advised the prisoner's lawyer to petition for a new trial and to make all the legal appeals he could. But on June 8, the Supreme Court ruled that it would not set Dunham's sentence aside.[36] Thus, as the year moved toward summer, Ashley still had not received any solid evidence from Dunham.

The convicted perjurer also claimed that he had information concerning the trial of John Surratt, an accused assassination conspirator. Ashley listened to Dunham's stories and relayed the information to Albert G. Riddle, the government prosecutor in the Surratt case. While visiting the jail, Ashley had occasion to speak with Dunham's former cellmate, William Cleaver, who also had information on Surratt, but who knew nothing about the so-called Johnson correspondence.[37]

At the same time that he was trying to get evidence from Dunham, Ashley, along with Butler, was attempting to ascertain whether John Surratt had any information on Johnson and the assassination. Matchett spoke to Dr. William J. Duhamel, the Old Capital Prison physician about this matter, insinuating that if Surratt could implicate someone in high office, he might be able to save himself. Matchett tried to see Surratt's sister Anne about this, but her lawyer Joseph P. Bradley would not allow it. Duhamel was an old friend of Johnson's and he kept the President constantly informed of Ashley's and Matchett's movements. Butler and Ashley also tried to interview Miss Surratt, but she refused to see them unless Bradley were also present. They declined to speak with her on this condition, since they believed that the attorney was working in the interest of the conspirators; thus an interview in his presence would have served no purpose.[38]

In April, Ashley had traveled to Philadelphia in what appears to have been an unsuccessful attempt at finding the elusive Mrs. Harris, who supposedly now possessed the Johnson letter about which General Baker had testified in February. Baker and Matchett were also trying to find the woman in an effort to persuade her to give up the letter. In New York City, Matchett subpoenaed Mrs. Harris, or a woman Baker identified as such. According to Baker, Mrs. Harris wanted to be paid for her information, and Ashley agreed to give the investigator a few thousand dollars. But this was insufficient, it seems, since the woman wanted $25,000; thus Baker was told to return the $1,000 already allotted to him. He complied. Mrs. Harris, like Adamson, was never found by the Committee on the Judiciary, nor was the letter.[39] Clearly the letter and the two people mentioned were fictitious.

Since all the so-called leads that had been brought to Ashley's attention had proved to be worthless, he now began to be extremely cautious. When a new bit of information was sent to him, he wrote to a friend that since he did not know anything about the character of the letter-writer, he had not yet replied. "I have," he wrote, "been too often imposed upon during the investigation in which I am engaged that I grow more cautious. Will you make some inquiry about the writer and advise me of your conclusions?"[40]

By July, Dunham saw that none of his schemes to get out of prison was going to succeed. He was physically sick and more desperate than ever to obtain his release, so he decided to appeal directly for a pardon. He sent his wife to see Riddle on July 23 to ask him to say a word in his favor. Since the prosecutor believed that Dunham's information concerning the Surratt case had been of value, he wrote to Johnson in his behalf. Mrs. Dunham had gone to see Ashley the day before, and he had written a letter to Riddle and Holt endorsing the idea of helping Dunham. Riddle later claimed that he never received the note, which may well have been true since the letter somehow wound up in Johnson's papers. Ashley never denied having written the letter. On July 24, the scheming Mrs. Dunham went to see Holt. After pleading for her husband, she persuaded the Judge Advocate to endorse Riddle's statement. But as he later indicated, this was in no sense a recommendation, "and neither contained nor was intended to contain any expression of confidence in the general integrity or truthfulness of Conover. . . . It was based solely on a principle of recognized public policy as applicable to the state of facts presented by Mr. Riddle . . . and . . . it neither urged nor suggested any definitive Executive action."[41]

On July 27, Dunham lost his last legal attempt to have his sentence stayed. Preparations to transfer him to the Albany Penitentiary began. Completely panic stricken, Dunham wrote to Johnson on July 29 asking for a pardon. He also enclosed a letter in which he claimed to have been suborned by Ashley and Butler to fabricate evidence, in an attempt to implicate Johnson in Lincoln's assassination. In return, they were to help him obtain a pardon.[42]

Dunham explained that "Ashley and Company" wanted him to help manufacture evidence which would show that Johnson had corresponded with Booth, that Booth had visited Johnson in his residence at Kirkwood House, that placing an armed George Atzerodt (one of the convicted conspirators) at Kirkwood House was a ruse to divert suspicion from the Vice President, and that just after March 4, 1865, Booth told a friend that he was acting with Johnson's knowledge and that the assassination had originally been planned for Inauguration Day, which accounted for Johnson's behavior on that occasion. Dunham stated that he told Ashley: "I should have no difficulty in finding persons of good standing and moral character to prove these matters." He also sent Johnson a memorandum of what the witnesses were supposed to swear, and he said that Ashley and Butler had inspected two men to see whether they were qualified to testify. Some innocuous Ashley notes to Dunham were included in the envelope. One letter asked Dunham for a statement of his supposed facts; one acknowledged receipt of such a statement; and another advised him to pursue all the legal avenues in an effort to stay his sentence. The last note indicated that if he gave Ashley the original Johnson-Booth letters which he claimed to have seen, nothing would be done with them except with Dunham's permission. The letter which Ashley wrote to Riddle and Holt was among the papers which Dunham sent to the President.[43]

Dunham wrote Johnson that as soon as he was released, he would prove what he said, "or lay before the public a complete exposure of the diabolical decision and most astounding proceedings."[44] In other words, he was playing his old game: "If you help me obtain a pardon, I will supply you with information against your enemies."

After a cabinet meeting on July 30, Johnson asked secretaries Gideon Welles, Hugh McCulloch, and Orville Browning, and Postmaster-General Andrew Randall to remain. He then presented the Dunham correspondence to them, and they proceeded to discuss the situation. They all agreed that the documents should be published, but Randall wanted to delay this until supporting evidence could be obtained. On the following day, it was decided that publication should be postponed until witnesses to substantiate Dunham's accusations could be found. Mrs. Dunham was to go to Albany to obtain the names of witnesses and Randall was to follow and hold an interview. But on August 2, Randall reported that Mrs. Dunham refused to proceed to Albany until her husband was pardoned. Johnson then sent the material to the Attorney General's office for study, and it was subsequently decided to publish the documents on August 10 without any corroborative evidence.[45]

The publication of this story naturally created a sensation throughout the country. Was there any truth to Dunham's allegations in respect to Ashley? Based on the available evidence, the answer is no.

Most important: there is no corroborative evidence to support the charges. The letters and statements which the executive department received from Duhamel, W.W. Moore, and prison officials Robert Ball, Robert Walters, and William Chandler reported only that Ashley came to see Dunham, and that Mrs. Dunham once visited Butler, but those statements contained absolutely no evidence that Ashley and Butler had required Dunham to manufacture evidence. Chandler clearly stated, "of what transpired at these meetings I know nothing except by hearsay, as they were always in the office and generally with the doors closed." On the other hand, the prison warden, T.B. Brown, declared on one occasion he heard Ashley tell Dunham "not to tell him anything which was not true."[46]

The only other pertinent documentary evidence is all unsubstantiated hearsay and rumor. The main body of this material is a letter written by William Rabe, convicted of defrauding the government in February, 1867, and mysteriously pardoned by Johnson in April, and a letter by "[unknown] to My Dear John" which appears to have been written by Rabe. While in prison, he was for a time a cellmate of Dunham. Both documents are vague and inconclusive and based simply on stories Dunham told Rabe. Neither letter ever explicitly stated that Ashley asked Dunham to fabricate evidence. In his May 10 memorandum, Rabe made it clear that he knew only what Dunham told him, which by itself proves nothing. Chandler unequivocally declared that Rabe's statements were fabrications, "for no prisoner was ever allowed an opportunity of hearing anything at those interviews" between Ashley and Dunham. Furthermore, Rabe's other corrrespondence with the executive department concerning the so-called conspiracy, often ended with a plea for a little money to help pay his expenses.[47] As long as he received money, Rabe appeared willing to produce alleged information.

A letter by another prison official, William H. Hughes, contains only hearsay and rumors; the statements by two other persons who claimed to have knowledge about the impeachment are unsubstantiated.[48]

Equally important for any evaluation of the truth of Dunham's statements is this: he was a convicted and admitted perjurer. To put it bluntly, he was a professional perjurer. Furthermore, the longer Dunham stayed in jail, the more desperate and outrageous his stories became. At one time he claimed that Ashley wanted him to help create evidence which would have implicated a dead man: New York politician, Preston King. Naturally, Dunham maintained that he could prove this, but he never did. A friend of Dunham, one Harrison, supposedly had the documents to prove all his allegations but, like the elusive "Mrs. Harris," Dunham's associate could never be found. Finally, he continually made pledges that "the public shall have the whole story in detail . . . as soon as I am at liberty." Yet, after he was pardoned, he never attempted to present any evidence in support of his allegations.[49]

All the letters which Dunham wrote to his wife found their way into Johnson's hands, so that the President was aware of all his accusations. Yet there is no evidence to suggest that the President had any of these charges investigated. If Johnson had believed Dunham's stories were true, it seems logical to assume that he would have attempted to prove them, in an effort to stop those who were trying to impeach him. But he never did. Such a lack of action indicates that he gave little, if any, credence to Dunham's incriminations. Johnson merely published the July 29 missives in what may well have been an effort to deflate the impeachment movement. He accomplished this, but only temporarily. Johnson also wanted to distract public attention from his impending move to suspend Secretary of War Edwin Stanton.[50]

Ashley went to see Dunham openly; his visits were public knowledge. Newspaper articles about their meetings appeared as early as May. Besides, Ashley was practiced in political maneuver. Had he really wanted to suborn Dunham, he would have gone to see him in secret. A conspiracy is simply not formed in public. Furthermore, Ashley was not a liar; he never denied having seen Dunham, but he did categorically deny having asked him to fabricate evidence.[51] If Ashley was guilty of anything, it was a lack of discretion, born of his intense desire to save the country from what he believed was a dangerous concentration of presidential power.

Finally, Ashley never directly accused Johnson, before the Committee on the Judiciary, or in any official capacity, of being involved in Lincoln's assassination, nor did Ashley ever attempt to present any evidence purporting to prove this. If he had truly wanted to destroy Johnson by any means, fair or foul, he certainly had ample opportunity to do so. Yet, he never presented any false information against the President. No doubt, blinded by his zeal to find legitimate evidence against Johnson, Ashley was willing to talk to anyone, whatever his reputation, who claimed to have some proof of Johnson's misconduct. Ashley's behavior was foolish, compulsive, and ruinous for his career, but it was not criminal. There is no evidence to support the allegation that in attempting to impeach Johnson, Ashley conspired to commit perjury.

On August 12, while the controversy over the Dunham communications was raging, Johnson suspended Secretary of War Stanton from his duties. This appeared to be a possible violation of the Tenure of Office Act, which had been passed in March. (The act required Senate approval for the removal of federal officials.) Ashley later argued that, had Congress been in session at the time, Johnson would have easily been impeached. The Chicago *Tribune* now came out for impeachment. The New York *Tribune*, which had been conservative in regard to impeachment, said that Johnson "has betrayed his party; he has betrayed his friends; he has betrayed his country."[52]

During the late summer and fall of 1867, Ashley was in Ohio vigorously campaigning for the Republican state ticket headed by gubernatorial candidate Rutherford B. Hayes. The campaign centered on a proposed state constitutional amendment calling for Negro suffrage. The election soon came to be regarded as a referendum on the future direction of congressional reconstruction. The issue of the impeachment was also prominent in the canvass, as Ashley clearly indicated on the eve of the election when he told a cheering rally that the contest was not merely local, but a vote which "would endorse or condemn the chief magistrate [Johnson] of the nation."[53]

The outcome of the election was a disaster for the radicals. The Negro suffrage amendment failed. Both houses of the legislature went to the Democrats, which meant that Wade would not win reelection, and Hayes won by fewer than 3,000 votes. Republicans also suffered setbacks in other states. All this was taken as a sign that the radicals were losing ground to their more conservative Republican colleagues. And that meant the immediate push toward impeachment would be weakened. The election returns depressed Ashley because the defeats dimmed the chances for impeachment. Carl Schurz accurately predicted that "whether or not Congress will go forward with the impeachment has become somewhat doubtful since the Ohio and Pennsylvania elections. The majority will possibly lack the courage."[54]

By mid-November, a weary Ashley was back in Washington for the final meeting of the first session of the Fortieth Congress. On November 23, he appeared before the Committee on the Judiciary to answer questions about his conduct in regard to the impeachment investigation. He admitted having gone to visit Dunham in order to obtain the incriminating Johnson letters, which Dunham claimed were genuine. But when these supposed letters could not be produced, and when he discovered that all Dunham's statements were vague and inconclusive, he never offered any evidence to the committee. Ashley emphatically denied all of Dunham's charges against him.[55]

Conceding that he suspected that Johnson was somehow connected with the assassination, he was asked why he had not presented evidence to support these suspicions. He answered: "I have no evidence that I regard as valid. . . .I have had no evidence which I regard as sufficient for the conviction of a criminal before a jury, and hence I never presented it." But Eldridge of Wisconsin was not satisfied, and he refused to let the matter rest. "What do you mean by saying that you had no evidence in your possession which you consider valid?" In his extreme frustration and depression over the failure of the Negro suffrage amendment in Ohio and haunted by the conviction that failure to impeach Johnson would destroy all chances for a successful reconstruction, Ashley replied:

> It was not the kind of evidence which would satisfy the great mass of men, especially the men who do not concur with me in my theory about this matter. I have had a theory about it. I have always believed that President Harrison and President Taylor and President Buchanan were poisoned, and poisoned for the express purpose of putting the Vice Presidents in the presidential office. In the first two instances it was successful. It was attempted with Mr. Buchanan and failed. . . . Then Mr. Lincoln was assassinated, and from my standpoint I could come to a conclusion which impartial men, holding different views, could not come. It would not amount to legal evidence.[56]

It was, of course, a bizarre theory and one he should have kept to himself. It was a mistake to have uttered such a statement publicly, and Ashley knew this immediately. But he had spent a year trying to impeach Johnson. He had followed up innumerable leads that went nowhere, and now the setbacks in the 1867 elections seemed to indicate a conservative resurgence. Ashley was exhausted and in a moment of extreme frustration he acted senselessly.

Yet the impression created by some historians that this was his only reason for moving an impeachment investigation is false. Ashley truly believed that Johnson had violated the Constitution, had acted in defiance of his oath of office, and had tried to subvert constructive reconstruction legislation. Johnson was also, according to Ashley, attempting to increase the power of the executive branch of government. All these presidential actions Ashley believed were dangerous to the nation, and for these reasons, he favored impeachment.

On November 25, the Committee on the Judiciary laid its majority and minority reports before the House. Since Churchill had changed his mind, the majority was now in favor of calling for articles of impeachment.[57] Convinced that the effort to remove him was going to be successful, Johnson prepared to resist the attempt at suspending him while the trial was in progress. His cabinet was prepared to back him on this. Logan believed that the majority report would carry. Ashley exclaimed that the impeachment would "be successful in spite of the cowards."[58]

But the results of the 1867 elections and the unstable financial conditions of the country had changed attitudes on impeachment. The Toledo *Blade*, for example, now concluded that the country could not endure the excitement of an attempt to remove Johnson. Other journals and individuals questioned the validity of the majority report, viewing it as a purely partisan document, with no real evidence that the President was guilty of "high crimes and misdemeanors." Ohio Congressman James Garfield, appalled by the majority report, was working hard to defeat the impeachers. By December 3, word of Ashley's theory had become public knowledge, and this further lowered the impeachment fever. Some of the staunchest advocates of impeachment soon became aware that the effort was going to fail. On December 7, the resolution calling for Johnson's impeachment was soundly defeated, 108 to 57. Over sixty Republicans had voted no.[59] The first attempt at impeachment had ended in failure.

Ashley's deportment in the whole matter was severely criticized. The Toledo *Blade* called his handling of the impeachment a "fiasco." His attempt to find evidence proving that Johnson was connected with Lincoln's assassination was, according to the *Blade*, "foolish and absurd." "His mistake was permitting his passion to get the better of his judgment . . . ." The whole affair had simply been "botched and boggled." Believing that he was being falsely accused, Ashley requested the opportunity to respond to his critics. He answered them in letters written to the Toledo *Blade* and the New York *Tribune*.[60]

He carefully pointed out that he had never publicly charged Johnson with complicity in Lincoln's assassination, although he admitted that he privately held such suspicions. This was true, since in his March 7 speech, he only intimated that he believed Johnson was involved. But his defense seems to beg the question, for such statements were impetuous and extravagant. He admitted having questioned criminals during the course of his investigation, but he declared that he would do it again, if he believed that documentary evidence could be placed in his hands which might unravel "the conspiracy which resulted in Mr. Lincoln's death. . . . Certainly, no one would expect to obtain such information from honest men. Honest men are not privy to premeditated murders." Once again he also unequivocally denied having manufactured evidence.[61]

Ashley conceded that the elections of 1867, and the unstable financial conditions of the country, had created a reaction which helped defeat the impeachment movement. Yet all this aside, he still believed that Johnson's conduct with regard to reconstruction, his violations of the Constitution, and his betrayal of principles warranted his removal. Ashley was convinced that history would vindicate those who favored impeachment.[62] But no defense could lessen the harm done Ashley by his admitted imprudence. No one seemed in the mood to heed him. The Ohio radical had become *persona non grata* to a number of Republicans. A fellow Toledoan, George Welles, wrote that Ashley's impeachment testimony had made him a laughing stock. "The fact is," Welles said, "this last move of Ashley's has annihilated him." It was time, thought Welles, for someone else to fill his shoes as congressman. Ashley's political enemies had been trying for a long time to defeat him, and it seemed that their chance had finally come. When a second attempt at impeachment was instituted in February, 1868, Ashley was discreetly omitted from the proceedings.[63] His actions had become extremely controversial, his standing among fellow Republicans went down, and his brilliant political career was severely damaged.

CHAPTER X

RECONSTRUCTION AND DEFEAT

Although the Republicans had achieved a great success in the elections of 1866, by December the party was still not unified. Ashley and his radical allies realized that they needed moderate support if they were to override Johnson's expected vetoes. Although many moderates were willing to go along with the ideas of the more advanced Republicans, if they had no other choice, for the moment they remained cautious. Further, the radicals were fragmented, often at odds among themselves about the proper course to pursue regarding reconstruction.

Ashley read the election results as a mandate for congressional action; he was prepared to stiffen the terms of reconstruction if the former Confederate states refused to ratify the Fourteenth Amendment.[1] Yet, except on impeachment, his thoughts and actions were neither doctrinaire nor unyielding during the Thirty-ninth and Fortieth Congresses. During this period, he was quite willing to accept compromises on short-term aims in an effort to achieve long-term goals. His dedication to radicalism did not diminish as he became a leader in the battle for Negro rights in the North as well as in the South. But his commitment to black suffrage and his impeachment activities lessened his influence; by the close of the Fortieth Congress, he was only a lame duck congressman looking for a political post.

Much of his time was committed to the impeachment during 1867, but he was also a major participant in struggles over Negro suffrage, the admission of new states, and the terms of reconstruction. During the opening day of the second session of the Thirty-ninth Congress, the Ohioan announced his intention to introduce a new reconstruction measure. The day after, John Broomall's resolution requiring the Committee on Territories to inquire into the expediency of reporting a bill establishing territorial governments, with universal manhood suffrage, in the defeated states, carried the House by a wide margin.[2] The relative ease by which the motion passed showed that the Republicans were united on one point: unless the Johnson governments ratified the Fourteenth Amendment, they would be declared null and void, and replaced by some congressional arrangement.

But the details of the congressional plan divided the Republicans. On the night of December 5, almost all the Republican members of the House and Senate attended a caucus. During the meeting, Ashley attacked Congressman Henry J. Raymond, publisher of the *New York Times*, for having supported Johnson in the 1866 National Union Convention. (Johnson tried to use this convention, which had been held in Philadelphia, as the basis for a new conservative political party, but the effort failed.) After an acrimonious debate about whether Raymond should be allowed to participate in a Republican caucus, the body decided to allow the New Yorker to remain.[3] But the actions of Ashley and his colleagues in the radical wing of the party gave clear warning that they would not stand for obstructionism from Johnson and his friends.

Immediately before Congress adjourned for the Christmas holidays, Stevens resurrected his April, 1866, reconstruction bill in the House. Instead of returning home during the interlude, Ashley remained in Washington to help with impeachment and to work on a new reconstruction bill, which he intended to introduce at the first opportunity. Before formally presenting it, he wanted to consult with the leading men in Congress, and he informed his friend Joseph Medill that "it embodied the opinion of a large majority of our friends."[4]

In December, 1866, the Supreme Court in *ex parte Milligan*, declared martial law invalid except in the actual theater of war, where civil courts were not open. The radicals were worried. If the decision was applicable to the South, it might hinder future efforts at reconstruction. Ashley believed that if the Court persisted in impairing legislative authority, it, like the President, could be circumvented. After all, he claimed, according to the Constitution, Congress was the dominant branch of government.[5] Thus it appeared that Congress was beginning to think that it needed to take more forceful action about reconstruction.

On January 3, Stevens offered a substitute for the pending reconstruction bill. The new proposal stipulated that the Johnson state governments were to be recognized as valid "for municipal purposes." (Radical opposition moved Stevens to eliminate this provision of the bill.) Conventions were to be held in the states to draw up new constitutions guaranteeing impartial laws "without regard to language, race or former condition." The bill called for Negro citizenship and suffrage and for the disenfranchisement of Confederate civil and military officials of all ranks for a minimum of five years. Anyone who swore that he favored ending the war by March 4, 1864, and who thereafter did not voluntarily aid the rebellion, would be exempt from forfeiture of citizenship. When a state had met all the requirements of the bill, it was up to Congress to decide on readmittance.[6] Ashley then moved to amend Stevens's bill, by substituting his own reconstruction proposal.

The Ohio radical's new measure was stronger than his December, 1865, bill, but most of its provisions had already been presented, and it was not really very extreme. The theory behind this bill was again territorialization. All the Johnson state governments, except Tennessee, were to be declared invalid and all the laws passed by their legislatures null and void. Until a constitutional state convention could meet and select a provisional governor, the state was to be governed by a five-man committee of public safety. The measure also provided for universal suffrage for all male citizens over twenty-one. *Citizens* were defined as "all persons, irrespective of race or former condition of servitude, born in the United States, or naturalized in pursuance of its laws." All military and civilian officeholders of the national or state governments of the Confederacy were to be disenfranchised, a stronger disability provision than Ashley had previously favored.[7]

A convention was to be empowered to form a new constitution, providing for the adoption of ordinances declaring "that all persons in the State are free and equal before the law," repudiating the rebel debt, and forbidding compensation for any emancipated slave. If the constitution were approved by a majority of the eligible voters, Congress would then decide whether the state had met all the conditions of the law, and was thus entitled to readmission to the Union. If the situation warranted, the measure provided for the establishment of military rule. The one completely new idea was that Texas be divided into two states.[8]

Ashley included in the bill a provision calling for establishment of "a well-organized system of free schools for all children in the State . . . from which no child shall be excluded because of race or color." A similar provision had been included in his March, 1862, bill. Although the 1867 measure has often been called extremely radical, it did not include the 1862 proposal for confiscation of rebel property, which might be given to freed slaves. On the whole, the provisions of this bill were moderate, or at the most slightly radical, and contained few new ideas. But the lack of unity among Republicans doomed it from the start, even though Ashley and some of his radical collaborators liked to think it was going to pass.[9]

For some time, Ashley had been aware that the battle with Johnson over reconstruction would be difficult, and thus realized the political importance of bringing Colorado and Nebraska into the Union. His Senate counterpart on the territorial committee, Wade, felt the same way and clearly summed up the feeling of many practical Republicans when he said that he wanted the senators-elect from the two territories seated, "because I want this body strengthened immensely by the reinforcement that these gentlemen will bring to bear upon every question you can get up." But a problem arose because the franchise in both areas was limited to whites.

Many Republicans wanted the people in the territories to vote directly on the question of impartial suffrage as a prerequisite to admission, but Ashley and Wade, eager to get these states into the Union as rapidly as possible, were both willing to settle for a provision which deleted the "white only" suffrage clause. Statehood bills incorporating this idea passed the Senate on January 9.[10]

But many House Republicans felt that such a simple guarantee of the franchise was not strong enough. Accordingly, the House voted its approval of George Boutwell's amendment to the Nebraska bill which required the territorial legislature to declare by public act that there would be no "abridgment or denial of the elective franchise or any other right to any person by reason of race or color." The amendment carried, with Ashley voting affirmatively. The bill then easily passed. Happy with this result, Ashley moved to have the Boutwell amendment added to the Colorado statehood bill. This was done, and that measure passed also. The Senate quickly concurred with the House changes, but Johnson vetoed both measures. Although the Nebraska veto was eventually overridden, Colorado had to wait another nine years for admittance.

Ashley's actions on the statehood bills show that he was not an ultra-radical unwilling to engage in parliamentary games; he was not trying to preserve doctrinal purity whatever the price.[11] Dedicated to the cause of human freedom, Ashley might be, but he was statesman enough to understand that sometimes halting steps were necessary to achieve any forward movement.

Having guided the two statehood bills through the House, Ashley again turned his attention to reconstruction. On January 16, he presented a modified substitute for his earlier reconstruction measure. For some reason he did not explain, perhaps in an effort to meet moderate Republican criticism of the bill, the provision defining citizenship no longer contained the statement, "irrespective of race or former condition of servitude," though it still stipulated that all persons born or naturalized in the United States were citizens. Other changes simply tightened the procedures of the enrollment process and provided for a secret ballot.[12]

During the next few weeks, both the Ashley and Stevens bills were severely attacked by moderate and conservative Republicans led by John Bingham and Henry Raymond. By January 26, neither side had accomplished anything, although Bingham had presented a motion to refer all reconstruction measures back to the Joint Committee. Stevens then requested Ashley to withdraw his bill and Bingham to withdraw his motion.[13]

Immediately after Stevens's request, Ashley rose to discuss the issue. Readily agreeing to withdraw his measure, he stated flatly: he did not

intend the Thirty-ninth Congress to adjourn without providing governments, justice, suffrage, and equality for the loyal men of the South. He
was in favor of mercy. He would have readmitted states if they had ratified
the Fourteenth Amendment. He could forgive the crimes of those who had
rebelled. But he was determined to see that loyal Southerners were protected. Ashley summed up his position:

> I want peace, I want unity, I want the Government restored, but I do
> not want the men who conquered the rebellion proscribed, and the gov-
> ernments of the rebel States carried on by men who have been waging
> bitter war against us for the last four years. . . . I say we are ready to
> forgive the great body of the Southern people, we are anxious to for-
> give them: but we are determined, by the grace of God, that these rebel
> States governments organized by Johnson shall not be reorganized, come
> what may; that disloyal Representatives shall not appear upon this floor,
> nor shall the electoral votes of such States be counted in any presidential
> election until constitutional governments have been organized and re-
> cognized by the Congress of the United States.[14]

The rest of his speech merely restated and defended his previously announced opinions on reconstruction.

Ashley was constantly interrupted by questions and comments from
the opposition. J. W. Chanler of New York asked him whether, if a state
contained only Negroes, he would recognize it? Ashley emphatically stated
his commitment to black suffrage by an unequivocal answer:

> If there were a single State in the American Union in which there was
> not a single white man and all were black men, I would clothe its popu-
> lation with the right of the franchise, and with every other right of an
> American citizen under this Government.[15]

This statement was greeted with ringing applause.

But Bingham refused to withdraw his motion. On January 28, the
House, much to Ashley's regret, voted to return the Stevens plan to the
Joint Committee. By early February, Stevens realized that his measure
would never pass. Reluctantly, he agreed to a plan of military restoration
drawn up by Senator George H. Williams of Oregon. During the next three
weeks, a complicated series of parliamentary maneuvers and compromises
took place in both the House and Senate, and a reconstruction bill passed
on February 20. On March 2, Johnson vetoed the bill. He was overridden,
and congressional reconstruction became a reality.[16]

The Reconstruction Act declared the Johnson governments illegal and
divided the South into five military districts. Each district was to be headed
by an officer not below the rank of brigadier general. The measure stipulated
a procedure for statehood which included Negro suffrage, disenfranchisement of leading Confederates, ratification of the Fourteenth Amendment,
and congressional approval of new written constitutions. On March 23,
Congress passed a second Reconstruction Act, spelling out procedures for

electing delegates, holding conventions, and adopting new constitutions.[17]

The first Reconstruction Act embodied the ideas of the moderate and conservative elements of the Republican party. The theory of territorialization was ignored. There was no guarantee of access to public schools for blacks. The disenfranchisement clause was limited and lenient in its application. The Johnson state administrations were not only not destroyed, but were recognized as provisional governments.

The radicals, including Ashley, had hoped for more, but they could not realize their hopes. Consequently, the term *radical Reconstruction* appears unjustified. The legislation did not confiscate land nor grant homesteads to Negroes. Republicans were mistaken in believing that, with suffrage, Southern blacks would have all the protection necessary for productive and stable lives. For the old Southern ruling class was bound to try to regain power. Without the economic strength rooted in land ownership, the freedmen would be unable to withstand the onslaught of the wealthy Bourbons against their political and civil rights. As Georges Clemenceau wrote in an article on Reconstruction: "There can be no real emancipation for men who do not possess at least a small portion of the soil."[18] Without land reform the so-called radical congressional plan was doomed from the start. It might be more appropriately named *moderate patchwork Reconstruction*.

During the spring of 1867, Ashley gave much of his time to the ongoing impeachment investigation. But his attention was also directed toward Ohio politics and, in particular, toward Negro suffrage.

After Ohio had ratified the Fourteenth Amendment, the Republicans in the state legislature sought to amend the state constitution by striking the word *white* from the document. The result of this movement was a Negro suffrage amendment tied to a proposal disenfranchising those who had fought against the Union, avoided the draft, or had not received an honorable discharge. The reasoning behind the latter proposal was that, since the amendment had to be approved by popular vote, disenfranchising Copperheads and deserters might win over voters who would otherwise oppose black suffrage. The Ohio Republican party supported the amendment. So did Ashley. Later he said he deeply regretted that impartial suffrage had been tied to disenfranchisement. Better, he believed, to have deferred state action on voting, since he was convinced that Negro suffrage could more easily be obtained by an amendment to the national Constitution. But once the legislature submitted the proposal, he courageously stumped the state for its ratification.[19]

Ashley's apprehensions about linking the amendment to disenfranchisement were well founded. It soon became known that over 27,000 Ohioans had deserted after Appomattox, some seeking to avoid further military service in the Indian wars or being stationed on the Mexican border; others eager to get home in time for spring planting; still others believing that the war was over and that they had fulfilled their commitment. These men had never received honorable discharges. A huge outcry against the amendment rapidly developed throughout the state. Ashley quickly tried to stem the force of the opposition, by pushing through Congress a bill which removed the stigma of desertion from all military personnel who left the armed forces without authorization after April 19, 1865.[20] Unfortunately, Ashley's bill came too late. Thousands of potential supporters of the impartial suffrage amendment had been permanently scared off by the ill-considered action of the Ohio legislature.

The Democrats immediately attacked Negro suffrage in the most vile ways. Wagonloads of young girls, with banners exclaiming, "Fathers, save us from Negro equality," appeared throughout the state. Appeals to racial superiority quickly surfaced. The Republicans tried to counter these tactics by waving the bloody shirt and denouncing Copperheads. Knowing that the election was being watched as a referendum on reconstruction and the impeachment, Ashley campaigned incessantly, averaging two speeches a day for over six weeks. Railing against the bigotry and prejudice which poisoned the campaign atmosphere, the Toledo radical declared that the "amendment simply proposed to incorporate in the State Constitution what had from the first been in the Declaration of Independence and the National Bill of Rights."[21] He was forcefully advocating Negro rights in the North as well as the South, for he truly believed all men were entitled to the ballot. Ashley felt that the amendment might carry, but his cautious optimism was not rewarded. The amendment was soundly defeated; voters seemed weary of war issues. The Republican nominee for governor, Rutherford B. Hayes, won by a narrow margin, but the state legislature went Democratic.[22]

In Pennsylvania, New York, New Jersey, Maryland, and Kansas, the Republicans also lost ground, causing many Union men to become more cautious. Although Ashley was discouraged and depressed by the results of the election, he was convinced that the fight for human rights should not lose momentum: "Instead of compromising or retreating because of our recent so-called reverses, I am for making an advanced movement upon the enemy. To retreat is impossible. . . . To encamp upon the late battle-field and attempt to remain there by entrenching is certain defeat. An advanced movement is our only hope."[23] But by the end of 1867, with the publication of his impeachment testimony and the subsequent defeat of the impeachment resolution, Ashley's power to influence events had seriously diminished. His advice went unheeded.

In July, 1867, he offered a joint resolution for a constitutional amendment, which would have given the ballot to all United States citizens. Ashley had first mentioned such a proposal on May 29, 1866, and his July amendment had included the stipulation that after July 4, 1876, all naturalized citizens would be required to read and write the English language as a qualification for voting. In July he had not expected to have any action taken on the proposal; he simply wanted to call the attention of the country to the question of suffrage as a national issue and to the need for all citizens to have the right to the ballot. He also believed that suffrage should be uniform in all the states. But his proposal for an educational qualification had evoked hostility among his German- and Irish-born constituents, and he was attacked for it during the 1867 campaign.[24]

In an effort to counter this criticism, Ashley revised his amendment in December. He denied that by requiring an educational test, he was trying to keep naturalized citizens from voting. On the contrary, his purpose was "to secure to every citizen born in this country or naturalized in pursuance of its laws the high privilege of the American ballot." The educational qualification was eliminated and replaced by a requirement that each state must establish and maintain, by taxation, an efficient system of free public schools. Since there was no racial requirement for admission, the schools were to be open to blacks. Ashley specifically said, "no child of the Republic shall be excluded." The Toledoan was thereby advocating equality of education in the North as well as in the South.

Ashley fervently believed that only an educated people could protect liberty. "No man," he said, "can overstate the inestimable value of education. I am confident that without the maintenance of free public schools in this country the people could not long be secure in civil or religious liberty." Arguing that if every citizen had the ballot, the piecemeal approach to reconstruction would be eliminated, he declared: "The most vital, all-important question of citizenship suffrage must be met and settled. No question of finance, or tariff, or taxation, nor even impeachment. . . must be permitted to supersede this."[25] But his colleagues were in no mood to listen to such ideas. The results of the recent elections made many Republicans believe that the suffrage issue should be avoided; therefore the movement toward a constitutional amendment was delayed until 1869.

The actual process of Reconstruction had not proceeded smoothly. In July Congress passed the Third Reconstruction Act, giving the military commanders additional powers in order to counteract Attorney General Henry S. Stanbery's narrow interpretation of previous measures. Further difficulties developed when Alabamians, for example, defeated their new constitution by registering as electors but then refusing to vote in the referendum, thus assuring that a majority of the legal voters would not approve the constitution.[26]

In order to cope with this problem, Ashley proposed a rather convoluted reconstruction measure on December 6; this included a section stipulating that only a majority of those actually voting was needed for ratification of state constitutions. On December 18, Ashley brought his bill before the House, but Stevens offered a simplified substitute, which retained the "majority of actual voters" idea and which passed quickly. After some slight Senate changes, and repassage over Johnson's veto, the measure became law on March 12, 1868.[27]

Johnson had fought congressional Reconstruction since its inception. The results of the 1867 elections only reinforced his belief that his obstructionism was effective. This was evident in the uncompromising tone of his December, 1867, message to Congress. During the next two months, his behavior further infuriated his congressional opponents. First, he asked Congress to vote thanks to General Winfield S. Hancock who sympathized with his positions, and who had replaced the radical favorite, Philip Sheridan, in Louisiana. Johnson also suspended General John Pope from command in Georgia and General O.C. Ord from command in Mississippi. Pope was replaced by the more conservative George G. Meade. Then, when the Senate refused to acquiesce in his suspension of Stanton, Johnson ordered Grant not to carry out any directives originating with the secretary of war. This led to a bitter dispute between the President and the general, and the radicals became enraged by Johnson's actions.[28]

Meanwhile, Republicans in Congress were being besieged by letters from Southern blacks and Unionists, deploring Johnson's appointments and consistently stating that unless his pernicious influence was diminished, Reconstruction would fail. Congress had to act if the cause of human freedom and the Republican program were to succeed in the South. As the Georgian Foster Blodgett said, if all was to go well, Congress had to stand firm, but "if Congress shows any weakness and fails to support our friends and allows the President to do as he pleases, then our party is in fact dead in Georgia and the entire South." Thus, when, on February 21, 1868, Johnson tried to remove Stanton from office and replace him with Lorenzo B. Thomas, the Republicans quickly seized the opportunity and passed a resolution of impeachment on February 24.[29]

Ashley had increasingly come to view Johnson's activities as usurpations of power. He became more and more convinced that the rights of all Americans and the safety of the government were "safer in the keeping of Congress than in the keeping of any President." On February 22, speaking directly to the issue of impeachment, the Ohioan bitterly attacked Johnson. Informing his audience that he was not approaching impeachment in the spirit of partisanship, he stated that for the good of the nation he wished only that removal had been attempted many months before. Accusing Johnson of forming alliances with former rebels, of deliberately violating the Tenure of Office Act, and of what amounted to maladministration in office, he pleaded for impeachment, both for the safety of the country and as a lesson to future presidents who might attempt one-man rule.

Ashley's speech presented a broad interpretation of the impeachment clause of the Constitution. Even if Johnson had not violated the Tenure of Office Act, he could be impeached, since the Ohio radical believed that removal from office by impeachment did not require commission of an indictable crime. "To assume that the President can be impeached only for 'treason' or 'bribery,'" he said, "is practically to assume that he cannot be impeached." In support of his position, Ashley cited the following passage from the constitutional scholar George Ticknor Curtis's *History of the Origin, Formation and Adoption of the Constitution of the United States*:

> The purposes of an impeachment lie wholly beyond the penalties of a statute or the customary law. The object of the proceeding is to ascertain whether cause exists for removing a public officer from office. Such a cause may be found in the fact that either in the discharge of his office or aside from its functions he has violated a law or committed what is technically denominated a crime. But a cause for removal from office may exist where no offense against positive law has been commited, as where an individual has from immorality or imbecility or maladministration become unfit to exercise the office.[30]

Ashley, like Curtis, interpreted the Constitution to mean that high crimes and misdemeanors not punishable by a court of law—such as nonfeasance in office, abuse of power, violation of public trust and neglect of duty—as well as indictable crimes, made a federal officer liable for impeachment. Recent studies indicate that the weight of precedent was on Ashley's side.[31]

Although Ashley had been in the vanguard of the fight for impeachment, that very position had made him the focus of too much controversy. He was too much the political maverick. He was completely left out of the impeachment proceedings, not asked to serve on the committee which drew up the articles of impeachment nor selected as one of the House prosecutors in the case.[32]

At the outset of the attempt to remove Johnson, Ashley and his radical colleagues were supremely confident of victory. They believed that tight party discipline would work to make the Senate convict the President. In a letter to his friend, newspaperman William H. Smith, Ashley wrote, "I think you may be prepared for A. J. disposition inside of 60 days. If not woe to the man who defeats it." But apprehension soon set in, and as the weeks passed, it became obvious that the final vote was going to be very close. Soon even the radical Cincinnati *Gazette* and the radical Worcester *Daily Spy* admitted that Johnson might be acquitted. On May 16, before a packed gallery, the Senate voted on the eleventh article of impeachment and by one vote failed to give the two-thirds needed for conviction. Seven moderate Republicans joined the conservatives and Democrats in voting for acquittal.[33]

Frustrated and humiliated by the Senate's action, Ashley tried to put up a brave front. "We have just felt the fatal power of a single vote," he wrote to his friend Denison Steele. "Do not suppose that we are discouraged or dismayed. Failure on the eleventh article, is to be our political Bull Run. . . . In such an hour let every Republican do his whole duty." But in reality he was extremely depressed, knowing perfectly well that they would never obtain the extra vote needed to remove Johnson and that the cause was lost. On May 26, the vote on the second and third articles remained unchanged, and the impeachment endeavor died.[34]

Ashley was naturally deeply disturbed by the final outcome. The action of the Senate was "indefensible and disgraceful." He believed that a victory for Grant in the upcoming presidental election was necessary to save the party from political disaster. But he felt the failure of impeachment was a defeat for democratic constitutional government, for he thought that the assumption of "kingly prerogatives" by Johnson might be carried further by future presidents. This, Ashley feared, could lead to the supremacy of the executive over the legislature, an idea which appalled him.[35]

In an effort to counter this dangerous trend, on May 30 Ashley introduced a constitutional amendment abolishing the Electoral College and the office of Vice President, and limiting the presidency to one term. He also wanted uniform rules of voter registration, and universal suffrage which would include blacks and women.[36]

In a speech explaining his purpose and aims, Ashley denounced executive usurpation of legislative and judicial prerogatives, criticized the presidential use of patronage and the power of appointment, portrayed the vice presidency as a useless office, denounced the caucus system of picking candidates for office, and called for direct primaries. In the course of his presentation, he summed up a lifelong goal by declaring, "I want citizenship and suffrage to be synonymous."[37] But he had little support, and the amendment died in committee.

The prospect of diminishing influence due to reverses in the 1867 elections, and the constant plea of Southern Unionists and Negroes that Johnson was an obstacle to Reconstruction put Ashley and his radical allies in a dilemma—impeach the President or stand pat. If they attempted impeachment and succeeded, then they were assured of dominance. Radical Republicanism would be safe. If they failed, their influence was over. But to do nothing in the face of presidential opposition to congressional legislation would have been an admission that their power was fading. Thus, they had no real choice. Many Republicans, including Ashley, firmly believed that Johnson was guilty of usurpation of legislative rights and powers, and of refusal to administer faithfully the law. They chose to fight against expanding executive power. But they lost the battle.

Johnson, by his constant support of Southern conservatives, by his narrow interpretation of the Constitution, and by his refusal to execute various laws, was attempting to obstruct legislation passed over his veto. Thus he was partly responsible for the ultimate failure of radical Reconstruction. But this after all was what he intended. Ashley had seen this almost from the beginning. By February, 1868, most Republicans reluctantly agreed; but it was too late. The Republican party remained as strong as ever after impeachment failed, but the radicals no longer counted. A new economic era was beginning. The day of the antislavery radicals was passing: their inability to impeach Johnson merely hastened the end. Yet, the Republicans' hesitant step was the correct one. Had they been victorious in their fight against Johnson, the chances for a successful reconstruction would have been improved and future social problems might have been avoided.

The erosion of Ashley's remaining power and influence came quickly. Since mid-1867 and his courageous, unpopular stand for Negro suffrage, quickly followed by his mistakes in the impeachment move, rumors had spread in Ohio that Ashley was finished politically and would not be renominated in 1868.[38] After the Senate failed to impeach Johnson, even Ashley's staunchest supporter, David Ross Locke, temporarily deserted him. In an editorial on July 27, Locke wrote that the Toledo area needed a new congressman, for times had changed:

> The questions upon which Mr. Ashley entered public life will be virtually settled with the election of Gen. Grant, and a new class of questions will come before the people. Mr. Ashley will go out of office with Mr. Johnson, and with a Republican President and a Republican Congress, slavery, and the evils it left will be quietly wiped out. Mr. Ashley dealt the monster effective blows in his day;—he can be of no use whatever in beating its dead carcass. The public good requires the consideration of new questions [economic ones] daily looming into importance, and which we believe other men, whose paths in life have been different, are more competent to deal with.[39]

But Ashley had always been a fighter, and he refused simply to move aside. The tenacity which characterized his public career helped him win renomination. Since Locke was a good Republican, he immediately endorsed Ashley and gave him his full support.[40]

Ashley knew that he faced a rough battle, and he tried to rally all the help he could muster. He implored Sumner to campaign in his behalf. He asked his old friend Friedrich Hassaurek to speak to the German Republicans, who were still angered by his 1867 proposal for an educational qualification for voting. He also sent Republican National Chairman William Chandler urgent pleas for speakers and money, since the Ohio Republican State Committee, perceiving him as a political liability, refused him any aid. But his pleas were not answered; the National Committee sent only minuscule aid.[41]

The Democrats, trying to capitalize on the concern with economic issues, especially improvements for the Toledo harbor, nominated as their candidate Truman H. Hoag, president of the National Insurance Company and the Toledo Gas Company. The old conservative Republican clique led by Clark Waggoner and Morrison R. Waite, which had opposed Ashley for so long, bolted the party and supported Hoag. Ashley fought back with literally everything he had, intellectually and financially, but to no avail. His stands on black suffrage, women's rights, his opposition to Pendleton's inflationary greenback plan, and his long-standing mistrust of special privilege branded him as radical, and a man of the past. With these views, he seemed too much the political maverick for the conservative businessmen of the area, who were looking for a new type of leader.

Ashley could not overcome the opposition of the foreign-born and the business community, and he went down to defeat. But he was not humiliated. Evidently many of his constituents did not see him as a discredited politican out of tune with the times. He had outspokenly backed unpopular ideas. He was closely associated with the impeachment fiasco. Yet he lost the district by only 912 votes out of over 30,000 cast.[42] Ashley paid for the serious political mistakes he had made in the last year. But he came very close to vindication.

Immediately after his defeat, Ashley urgently asked all loyal Republicans, whether they had voted for him or not, to unite behind Grant and Colfax. He then proceeded to New York to campaign for the national ticket. When he heard that Grant had won, he was delighted. "A bright political morning now succeeds our long, dark and stormy political night," he wrote to Sumner.[43]

Campaigning had cost Ashley a great deal of money; he admitted that he was almost broke. Now the father of four (his third son Charles had been born in 1864, and Mary, his only daughter, in 1866), he was desperate for a job. He wrote to leading Republicans, sounding them out about a Cabinet appointment, but he apparently received no encouragement. As Jacob M. Howard of Michigan wrote on the back of Ashley's letter of inquiry: "Answered. . . that I know nothing of the situation."[44]

Returning to Congress as a lame duck representative, Ashley accomplished little. Still firmly committed to universal suffrage, he introduced a constitutional amendment providing for it. But the proposal was sent to the Committee on the Judiciary, where it died. During this session, Congress passed the Fifteenth Amendment giving Negroes the right to vote. Although Ashley voted for it, he took little part in the discussions and parliamentary maneuvers concerning the amendment.[45]

On March 4, 1869, his congressional duties came to an end. He had devoted a good portion of his career to the antislavery cause, and to trying to translate the phrase "liberty for all" into action. He could be proud that he had been at the center of activity during some of the finest political moments in his country's history. But his power as a party leader had eroded. His time had passed. Popular interests had already begun to change, and like other radical Republicans, Ashley saw himself bypassed in the new era.

CHAPTER XI

GOVERNOR AND BUSINESSMAN

As Ulysses S. Grant began to organize his administration, Ashley still had no position in government, but his friends quickly acted on his behalf. His long tenure as chairman of the Committee on the Territories had made him an expert on territorial affairs. When no cabinet post was forthcoming, he was willing to settle for a territorial governorship. As a matter of courtesy, recommendations for Ashley's appointment as governor of Montana were sent to Grant from many quarters, including a letter signed by ninety-eight members of the House and a note signed by fifteen senators. Rutherford B. Hayes, N.P. Banks, John A. Logan, George W. Julian, James G. Blaine, and William Chandler all wrote Grant to recommend Ashley's appointment. After discussing the matter with his cabinet, Grant sent Ashley's nomination to the Senate on April 25.

It was rumored that the President did not want to appoint Ashley, but that he yielded to the requests of Republican members of Congress. After a bitter debate, in which Democrats and anti-impeachment Republicans spoke against the Ohioan, Ashley was confirmed, but by only one vote. The radical senators voted solidly for the Toledoan.[1]

Ashley immediately accepted the position and requested a sixty-to-ninety-day leave of absence in order to prepare his family for the move, to fulfill previously arranged political commitments, and to tie up some loose ends in business. His Ohio political enemies quickly began to complain about his delay in leaving for Montana. Worried that the old Waggoner clique, in league with the Sherman machine, might attempt to have him removed from office, Ashley (before leaving for Montana) asked Secretary of State Hamilton Fish to assure him that he would be granted a full hearing if such a movement were initiated.[2]

After fulfilling his obligations, Ashley set out for Montana in late July. He left with high hopes for making a new life in the West. Confident that he could handle the governorship and build a Republican party in the territory, he wrote Sumner, "I expect when we secure a Republican Legislature in Montana, to honor our Territory with the names of Whittier, Garrison, Phillips, and Sumner. Whenever I have the power, you may trust me to perpetuate the names of the old Anti Slavery Guard."[3] But as far as politics were concerned, events would no longer conform to Ashley's vision of them and his purposes were to be thwarted.

Upon arriving in Montana, he began traveling around the territory in an effort to familiarize himself with the conditions of the area and the problems of the residents. Believing that the territory had good economic growth potential, he promised the inhabitants that he would try to have the Northern Pacific Railroad built through Montana within three years. He also appointed Benno Speyer of New York Commissioner of Territorial Emigration, in an effort to attract new settlers.[4] After his survey of the area, the new governor turned his attention to politics. But though he was initially well received, the political situation in Montana was really not congenial to someone with Ashley's radical background and ideas.

Many of the original settlers of the territory were Southerners or Confederate partisans from the border states. A substantial contingent of Missourians had emigrated to Montana in 1862 after the Confederate defeat at Pea Ridge. Among them were a group of men who had fought under the command of General Sterling Price. These men and the other pro-Southern elements became known in Montana politics as the "left wing of Price's Army." Most of the new settlers were attracted to the Democratic party, and since 1864 Democrats had dominated Montana politics. As the first secretary of the territory, General Thomas F. Meagher explained, "Outnumbering largely the loyal portion of the population, the sympathizers with the rebellion acquired not only a strong majority in the Territorial Legislature, but the mastery, moreover of the political action of the Territory in the election of county and other officers."[5] These Democrats were still powerful in 1869, and they were dismayed at the selection of a leading radical Republican as governor. Ashley thus faced a difficult situation.

In late September, while speaking in Helena, Ashley said that he was still a friend of the Negro, but that he was an enemy of amalgamation. Accordingly he would not ask the settlers of Montana to promote the immigration of people "with whom they cannot properly intermarry." He was immediately attacked for these statements and accused of turning his back on the Negro and adopting the idea of a "white man's government."[6]

Ashley quickly denied that this was his intention. He was for a government for all the people; he did not favor legislation which would exclude any race from emigrating to Montana, nor would he ever vote for any law which was unequal or unjust to any group. But, he said:

Because I will not oppress a race, it does not follow that I should have
no preference as to who should be my friends and neighbors. I voted
for the 15th Amendment, and am as anxious for its adoption as any
man. . . . I never have favored, and never expect to favor, the amalgamation of "barbarians," whether of the Mongolian, Indian or Negro races,
with the white race. In aiding immigration to Montana from the civilized nations of Europe, I would prefer those of Great Britain, Germany
and Northern Europe. . . .7

There can be no doubt that these opinions express racial prejudice and
bias, but they were not new ideas now being conveniently brought forth. In
his first major congressional speech in May, 1860, Ashley had clearly stated
his strong opposition to miscegenation. The governor had always been uncer-
tain whether blacks could assimilate into American society. Ashley's hesi-
tancy came from the commonly accepted view that a deeply racist white
population would never accept blacks as equals. (Other radical Republicans
held similar opinions. Benjamin Wade, for example, had private prejudices
against Negroes, but maintained that he would not allow his bias to interfere with his public responsibility.)

Ashley's Helena statement did not mean that he was deserting his basic
principles; he was still committed to full political and civil rights for all
Americans regardless of race or class. "I am not," he wrote to a friend in
Toledo, "for a white man's government; either in Montana or elsewhere.
Nor am I for excluding any race of men by positive law or by *'unfriendly
legislation'* from Montana. As I have often said, *'the protection I ask of
government for myself and mine I demand for every race and condition of
men:'* not only in Montana, but throughout the nation."8 Since Ashley
had to deal with a hostile pro-Southern white population in Montana, it
was prudent for him to try to promote white migration to the territory.
But if Negroes came, he was prepared to fight for their rights, and he
would soon prove it in his message to the Montana legislature.

The Helena speech was unfortunate, however, because it left Ashley
open to attack from his political enemies who were looking for a way
further to tarnish his already clouded reputation. Faced with a hostile
opposition unsympathetic to the Negro, and wanting to turn Montana into
a Republican territory, the new governor tried to walk the political fence.
But in trying to win over his Democratic opponents by his statements on
immigration while still maintaining his real goal of political and civil freedom for all, Ashley pleased no one.

In December, the governor was unexpectedly faced with an assembled
legislature. Federal laws in 1868 and 1869 called for biennial rather than
annual sessions of territorial representative bodies. The Montana legislature,
controlled by Democrats (there were no Republicans in the upper house,

or Council, and only three in the lower house), believed the body should meet in 1869 and in 1870, and after that biennially. Ashley, on the other hand, insisted that since Congress had not appropriated funds for a legislative meeting, the current session was unnecessary. But since a quorum was present, he accepted the situation, recognized the assembly, and decided to let the courts rule on the legality of the session.[9]

In his message to the legislature, Ashley discussed territorial appointments, election laws, biennial sessions, gerrymandering (he was opposed to it), tax reform, the Northern Pacific Railroad, and the general conditions of mining and agriculture in Montana. He also reasserted his opinions on immigration, maintaining that people from northern Europe were better suited to the climate and conditions of the territory than "any race from a tropical climate, whether white or black."[10]

One of the social problems facing the area was the importation of Chinese coolies. The governor was against this practice. Comparing it to slavery, he condemned the use of cheap coolie labor as a vicious crime which drove wages down and thus hurt the average American workingman, both white and black. The only people who would benefit from this pernicious practice would be the "capitalists and monopolists." Yet, Ashley was against discrimination and unfair taxation directed against the Chinese living in Montana, and he asked for equal protection of the law for all people.[11]

Some clear indications that Ashley had not receded from his basic political beliefs were his plea for a free public school system, open to children of all races and classes, and his request that the legislature change the election laws to conform to the exact wording of the Fifteenth Amendment. Finally, he clearly showed his Jackson Democratic background when he came out against special business legislation which benefited the few at the expense of the many. "The first and highest duty of the legislature [he stated] is to protect the laboring man from the grasping avarice of capital. I have looked in vain for any general or specific act of the Legislative Assembly . . . to secure the benefit of association or organization of any class of laboring men . . . . If labor cannot be helped by legislation, it has, at least, the right to demand that it shall not be taxed for the benefit of a favored few."[12] Statements such as these were bound to alarm the business-minded Stalwarts who were beginning to control the national Republican party.

Ashley's relationship with the Democratic legislature quickly degenerated into mutual hostility. Almost immediately, the governor became embroiled in a controversy over territorial appointments. An 1867 Montana law had stipulated that the territorial auditor, treasurer, and superintendent of public instruction be chosen by general elections, and then commissioned by the governor. Elections for these offices had recently been held, but Ashley refused to accept them as legal. He pointed out that the Organic Act of 1864 establishing Montana provided that the governor nominate, and with the advice and consent of the Council, appoint all territorial officers. Ashley nominated his own candidates for the three disputed offices, but when he rejected a Democratic compromise to divide all territorial appointments evenly between Republicans and Democrats, the Council refused to confirm any of his appointees. Relations between the two branches of government then became exceedingly antagonistic. Of the sixty-three pieces of legislation enacted during the session, three were passed over Ashley's veto; thirty-eight became law without his signature. The governor's ability to deal with the Democrats had been severely weakened. Then in the middle of the session he suddenly received word that Grant had removed him from office.[13] As if to humiliate him further, Grant nominated General B.F. Potts as his replacement. Potts had originally been the choice for governor of the Sherman forces in Ohio.

No official reason for his dismissal was offered. He was shocked by the implication that he was removed for betraying the Republican party. Stating that he had just finished settling his family in Montana at great expense, and that he had staked his political future on converting the territory to the Republican party, Ashley wrote to various Republicans asking them to come to his aid. In each letter he emphatically denied having deserted the basic principles of Republicanism. Ashley also wrote to Grant and Fish, asking for his promised hearing, and he stated that his actions as governor had the full support of Republicans in Montana. The administration never did grant him a hearing, although his claim of Republican support was sustained by the letters and petititons presented in his behalf and by editorials in the Republican Helena *Daily Herald*.[14]

Charles Sumner tried to help his old friend when, in early January, 1870, Grant called at the senator's residence to discuss the Santo Domingo annexation treaty. Two newspapermen, Ben Perley Poore and John W. Forney, were having dinner with Sumner and were talking about Ashley when the President unexpectedly arrived. Before Grant could begin to talk about the treaty, Forney and Sumner brought up the subject of Ashley's removal. Grant became extremely upset. He called Ashley "a mischief-maker and a worthless fellow," and he hoped that the senator would not oppose Potts's appointment. Grant and Sumner then informally discussed Santo Domingo, and as the President was preparing to leave, the senator again mentioned Ashley's case, but Grant simply ignored the remark.[15]

Although Ashley's friends talked to Grant and were able to delay Potts's confirmation by having it postponed and held up in committee, they could not overcome the President. On July 13, the Senate by a vote of 27 to 13 approved Potts's nomination.[16]

What caused Ashley's removal has never been entirely clear. Charles Sumner Ashley attributed it to his father's close association with Sumner, who was at odds with Grant. But the evidence does not support this assumption, since when he removed Ashley, Grant still had a working relationship with Sumner. Only after the dispute over Santo Domingo became bitter in the spring of 1870 did the two men split completely.[17]

From the available evidence, it appears that the governor was removed for two reasons: he had offended Grant and he was at odds with the Sherman machine in Ohio. Before leaving for Montana, Ashley had remarked that the Republican party was "acting dumb in the presence of a dummy." Ashley resented Grant's failure to consult party leaders before appointing his cabinet. Grant heard about Ashley's comment only much later, but he was none the less enraged.

In 1866 Senator John Sherman had shown his hostility to Ashley by giving his patronage positions to Johnson Republicans in Ohio, although the President was working to get Ashley out of the House. In March, 1869, Potts had been Sherman's preferred candidate for the Montana post, but the senator had voted to confirm Ashley rather than appear responsible for rejecting a fellow Ohio Republican. Now in 1870, Sherman was only too happy to take advantage of Grant's pique and work to have Ashley dismissed. Ashley believed that the combination of Sherman's opposition and his own comment about Grant led to his downfall, and the facts appear to support this view.[18]

Undecided about what to do after losing his post, Ashley stayed in Montana until late November, 1870. He then decided to go East, in order to find a new means of livelihood; his family would follow later. For a time he thought of becoming a candidate for Clerk of the House of Representatives, but Carl Schurz and Sumner seem to have dissuaded him. Badly in need of money, Ashley joined an organized lecture tour and spent most of the winter of 1871 presenting his "Recollections of Men and Measures during Ten Years in Congress." He also made some speeches in behalf of the Northern Pacific Railroad, but he apparently did not like the association, since he ended the arrangement within six weeks. During the spring and summer, 1871, he was in Kansas negotiating a boundary line between Indians and the state. For some unexplained reason (though it was rumored that Grant had told Ashley he had done him an injustice), the President appointed him to the boundary commission, but relations between the two men continued to be frosty.[19]

Toward the end of the summer, Ashley's family left Montana for Yellow Springs, Ohio, where it had been decided they would reside, as the oldest children were to be enrolled in Antioch College. Ashley appears to have played no significant role in the Ohio elections of 1871, except to let it be known that he was opposed to John Sherman's reelection as senator by the state legislature. The fall elections had left the Republicans with only an eleven-vote majority in the assembly. Thus if the Sherman forces could not maintain party discipline, the senator might be defeated. Ashley was very willing to manage the dump-Sherman movement.[20]

Ashley's strategy was to try to eliminate the closed caucus nomination by Republicans before the actual voting took place in the assembly. In an open vote, with three or four Republicans being nominated, Ashley hoped that, with the support of a few Democrats, another candidate might be elected. Among the men considered as alternatives to Sherman were ex-Governor Jacob Cox, Congressman James Garfield, and Governor Rutherford B. Hayes. Accordingly, Ashley wrote letters and articles denouncing the senatorial caucus nominating system and traveled around the state in an effort to win support for his position. But he failed. Hayes and Garfield refused to challenge Sherman, and he easily won the endorsement of the legislature. Thus once again, the Sherman machine had defeated Ashley.[21]

During Grant's first term of office, hostility among various factions within the Republican party grew. Splits developed over monetary policy, the tariff, reconstruction, Negro rights, foreign affairs and the rights of labor. By the end of 1870, a group of "liberal" Republicans led by B. Gratz Brown and Carl Schurz had won control of the Missouri Republican party. Schurz soon became the leading advocate of forming a coalition of civil service reformers, currency reformers, low tariff men, and all others who might be in opposition to Grant. In Ohio, four Republicans, Jacob Cox, George Hoadly, Stanley Matthews, and Friedrich Hassaurek, distressed by the immoral opportunism and greed which surrounded the Grant administration, began a reform movement. Charles Sumner had also broken with the President; the old antislavery leader was very bitter over his removal as chairman of the Senate Foreign Affairs Committee; and Ashley was unhappy about the treatment accorded his old friend.[22] By late 1871, it had become obvious that a new party was needed to stop Grant, since the Republicans were going to renominate him. Ashley was among those who joined the new Liberal Republican movement.

He seems to have been attracted to the Liberal Republicans for a number of reasons. He disliked and distrusted the man who had dismissed him as governor of Montana, and who was mistreating his friend Charles Sumner. Resentment and loyalty would have drawn Ashley into almost any anti-

Grant movement. But the Ohioan also approved of the Liberal Republicans' stand on civil service reform and hard money. Though Grant himself was not an inflationist, he had support from that faction of the party. Moreover, as the Republicans became the defenders of business and upholders of the status quo, it became evident that they had no place for a man of Ashley's advanced beliefs. Desire for political power and influence also moved Ashley to join the new party. Finally, like some other former radicals, Ashley seems to have deluded himself into believing that the Democrats (who joined the Liberal Republicans during the campaign) had adopted old antislavery Republican ideas and that Negro civil and political rights would be better protected if Grant were defeated.

Throughout the spring of 1872, the Ohioan tried to muster support for the new movement. He traveled to Massachusetts to talk to newspaperman Samuel Bowles and businessman Edward Atkinson; he corresponded with the New York *Tribune*'s Whitelaw Reid. But the stigma of the impeachment still clung to him, and although he tried to obtain a position of importance in the emerging party, he was unable to accomplish this.[23]

Although Ashley hoped that Sumner would strongly endorse the movement before the scheduled May 1 convention, the senator played a waiting game. Sumner consented only to draft a series of resolutions on civil rights, which he hoped would be incorporated into the party platform. He entrusted these resolutions to his friend, the Massachusetts abolitionist Francis W. Bird. At the convention in Cincinnati, Ashley (who was not a delegate) helped Bird round up support for Sumner's ideas, and the platform did include a call for equal rights.[24] The Liberal Republicans then nominated the erratic and at times eccentric New York newspaperman Horace Greeley for President. In July, the Democrats also nominated Greeley.

The decision to support Grant or Greeley shattered what was left of the old radical Republican and abolitionist ranks. Benjamin Wade and Zachariah Chandler came out for Grant, as did Wendell Phillips, Gerrit Smith, and most of the old abolitionists. They supported the President, because they believed he stood for federal enforcement of the freedmen's rights in the South and because they did not want to turn this task over to the former slaveholders who were campaigning for Greeley. Ashley, Schurz, Sumner, Trumbull, and Julian all endorsed Greeley.[25]

Ashley campaigned for the ticket in New York, Ohio, and Illinois, and he made a major speech in Toledo on June 28.[26] Condemning the corruption, manipulation, and "ring rule" of the Grant administration, he asked his old friends to support the Liberal Republicans. He also went over his own career as an antislavery man, found fault with Secretary of the Treasury George

Boutwell, and demanded that government bonds be redeemed in gold. In his address Ashley criticized what he believed was Grant's obsequiousness toward Great Britain, and he attacked the President for his behavior toward Sumner. Asking everyone to forget the past, he advised Negroes to support Greeley. He believed that the Democrats had now adopted all the old radical positions; thus the interests of the freedmen would be safe under an old anti-slavery leader like Greeley. But like Sumner and Julian, Ashley was really deceiving himself on this point, since Greeley's intention to work with the "better classes" of Southern white society did not offer much protection for Negro civil and political rights. In fact, Ashley seems to have made this speech with a notable lack of passion, and a reporter for the Toledo *Blade* commented that "the most uncomfortable man within the city limits last night was Jas. M. Ashley."[27]

Though Greeley himself took a prominent part in the campaign, the odds were against him, and he was soundly defeated. Ashley no longer had a home among Republicans nor was he welcomed by Democrats. Once more he was adrift. His political career ended.

After the election Ashley returned to the practice of law in Toledo, establishing a firm specializing in patent cases. Free from political obligations, he now had more time to devote to his family. Since he believed that he had been handicapped by his lack of formal education, he was determined to educate his children whatever material sacrifice that might entail. He sent all four of his children to college, including his daughter Mary, which was quite remarkable for the time, but not for a man who believed in women's suffrage. He enjoyed being with his children, and unlike his own father, he did not try to force his opinions on his offspring. Ashley was a liberal parent; in many ways, he was indulgent with his children, and they in turn adored him. Having been away from home so often in the past, Ashley now wanted the family to stay together. Thus, in 1875, he moved the family to Ann Arbor, Michigan, where his eldest son James was to attend the University of Michigan Law School, and another son Henry was to be enrolled as an undergraduate. Ashley and his wife Emma quickly established themselves in the community. Emma became a leading member of the Unitarian Church; the former congressman entered the railroad business, in 1877.[28]

As early as 1845, there had been discussion about the need for a rail link between Toledo and Ann Arbor, but the project went no further than discussion until after the Civil War. A company to build the railroad was incorporated in 1869. It did some preliminary work; then, in 1874, the firm went bankrupt. Another company was then formed, and it suffered the same fate. In July, 1877, Ashley, having become interested in the project, purchased the Toledo and Ann Arbor Railroad with borrowed money. Included in the purchase agreement were the rail bed, the franchise, the right of way, property in Ann Arbor, and 72,000 railroad ties.[29]

Approaching the task of running a railroad with the same passion, skill, and tenacity with which he had approached his congressional duties, Ashley managed to raise the money needed to build and operate the line. By June 3, 1878, the connection between Ann Arbor and Toledo was completed. Regular service began on July 1. He was aided in the business by his sons James and Henry. During the next decade the Ashleys continued to build the railroad through the lower peninsula of Michigan until by 1889 the road extended to Frankfort, on the Lake Michigan shore. During the 1880s the name of the company was changed to the Toledo, Ann Arbor and Northern Michigan Railroad.[30]

Reaching Lake Michigan which had hitherto been a barrier to railroad transport, did not prevent the Ashleys from expanding their business. With the aid of the Craig Shipbuilding Company of Toledo, a ferry capable of carrying loaded railroad cars across open water and fitted with ice-breaking equipment was built by 1892. Within a short period a ferry-freight service was established between Frankfort and Kewaunee, Wisconsin, where rail connections were made for Green Bay. In 1890, Ashley retired, and turned over operation of the company to his sons. The Panic of 1893, and a crippling strike during the same year proved to be disastrous for the business, and the Ashley family lost control of the railroad when it was forced into receivership.[31]

Considering his radical background, his various anti-monopoly and anti-corporation statements, and his genuine concern for the plight of the workingman, it comes as no surprise that Ashley's ideas about the rights of labor were not those of the average late nineteenth-century businessman. Ashley feared that the growing power of what he called "the monster of iron, steam and electricity," if not properly controlled, would crush all toilers. But he believed man was capable of harnessing "the monster" and making "it do our bidding." His remedy for the danger was "arbitration and co-operation."

In 1887, he introduced the idea of profit-sharing for his workers, which he believed was an improvement over the wage system. According to Ashley, "wageworkers of the world must co-operate with capital on a stipulated agreement for a portion of the net profits, and thus secure beyond question an equitable division of the wealth produced by the united efforts of labor and capital." Co-operation and profit-sharing, he felt, would make strikes inexcusable. Believing that everyone would work together in harmony under such a plan, he stipulated that five years of continuous employment was a prerequisite for inclusion in profit-sharing. His plan also contained provisions for death benefits for widows of company employees, and for a limited form of accident insurance. Unfortunately the company never earned a large enough profit to make it feasible to put his ideas into practice.[32]

Ashley also recognized that labor had the right to organize a national federation (union) of railroad workers. He believed that such an organization should have a written constitution, elections by secret ballot, and rank-and-file control of policy. Although he favored the principle of labor organizations, Ashley was a lifelong believer in individual liberty and thus felt that no worker should be compelled to join a union against his will, or as a prerequisite for employment in a particular industry.[33]

After retiring from business, Ashley attempted a political comeback in 1890 by running as the Republican candidate for Congress from his old district. He campaigned on a platform advocating direct election of the President and United States senators, abolition of the office of Vice President, and phasing out nominating conventions in favor of direct primaries. At the same time he also tried to promote his ideas on industrial cooperation and profit-sharing and pledged to work for the rights of the laboring man in Congress. But the major issue of the campaign was the tariff. Ashley declared that he was in favor of a revenue tariff, which would benefit new industries. Clark Waggoner—Ashley's lifelong political opponent, a man who seemed totally incapable of forgetting the past—had pamphlets attacking Ashley printed at his own expense. They were simply rehashes of old and untrue charges that had been made against Ashley almost thirty years before. Ashley lost the election by a narrow margin. Two years later he ran again with the same results.[34]

Ashley now formally retired from public life, and he spent his time traveling, fishing, and swimming, three activities he dearly loved. In 1893 his health began to deteriorate. The following year he suffered a severe attack of diabetes, which continued to plague him through the remainder of his days. In the summer of 1896 he went on a fishing trip in Michigan, and not watching his diet, he took sick. Rushed to a sanitarium in Ann Arbor, he suffered a fatal heart attack on September 16, 1896. His body was brought to Toledo where he was buried a few days later.[35]

Ashley's death came when the national government was abandoning the Negro, and Jim Crow laws were becoming the rule in the South. Such ideas had always been abhorrent to him. His guiding principles as a public man had been opposition to slavery and a strong commitment to equal political and civil rights for all. Like all men he had faults; he could be intemperate in language and indiscreet in action. Yet he was one of the most important political figures of his era. Hardworking, intelligent, compassionate, and principled, he became a leader of the antislavery forces in the

1850s. He was deeply concerned with the problems of reconstruction as early as 1861. The passage of the Thirteenth Amendment owes more to him than to any other man. His zeal for impeachment has blinded historians to his achievements. But the black men of America suffered no such failure of vision. Three years before he died he was honored by the Afro-American League of Tennessee. In paying tribute to him, the president of the league, William H. Young, said:

> We come to snatch from the consummate statesman, patriot, philanthropist and benefactor, the chill and gloom of ingratitude and to reinvest his being with new life.
>
> We come to reassure him that the years of strife, turmoil, and self-abnegation spent for a despised race were "as bread upon the water."
>
> We come to remind him that we to-night intend that his name and life-work shall be a precious legacy to our children's children.
>
> That they shall rise up and call him blessed.
>
> We have come to announce to the world that henceforth he who shall merit our gratitude shall not go unrewarded. [36]

Young's moving tribute gives appropriate recognition to a principled, yet pragmatic champion of human freedom.

ABBREVIATIONS

AASL	AMERICAN ANTIQUARIAN SOCIETY LIBRARY
AHR	AMERICAN HISTORICAL REVIEW
AJ	ANDREW JOHNSON PAPERS
CWH	CIVIL WAR HISTORY
IMH	INDIANA MAGAZINE OF HISTORY
JAH	JOURNAL OF AMERICAN HISTORY
JNH	JOURNAL OF NEGRO HISTORY
JSH	JOURNAL OF SOUTHERN HISTORY
LC	LIBRARY OF CONGRESS
MMWH	MONTANA THE MAGAZINE OF WESTERN HISTORY
MVHR	MISSISSIPPI VALLEY HISTORICAL REVIEW
NOQ	NORTHWEST OHIO QUARTERLY
NYHS	NEW YORK HISTORICAL SOCIETY
NYPL	NEW YORK PUBLIC LIBRARY
OAHQ	OHIO STATE ARCHAEOLOGICAL AND HISTORICAL QUARTERLY
OH	OHIO HISTORY
OHS	OHIO HISTORICAL SOCIETY
RHL	RUTHERFORD B. HAYES LIBRARY
RTL	ROBERT TODD LINCOLN COLLECTION
SP	CHARLES SUMNER PAPERS
WPHM	THE WESTERN PENNSYLVANIA HISTORICAL MAGAZINE

NOTES

PREFACE

1. Claude G. Bowers, *The Tragic Era: The Revolution After Lincoln* (Cambridge, Mass., 1929), 157,158, 240, 459; George Fort Milton, *The Age of Hate: Andrew Johnson and the Radicals* (New York, 1930), 382, 401; C. Vann Woodward, "That Other Impeachment," *The New York Times Magazine* (Aug. 11, 1974), 28.

I: EARLY LIFE

1. Benjamin W. Arnett, ed., *Duplicate Copy of the Souvenir from the Afro-American League of Tennessee to Hon. James M. Ashley* (Philadelphia, 1894), 695-96. This volume is sometimes cited as *Orations and Speeches*; in this study it will be cited as *O & S*.

2. Charles S. Ashley, "Governor Ashley's Biography and Messages," *Contributions to the Historical Society of Montana*, VI (1907), 210; Toledo *Commercial*, Feb. 3, 1865; New York *Tribune*, Feb. 1, 1865; New York *Independent*, Feb. 9, 1865; George W. Julian, *Political Recollections, 1840-1872* (Chicago, 1884), 364.

3. The exact date of Ashley's birth is not certain. *The Dictionary of American Biography* (New York, 1927), I, 389; *Biographical Directory of American Congress, 1774-1949* (Washington, D.C., 1950), 793; New York *Tribune*, Sept. 17, 1896, all give Nov. 14, 1824 as the date of birth. C.S. Ashley, "Governor Ashley's Biography," 143; Nelson W. Evans, *A History of Scioto County, Ohio* (Portsmouth, Ohio, 1903), 289; Nevin O. Winter, *A History of Northwest Ohio* (Chicago, 1919), I, 294, all use Nov. 24, 1822. In his speeches and letters, Ashley always gave his age in accordance with the 1824 date. See for example James M. Ashley to Hamilton Fish, April 27, 1869, Grant Administration 1869-77, State Department Appointment Papers, Box 2 James M. Ashley, National Archives. This study will use the 1824 date. There is also confusion about whether the initial M stood for Monroe, Mansfield, or Mitchell. Since Ashley always signed his letters, J.M. or James M. Ashley, it is best to let the initial stand by itself.

4. Oliver Haught to Irene McCreary, March 20, 1955, Ashley File, Toledo Public Library; Evans, *History of Scioto*, 646.

5. *Ibid.*, 289, 635; C.S. Ashley, "Governor Ashley's Biography," 143; *Dictionary of American Biography*, I, 389; Ben Perley Poore, *The Federal and State Constitutions, Colonial Charters and Other Organic Laws of the United States* (Washington, D.C., 1878), II, 1894.

6. Evans, *History of Scioto*, 635, 696; C.S. Ashley, "Governor Ashley's Biography," 144; Alonzo W. Fortune, *Origins and Development of the Disciples* (St. Louis, 1944), 1-116; *Dictionary of American Biography*, II, 447-48, 463.

7. Evans, *History of Scioto*, 635, 696; C.S. Ashley, "Governor Ashley's Biography," 144.

8. *Ibid.*; Winter, *History of Northwest Ohio*, II, 309; Evans, *History of Scioto*, 646.

9. *Ibid.*

10. James M. Ashley, "Memoir," chapters I and II, University of Toledo Library. Ashley wrote the "Memoir" in July, 1896. The manuscript deals with his early life and has one chapter on his political campaigns. The pagination of the "Memoir" is confused, thus requiring some unusual citations. The "Memoir" was for many years

in the possession of Edward R. Hewitt, Ashley's son-in-law. Upon Hewitt's death, his daughter, Mrs. Gordon Stevenson, gave the manuscript to Mr. John Morgan, of the University of Toledo Library. While the author was doing research in Toledo, Mr. Morgan showed him the "Memoir" with the permission of the present Ashley family. There are two copies of it, one handwritten, the other typed. The citations in this study are from the typed copy.

As often as possible, the manuscript has been scrutinized for accuracy. In many instances, especially on political campaigns, contemporary newspapers, speeches and letters were used to corroborate Ashley's statements. The accuracy of those parts which could be checked gave me confidence to believe the portions for which no other evidence was available.

11. Winter, *History of Northwest Ohio*, II, 309; C.S. Ashley, "Governor Ashley's Biography," 144-45; *Dictionary of American Biography*, I, 389; Judge H. Harriman, "Address Upon Governor Ashley, January 10, 1897," (Pamphlet, University of Michigan Library), 4; Ashley, "Memoir," chapter I, II; *O & S*, 336-37; 609, 615-16;

12. *Dictionary of American Biography*, I, 389; Margaret Ashley Paddock, "An Ohio Congressman in Reconstruction," Master's essay, Columbia University, 1916, 1; *O & S*, 605-606, 620-21, 695, 696; Ashley, "Memoir," 1st chapter, 2, 1st chapter (part 2nd), no page number given.

13. *Dictionary of American Biography*, II, 447-48; Ashley, "Memoir," 1st chapter, 2-3, 8; *O & S*, 696.

14. *Ibid.*, 615; Ashley, "Memoir," 1st chapter 3-14; Thomas H. Johnson and Harvey Wish, *The Oxford Companion to American History* (New York, 1966), 246; C.S. Ashley, "Governor Ashley's Biography," 144.

15. Ashley, "Memoir," 1st chapter, 13-14, chapter 2, 26 or 6 [Ashley used both numbers]; Leland W. Meyer, *The Life and Times of Colonel Richard M. Johnson of Kentucky* (New York, 1932), 317-22.

16. Ashley, "Memoir," 1st chapter, 3, 6, 14; Harriman, "Address Upon Governor Ashley," 4; *O & S*, 696.

17. Ashley, "Memoir," insert in 1st chapter (2nd part), 1 2, or if the pages of this chapter are numbered consecutively, 12, 13.

18. *Ibid.*, 2nd chapter, 25, 35/32. For some reason Ashley numbered page 29 as 27, and for the rest of the chapter the pages are two and sometimes three figures behind what they should have been. C.S. Ashley, "Governor Ashley's Biography," 145, 214, 215; Edward R. Hewitt, *Those Were The Days* (New York, 1943), 177; Harriman, "Address Upon Governor Ashley," 4; Evans, *History of Scioto*, 646; Letter of Benjamin W. Arnett, in *O & S*, 650; Rev. Dr. J.T. Sutherland, "Introductory Address," (Pamphlet, University of Michigan Library), 2. Ashley later joined the Unitarian Church.

19. Ashley, "Memoir," Introduction, 2, 3, 2nd chapter, 35/32; C. S. Ashley, "Governor Ashley's Biography," 145; Evans, *History of Scioto*, 289; Harriman, "Address Upon Governor Ashley," 4.

20. Ashley, "Memoir," 2nd chapter. Here again the pagination is confusing. Ashley first started to number the pages 1, 2, etc.; then he changed his mind and the first page of the chapter became 21; 21-22.

21. *Ibid.*, 22, 23; C. S. Ashley, "Governor Ashley's Biography," 146-47; Paddock, "An Ohio Congressman," 2; *O & S*, 717; Evans, *History of Scioto*, 289.

22. Ashley, "Memoir," 2nd chapter, 22-24, 1st chapter (2nd part), 5-6; C.S. Ashley, "Governor Ashley's Biography," 145-46; Paddock, "An Ohio Congressman," 1: *Dictionary of American Biography*, I, 389-90; Winter, *History of Northwest Ohio*, I, 294; Evans, *History of Scioto*, 289. By the time Ashley returned to Portsmouth, his parents no longer lived in Scioto County.

23. Ashley, "Memoir," 2nd chapter, 25, 27, 29/27, 30/28; *O & S*, 718; C.S. Ashley, "Governor Ashley's Biography," 148; Evans, *History of Scioto*, 289.

24. Ashley, "Memoir," 2nd chapter, 30/28, 36-33.

25. Glyndon G. Van Deusen, *The Jacksonian Era, 1828-1848* (New York, 1959), 156-57; Ashley, "Memoir," 2nd chapter, 30/28-32/30.

26. He worked as a printer for the Portsmouth *Weekly Tribune*, the Maysville (Kentucky) *Eagle*, the Columbus *Ohio Statesman*, and newspapers in Wheeling, Virginia; Louisville, Kentucky; St. Louis, and New Orleans. He then cut lumber in western Virginia, bought and sold grain, and studied, but did not practice medicine in Portsmouth. *Ibid.*, 30/28-32/30, 30½, 34/31, 35/32, 36/33; C. S. Ashley, "Governor Ashley's Biography," 147; Evans, *History of Scioto*, 97; Paddock, "An Ohio Congressman," 2; Toledo *Blade*, Nov. 8, 1860.

27. Evans, *History of Scioto*, 287-89, 519; C. S. Ashley, "Governor Ashley's Biography," 147; Harvey Scribner, *Memoirs of Lucas County and the City of Toledo* (Madison, 1910), II, 38; Ashley, "Memoir," 2nd chapter, 36/33. Ashley claimed that he published the newspaper regularly during the presidential campaign of 1848. He said he would have voted the Free Soil ticket if he lived in New York; he was forced to stop publication because of his antislavery views. A speech by Edward Jordan, on March 12, 1863, supports the contention that Ashley's views were antislavery in 1848, but offers no indication about how long the paper was published. Toledo *Commercial*, March 23, 1863.

28. Ashley, "Memoir," 2nd chapter, 37/34½. Ashley began telling this part of his story in what he called the second chapter and numbered the page 1; but it is really 38 of the second chapter.

29. Evans, *History of Scioto*, 290, 617; C. S. Ashley, "Governor Ashley's Biography," 149.

30. Ashley, "Memoir," 2nd chapter, 38-39; *O & S*, 611-13, 623-25.

31. Wilbur Siebert Papers, OHS, interview with James M. Ashley, July 1894; Delorus Preston, "The Underground Railroad in Northwest Ohio," *JNH*, XVII (1932), 411, 434-35; Dorothy Stafford, "Men Who Made Toledo," James M. Ashley—Slavery and a Railroad," Toledo *Blade*, March 26, 1950; Ashley, "Memoir," 2nd chapter, 39-41; C. S. Ashley, "Governor Ashley's Biography," 148; Eric Foner, *Free Soil, Free Labor, Free Men* (New York, 1970), 283.

32. Ashley, "Memoir," 2nd chapter, 38; Toledo *Blade*, Sept. 17, 1860.

33. C. S. Ashley, "Governor Ashley's Biography," 148, 214-16; Toledo *Blade*, Nov. 13, 1851; *Dictionary of American Biography*, I, 389; Sunderland, "Introductory Address," 2; Hewitt, *Those Were the Days*, 174; Randolph C. Downes, *Lake Port*, (Toledo, 1951), 391-92; Toledo *Commercial*, March 10, May 18, Dec. 28, 1869; Howard Glydon [Laura Searing], *Notable Men in the House* (New York, 1862), 45-49.

34. Toledo *Blade*, Nov. 13, 29, 1851, Feb. 18, March 4, 25, May 14, 1852, Feb. 28, March 5, April 19, 1853, Jan. 2, 1855; Letter of James M. Ashley, April 1, 1853, *Ibid.*, May 3, 1853.

35. Evans, *History of Scioto*, 646; C.S. Ashley, "Governor Ashley's Biography," 149-50; Toledo *Blade*, Feb. 25, 1856, June 8, Oct. 2, 1858. Ashley's political activities during this period will be discussed in Chapter II.

36. James M. Ashley to Salmon P. Chase, April 12, 1858, Salmon P. Chase Papers, LC; Toledo *Blade*, April 20, July 28, 1858.

II: TOLEDO POLITICIAN

1. James M. Ashley-James B. Steedman Debate, Sept. 14, 1860, Defiance, Ohio, Toledo *Blade*, Sept. 17, 1860.

2. Ashley, "Memoir," chapter X, 1; Ashley-Steedman Debate, Sept. 24, 1860, Toledo, Ohio, Toledo *Blade*, Sept. 26, 1860; Ashley to A. Sankey Latty (Sept. 25, 1854), *Ibid.*, Sept. 27, 1854; Ashley to D.B. Smith (March 1866), *Ibid.*, March 30, 1866, *Ibid.*, July 3, 1854, Oct. 18, 1858, Sept. 17, 1860; Ashley, Interview, Toledo *Commercial*, Dec. 22, 1892; *O & S*, 33-35, 622.

3. Foner, *Free Soil, Free Labor, Free Men*, 149-85, 144.

4. Ashley, Interview, Toledo *Commercial*, Dec. 22, 1892; *O & S*, 753; Ashley to Schuyler Colfax, Feb. 28, 1870, Schuyler Colfax Papers, University of Rochester; Ashley to Charles Sumner, Dec. 19, 1869, SP, Harvard University; Ashley to James A. Garfield, Dec. 24, 1869, James A. Garfield Papers, LC; Ashley to U.S. Grant, State Department Territorial Papers, Montana, 1864-72, Official Correspondence, October 14, 1864 to July 16, 1872, National Archives; Evans, *History of Scioto*, 290; C.S. Ashley, "Governor Ashley's Biography," 151; Ashley-Steedman Debate, Toledo *Blade*, Sept. 17, 26, 1860.

5. *Ibid.*; Clark Waggoner, *A History of Toledo and Lucas County* (New York, 1888), 127.

6. Eugene H. Roseboom, *The Civil War Era, 1850-1873*, vol. IV in Carl Wittke, ed., *The History of the State of Ohio* (Columbus, 1944), 267-73; William O. Lynch, "Anti-Slavery Tendencies of the Democratic Party in the Northwest, 1848-1850," *MVHR*, XI (Dec. 1924), 331; Glyndon G. Van Deusen, *Horace Greeley, Nineteenth Century Crusader* (Philadephia, 1953), 168-72.

7. Toledo *Blade*, Sept. 17, 26, 1860; Foner, *Free Soil, Free Labor, Free Men*, 155.

8. *Ibid.*, 277; Roseboom, *Civil War Era*, 220; Downes, *Lake Port*, 396; Louis Filler, *The Crusade Against Slavery, 1830-1860* (New York, 1960), 38-40; Toledo *Blade* March 4, 1852; Ashley to Editor Toledo *Blade*, Sept. 27, 1853, *Ibid.*, Sept. 27, 1853; Ashley, "Memoir," 2nd chapter, 34/31; Evans, *History of Scioto*, 646.

9. Roseboom, *Civil War Era*, 222-24.

10. O. White to Chase, Sept. 9, 1853, Chase Papers, LC; Toledo *Blade*, Sept. 16, 1853.

11. *Ibid.*; Ashley, "Memoir," chapter X, 10-11.

12. Toledo *Blade*, Sept. 17, 21, 22, Oct. 1, 1853.

13. *Ibid.*, Sept. 16, Oct. 10, 1853; Ashley, "Memoir," chapter X, 10-11; Roseboom, *Civil War Era*, 224-25, 276.

14. *Ibid.*, 225-26; Downes, *Lake Port*, 396; Toledo *Blade*, May 18, 1854.

15. *Ibid.*, Sept. 17, 1860; Roseboom, *Civil War Era*, 136; Ashley, "Memoir," chapter X, 10-11; *O & S*, 19, 603; Foner, *Free Soil, Free Labor, Free Men*, 150, 158, 171, 177-78.

16. Hans L. Trefousse, *The Radical Republicans: Lincoln's Vanguard for Racial Justice* (New York, 1969), 67; *O & S*, 602-604.

17. David H. Bradford, "The Background and Formation of the Republican Party in Ohio, 1844-1861," (Ph.D. dissertation, University of Chicago, 1947), 136-37; Joseph P. Smith, ed., *History of the Republican Party in Ohio* (Chicago, 1898), I, 9; Roseboom, *Civil War Era*, 282; *Ohio State Journal*, Feb. 15, 16, 1854; Toledo *Blade*, March 4, 9, 1854.

18. Smith, *History of the Republican Party*, I, 11-14; Bradford, "The Republican Party in Ohio," 138; Roseboom, *Civil War Era*, 282-83; *Ohio State Journal*, March 23, 23, 1854.

19. Salmon P. Chase to E.S. Hamlin, April 25, 1854, in Edward G. Bourne, ed., *Diary and Correspondence of Salmon P. Chase, Annual Report of the American Historical Association*, 1902, II (Washington, D.C., 1903), 261; Bradford, "The Republican Party in Ohio," 139; Smith, *History of the Republican Party in Ohio*, I, 19; Toledo *Blade*, June 23, 1854.

20. Bradford, "The Republican Party in Ohio," 133-36.

21. Toledo *Blade*, June 23, July 3, 1854; Ashley, "Memoir," chapter X, 11; C.S. Ashley, "Governor Ashley's Biography," 152. The younger, more radical Democrats left the party for good in 1854 or 1855. Foner, *Free Soil, Free Labor, Free Men*, 159.

22. Downes, *Lake Port*, 112.

23. Toledo *Blade*, July 3, 1854; Foner, *Free Soil, Free Labor, Free Men*, 98.

24. Toledo *Blade*, July 3, 1854.

25. *Ibid.*

26. *Ibid.*; Foner, *Free Soil, Free Labor, Free Men*, 73-102.

27. *Ibid.*, 169; Toledo *Blade*, July 3, 1854.

28. *Ibid.* Ashley's connection with the Know-Nothings will be discussed later in the chapter.

29. *Ibid.*; *O & S*, 300; Foner, *Free Soil, Free Labor, Free Men*, 105. Although Ashley wanted slavery completely abolished, he and other radicals in the 1850s accepted the view that the Constituion forbade interference with the domestic institutions of a state. But he still wanted the South to move toward emancipation as quickly as possible.

30. Toledo *Blade*, July 15, 1854; Bradford, "The Republican Party in Ohio," 140-41; Roseboom, *Civil War Era*, 285-86; *Ohio State Journal*, July 15, 1854.

31. Trefousse, *The Radical Republicans*, 84; Foner, *Free Soil, Free Labor, Free Men*, 233.

32. Roseboom, *Civil War Era*, 177, 286-93.

33. Clark Waggoner, "James M. Ashley and His Record," Oct. 29, 1890, "James M. Ashley and His Record," second article, Nov. 1, 1890, "James M. Ashley and His Defeat," Nov. 17, 1890, Rutherford B. Hayes Papers, RHL; Downes, *Lake Port*, 119, 284; Randolph Downes, *History of Lake Shore Ohio* (New York, 1952), 517.

34. Toledo *Blade*, Sept. 17, 26, 1860; O. White to Editor Toledo *Blade*, Sept. 28, 1860, *Ibid.*, Sept. 28, 1860.

35. *Ibid.*, July 3, 1854; Ashley to Latty, Sept. 25, 1854, *Ibid.*, Sept. 27, 1854.

36. *Ibid.*, Sept. 17, 26, 1860, Sept. 26, 1868.

37. Ashley, Interview, Toledo *Commercial*, Dec. 22, 1892; Ashley, "Memoir," chapter X, 15-17; *O & S*, 14.

38. Ashley to A. Latty (Sept. 25, 1854), Toledo *Blade*, Sept. 27, 1854. In this letter Ashley stated that he was in favor of changing the corrupt caucus and convention systems of nominating candidates for political office.

39. Ashley, "Memoir," chapter X, 20-33; Ashley, Interview, Toledo *Commercial*, Dec. 22, 1892; Ashley to A. Latty (Sept. 25, 1854), Toledo *Blade*, Sept. 27, 1854; Roseboom, *Civil War Era*, 293-95.

40. Eugene H. Roseboom, "Salmon P. Chase and the Know-Nothings," *MVHR*, XXV (Dec. 1938), 335-38; Bradford, "The Republican Party in Ohio," 144.

41. Ashley, "Memoir," chapter X, 23; Ashley, Interview, Toledo *Commercial*, Dec. 22, 1892; Roseboom, "Chase and the Know-Nothings," 340; Chase to E.S. Hamlin, Nov. 1, 1854, Jan. 22, Feb. 8, 1855, Chase to L.D. Campbell, May 25, 1855, in Chase, *Diary and Correspondence*, 265-70, 273-74; Joshua R. Giddings to George W. Julian, May 30, 1855, Julian-Giddings Papers, LC; Toledo *Blade*, June 18, 1855.

42. Ashley to Chase, Jan. 21, 1855, Chase Papers, LC. The term *Hunker* emerged from the charge that this group "hankered" or "hunkered" after political office.

43. *Ibid*.

44. Roseboom, "Chase and the Know-Nothings," 340-41; Chase to L. D. Campbell, May 25, 1855, in Chase, *Diary and Correspondence*, 273-74.

45. Ashley to Chase, May 29, June 16, 1855, Chase Papers, LC.

46. Roseboom, "Chase and the Know-Nothings," 341; *New York Times*, June 14, 15, 16, 1855; Sister M. Evangeline Thomas, *Nativism in the Old Northwest, 1850-1860* (Washington, D.C., 1936), 185-86; Carl F. Brand, "History of the Know-Nothing Party in Indiana," *IMH*, XVIII (March, June 1922), 196.

47. Roseboom, "Chase and the Know-Nothings," 341-42.

48. Ashley to Chase, June 16, 1855, Chase Papers, LC; Ashley, "Memoir," chapter X, 3; Toledo *Blade*, Sept. 17, 1860; *New York Times*, June 16, 1855.

49. Toledo *Blade*, July 14, 15, 1855. Bradford, "The Republican Party in Ohio," 146-48; Smith, *History of the Republican Party in Ohio*, I, 33-37; Roseboom, "Chase and the Know-Nothings," 344-45; Ashley to Horace Greeley, April 26, 1859, Horace Greeley Papers, NYPL.

50. Bradford, "The Republican Party in Ohio," 149; Robert F. Horowitz, "James M. Ashley and the Presidential Election of 1856," *OH*, 83 (Winter 1974), 4-9.

51. Toledo *Blade*, Sept. 27, Oct. 12, 13, 15, 16, 1855; Ashley, "Memoir," chapter X, 24; Ashley to Chase, Oct. 21, 1855, Chase Papers, LC; Bradford, "The Republican Party in Ohio," 150-51; Roseboom, "Chase and the Know-Nothings," 347.

52. Ashley to Chase, Oct. 21, 1855, Chase Papers, LC.

III: PRESIDENTIAL POLITICS AND ELECTION TO CONGRESS

1. Ashley to Chase, Jan. 21, May 29, June 16, 1855, Chase Papers, LC; J. W. Schuckers, *The Life and Public Services of Salmon Portland Chase* (New York, 1874), 156-58; Albert Bushnell Hart, *Salmon P. Chase* (Boston, 1899), 153-55.

2. *Ibid*.; Chase, *Diary and Correspondence*, 267-72; Oran Follett to Chase, Jan. 7, May 29, 1855, Chase Papers, LC.

3. Ashley to Chase, June 16, 1855, Chase Papers, LC; Andrew W. Crandall, *The Early History of the Republican Party, 1854-1856* (Gloucester, Mass., 1960), 48-49, 62, n34.

4. Ashley to Chase, June 16, 1855, Chase Papers, LC.

5. *Ibid.*, Oct. 21, 1855, Thomas Spooner to Chase, Feb. 5, 1856, Chase Papers, LC; Horowitz, "James M. Ashley and the Presidential Election of 1856," 9-10; James B. Stewart, *Holy Warriors, The Abolitionists and American Slavery* (New York, 1976),171.

6. Ashley to Chase, Oct. 21, 1855, Chase Papers, LC; Crandall, *Early History of the Republican Party*, 33, 43, 49; Glyndon G. Van Deusen, *William Henry Seward* (New York, 1967), 163-64.

7. Ashley to Chase, Oct. 21, 1855, Chase Papers, LC.

8. *Ibid.*

9. Ashley, Interview, Toledo *Commercial*, Dec. 22, 1892; Ashley, "Memoir," chapter X, 24.

10. Russell Errett to Chase, November 16, 1855, Chase Papers, LC; Charles G. Going, *David Wilmot, Free-Soiler* (New York, 1924), 477-84.

11. Ashley to Chase, Jan. 18, 1856, Chase Papers, LC; Crandall, *Early History of the Republican Party*, 51-52; Ashley to Chase, Feb. 26, 1856, Chase Papers, OHS.

12. Ashley to Chase, Jan. 18, 1856, Chase Papers, LC; Ashley to Chase, Jan. 23, Feb. 19, March 12, 1856, Chase Papers, OHS.

13. *Ibid.*, Feb. 19, 1856.

14. Trefousse, *The Radical Republicans*, 98; Bradford, "The Republican Party in Ohio," 161; Roseboom, *Civil War Era*, 316; Crandall, *Early History of the Republican Party*, 51, 60-61, 156; Leonard H. Bernstein, "Convention in Pittsburgh," *WPHM*,XLIX (Oct. 1966), 289-300; *Official Proceedings of the Republican Convention in the City of Pittsburgh, Pennsylvania on the Twenty-Second of February, 1856* (New York, 1956), 12-13; *New York Times*, Feb. 24, 1856; Smith, *History of the Republican Party in Ohio*, I, 52.

15. Ashley to Chase, Feb. 26, 1856, Chase Papers, OHS.

16. *Ibid.* Another Chase supporter, John Heaton, also felt the governor could have received the nomination here. Crandall, *Early History of the Republican Party*, 156, 174, *n*7.

17. Ashley to Chase, Feb. 26, 1856, Chase Papers, OHS.

18. Trefousse, *The Radical Republicans*, 96, 100; Crandall, *Early History of the Republican Party*, 155-61; Bradford, "The Republican Party in Ohio," 230; Roseboom, "Chase and the Know-Nothings," 341; Roseboom, *Civil War Era*, 317.

19. Toledo *Blade*, May 9, 1856, Nov. 17, 1868; *New York Times*, June 17, 20, 1856; Roseboom, *Civil War Era*, 317-18; Ashley, "Memoir," chapter X, 26; *O & S*, 617; Allan Nevins, *Ordeal of the Union* (New York, 1947), II, 469-70; Smith, *History of the Republican Party in Ohio*, I, 58.

20. Kirk H. Porter and Donald B. Johnson, *National Party Platforms, 1840-1956* (Urbana, 1956), 27-28; Chase to Julian, July 17, 1856, Julian-Giddings Papers, LC; Horowitz, "James M. Ashley and the Presidential Election of 1856," 11-13.

21. Ashley, "Memoir," chapter X, 26; Toledo *Blade*, July 14, Sept. 15, 23, 1856.

22. *O & S*, 605.

23. *Ibid.*, 605, 613, 614-15.

24. *Ibid.*, 606, 615-17.

25. *Ibid.*, 616, 623.

26. *O & S*, 615.

27. *Ibid.*, 611-13, 623-24, 625.

28. *Ibid.*, 622; Foner, *Free Soil, Free Labor, Free Men*, has shown that this was among the main tenets of Republican ideology, 22, 38.

29. *O & S*, 616, 627.

30. *Ibid.*, 617, 618.

31. *Ibid.*, 616.

32. C. S. Ashley believed that this was a clear call for Negro suffrage, and I think he is correct. C. S. Ashley, "Governor Ashley's Biography," 161.

33. *O & S*, 628.

34. Frederick Douglass, "Introduction," *O & S*, 6-7; David M. Potter, *Lincoln and His Party in the Secession Crisis* (New Haven, 1942), 22.

35. Roseboom, *Civil War Era*, 319-20, 322, 323; Bradford, "The Republican Party in Ohio," 162-63; David Donald, *Charles Sumner and the Coming of the Civil War* (New York, 1960), 294-97, 317-19; Victor B. Howard, "The 1856 Election in Ohio: Moral Issues in Politics," *OH*, 80 (Winter 1971), 43, 44; Ashley, "Memoir," chapter X, 26; Foner, *Free Soil, Free Labor, Free Men*, 130.

36. Ashley to Chase, Nov. 27, 1857, Chase Papers, LC.

37. Roseboom, *Civil War Era*, 325-26; Ashley to Chase, Nov. 27, 1857, Chase Papers, LC.

38. *Ibid.*, June 16, 1857, Chase Papers, LC.

39. Roseboom, *Civil War Era*, 326-29; Smith, *History of the Republican Party in Ohio*, I, 69-74; Ashley, "Memoir," chapter X, 26-27.

40. *Ibid.*, chapter X, 26.

41. Ashley to Chase, Feb. 17, 1858, Chase Papers, LC.

42. *Ibid.*

43. Ashley to Chase, Feb. 17, April 12, 1858, Chase Papers, LC; Foner, *Free Soil, Free Labor, Free Men*, 130-32; Trefousse, *The Radical Republicans*, 111-20.

44. Ashley to Chase, April 12, 1858, Chase Papers, LC; Toledo *Blade*, April 20, 1858.

45. *Ibid.*, July 6, 16, 23, 1858; Ashley to Chase, July 30, 1858, Dec. 18, 1860, A. Latty to Chase, July 30, 1858, Chase Papers, LC; Smith, *History of the Republican Party in Ohio*, I, 79; Ashley, Interview, Toledo *Commercial*, Dec. 22, 1892; Ashley, "Memoir," chapter X, 27-31.

46. Toledo *Blade*, July 23, 27, 29, Aug. 10, 23, 1858; Latty to Chase, July 30, 1858, Chase Papers, LC.

47. Toledo *Blade*, Aug. 10, Sept. 7, Oct. 1, 18, 1858; Ashley to Chase, Feb. 19, 1856, Chase Papers, OHS.

48. Ashley, "Memoir," chapter X, 30-33; C.S. Ashley, "Governor Ashley's Biography," 165; Paddock, "An Ohio Congressman," 4.

49. *O & S*, 16-17; Ashley, "Memoir," chapter X, 33-36; C. S. Ashley, "Governor Ashley's Biography," 165-66; Toledo *Blade*, Oct. 1, 1858.

50. Ashley, "Memoir," chapter X, 36-39; Toledo *Blade*, Oct. 1, 1858.

51. *Ibid.*, Sept. 24, Oct. 14, 1858; *Congressional Quarterly's Guide to U.S. Elections*, (Washington, D.C., 1975), 605.

52. *O & S*, 17-18, 747-48; Toledo *Blade*, Oct. 18, 1858; Foner, *Free Soil, Free Labor, Free Men*, 132; Ashley to Chase, Nov. 28, 1858, Chase Papers, LC.

53. *Ibid.* This was really the first round of a bitter political fight between Ashley and Waggoner that lasted for forty years.

IV: FRESHMAN CONGRESSMAN

1. *O & S*, 13-21, 22-30, 16.

2. *Ibid.*, 20, 29-30.

3. *Ibid.*, 15, 17-18.

4. *Ibid.*, 17-18, 25-26, 28.

5. Roseboom, *Civil War Era*, 342-43; Foner, *Free Soil, Free Labor, Free Men*, 133-34; Ashley, "Memoir," 2nd chapter, 38-39; *O & S*, 15.

6. Roseboom, *Civil War Era*, 345-46; Downes, *Lake Shore*, 379; Bradford, "The Republican Party in Ohio," 181.

7. Jacob R. Shipherd, comp., *History of the Oberlin-Wellington Rescues* (New York, 1969), 247-53; William C. Cochran, "The Western Reserve and the Fugitive Slave Law," Western Reserve Historical Society *Collections*, CI (1920), 180-85; Downes, *Lake Shore*, 379-80; James B. Stewart, *Joshua R. Giddings and the Tactics of Radical Politics* (Cleveland, 1970), 269.

8. Roseboom, *Civil War Era*, 346-47.

9. *Ibid.*, 347-50; Bradford, "The Republican Party in Ohio," 181, 183-84.

10. Smith, *History of the Republican Party in Ohio*, I, 90-91; Toledo *Blade*, June 4, 1859; Foner, *Free Soil, Free Labor, Free Men*, 137; Trefousse, *The Radical Republicans*, 128-29; Giddings to Chase, June 7, 1859, Chase Papers, Historical Society of Pennsylvania.

11. Toledo *Blade*, Sept. 13, 14, 16, 23, Oct. 13, 1859; Roseboom, *Civil War Era*, 353-57.

12. Ashley to Chase, March 28, 1859, Chase Papers, OHS.

13. Ashley to Greeley, April 26, 1859, Greeley Papers, NYPL.

14. Ashley to Chase, July 29, Aug. 26, 1859, Chase Papers, LC; Donnal V. Smith, *Chase and Civil War Politics* (Columbus, 1931), 14; Charles A. Dana to James Pike, Aug. 26, 1859, in James S. Pike, *First Blows of the Civil War* (New York, 1879), 443.

15. Ashley to Chase, July 29, 1859, Chase Papers, LC.

16. *Ibid.*, Aug. 26, 1859, Chase Papers, LC.

17. *Ibid.*, Dana to Pike, Aug. 26, 1859, in Pike, *First Blows*, 443.

18. Ashley to Chase, Aug. 26, 1859, Chase Papers, LC; William E. Baringer, *Lincoln's Rise to Power* (Boston, 1937), 145, 149.

19. Ashley to Editor *National Era*, July 29, 1859, Toledo *Blade*, Oct. 25, 1859; Ashley to Chase, July 29, Aug. 26, 1859, Chase Papers, LC; Ashley to Gideon Welles, Nov. 18, 1859, Gideon Welles Papers, Connecticut Historical Society.

20. *O & S*, 14-16, 20, 25-29, 31-36, 41; Ashley to Editor Toledo *Blade*, Oct. 29, 1859, Toledo *Blade*, Oct. 29, 1859.

21. *Ibid.*, Dec. 8, 1859; Ashley to his family (Dec. 2, 1859), in *Ibid.*, Dec. 9, 1859; Robert L. Stevens, ed., "John Brown's Execution—An Eye Witness Account," *NOQ*, 21 (Autumn 1949), 140-48; *National Anti-Slavery Standard*, June 16, 1860.

22. *Congressional Globe*, 36th Cong., 1 Sess., 2, 21; Trefousse, *The Radical Republicans*, 131.

23. Ashley to Chase, Dec. 19, 1859, Chase Papers, LC; *Cong. Globe*, 36th Cong., 1 Sess., 634, 650; *New York Times*, Feb. 1, 3, 1860.

24. *Cong. Globe*, 36th Cong., 1 Sess., 726; Toledo *Blade*, Feb. 10, 1860.

25. Glydon, *Notable Men in the House*, 48.

26. Paddock, "An Ohio Congressman," 2; C. S. Ashley, "Governor Ashley's Biography," 169, 194; Toledo *Blade*, March 13, 1861.

27. *Cong. Globe*, 36th Cong., 1 Sess., 2056, 3179; Chase to Spooner, Dec. 18, 1859, in Chase, *Diary and Correspondence*, 283-84; Ashley to Chase, Dec. 19, 1859, Jan. 14, 1860, Chase Papers, LC; Toledo *Blade*, Dec. 22, 27, 1859.

28. Ashley to Chase, Dec. 19, 1859, Jan. 14, 1860, Chase Papers, LC; Roseboom, *Civil War Era*, 361; Chase to Sumner, Jan. 20, 1860, in Chase, *Diary and Correspondence*, 284-85.

29. Ashley to Chase, Dec. 19, 1859, Chase Papers, LC.

30. *Ibid.*, Jan. 14, April 5, 1860, Chase Papers, LC.

31. Roseboom, *Civil War Era*, 361-62; Bradford, "The Republican Party in Ohio," 204; Hans L. Trefousse, *Benjamin Franklin Wade: Radical Republican from Ohio* (New York, 1963), 120-23.

32. Ashley to Chase, April 5, 1860, Chase Papers, LC; Smith, *Chase and Civil War Politics*, 16.

33. Bradford, "The Republican Party in Ohio," 204-10; Smith, *Chase and Civil War Politics*, 15-20; Trefousse, *Wade*, 125-28; *Proceedings of the First Three Republican National Conventions* (Minneapolis, 1893), 147-53, 168; Nevins, *The Emergence of Lincoln*, IV, 251, 254-60; James Elliott to Chase, May 21, 1860, Chase Papers, LC; Benjamin P. Thomas, *Abraham Lincoln* (New York, 1952), 208-213.

34. Reinhard H. Luthin, "Salmon P. Chase's Political Career before the Cvil War," *MVHR*, XXIX (March 1943), 531; Smith, *Chase and Civil War Politics*, 8-15; Ashley to Chase, March 28, 1859, Chase Papers, LC; David M. Potter, *The Impending Crisis, 1848-1861*, completed by Don E. Fehrenbacher, ed. (New York, 1976), 422-30.

35. *Proceedings of the First Three Republican National Conventions*, 160-61; Foner, *Free Soil, Free Labor, Free Men*, 132-133, 175-76; Stewart, *Giddings*, 271-73.

36. *O & S*, 45-47, 48, 59, 84, 92-93; Foner, *Free Soil, Free Labor, Free Men*, 98, 117.

37. *O & S*, 48, 48-53, 54-57, 57-62, 88.

38. *Ibid.*, 65, 68-79, 76.

39. *Ibid.*, 47, 98-101; Foner, *Free Soil, Free Labor, Free Men*, 119-20.

40. *O & S*, 63, 78-81, 92, 93, 97, 111-12.

41. *Ibid.*, 94, 105; *Cong. Globe*, 36th Cong., 1 Sess., Appendix, 373, 376; Foner, *Free Soil, Free Labor, Free Men*, 267-76; V. Jacque Voegeli, *Free But Not Equal—The Midwest and the Negro during the Civil War* (Chicago, 1967), 3-4.

42. George M. Frederickson, "A Man but Not a Brother: Abraham Lincoln and Racial Equality," *JSH*, XLI (Feb. 1975), 42-43, 48.

43. *O & S*, 53, 58, 107.

44. *Ibid.*, 53.

45. *Ibid.*, 47, 92-93, 113.

46. *National Anti-Slavery Standard*, June 16, 1860; Toledo *Blade*, June 14, July 7, 9, 10, 1860.

47. *Ibid.*, July 14, 25, 26, 28, 1860; Bradford, "The Republican Party in Ohio," 231; Roseboom, *Civil War Era*, 367-70.

48. Toledo *Blade*, Aug. 3, 1860; John M. Morgan, "The People Choose Freedom, The Congressional Election of 1860 in Northwestern Ohio," *NOQ*, 22 (Summer 1950), 114-15.

49. Ashley to Sumner, Aug. 7, Oct. 13, 1860, SP; Ashley to J. Giddings, Sept. 12, 1860, Giddings Papers, OHS; Sumner to Mr. Haynes, in Toledo *Blade*, Aug. 17, 1860; *Ibid.*, Sept. 7, 10, 17, 18, 19, 26, 1860.

50. *Ibid.*, Sept. 18, 19, 1860; Morgan, "The People Choose Freedom," 116, 117; Downes, *Lake Port*, 141-42; *Congressional Quarterly's Guide to U.S. Elections*, 608.

51. *O & S*, 38, 39; Toledo *Blade*, Nov. 6, 1860; Roseboom, *Civil War Era*, 371.

V: STANDING FIRM

1. Ashley to F. Hassaurek, Nov. 19, 1860, Friedrich Hassaurek Papers, OHS; Toledo *Blade*, Nov. 12, 22, 1860; Trefousse, *The Radical Republicans*, 140-41.

2. *Cong. Globe*, 36th Cong., 2 Sess., 6; Foner, *Free Soil, Free Labor, Free Men*, 178-80.

3. *O & S*, 118.

4. Ashley to Frank Case, Dec. 29, 1860, in 37th Cong., 3 Sess., House Report No. 47, 23.

5. Ashley to Chase, Dec. 18, 1860, Chase Papers, LC; Toledo *Commercial*, July 13, 1863.

6. Ashley to Chase, Dec. 18, 1860, Chase Papers, LC.

7. *Ibid.*; Trefousse, *The Radical Republicans*, 147-49; Ashley to William Schouler, Feb. 17, 1861, Schouler Papers, Massachusetts Historical Society.

8. Latty to H. C. Blake, Dec. 23, 1862, in 37th Cong., 3 Sess., House Report No. 47, 50; Ashley to the Electors of the 10th Congressional District, Sept. 18, 1862, Toledo *Blade*, Sept. 19, 1862; Ashley to Abraham Lincoln, Dec. 22, 1860, Lyman Trumbull to Lincoln, Dec. 18, 1860, RTL, LC; Stanley P. Hirshson, *Grenville M. Dodge, Soldier, Politician, Railroad Pioneer* (Bloomington, 1967), 24, 30; Trefousse, *The Radical Republicans*, 150; William E. Smith, *The Francis Preston Blair Family in Politics* (New York, 1933), I, 513-14.

9. *O & S*, 730-32; Van Deusen, *Seward*, 241, 244-46.

10. *O & S*, 117, 119-27, 136.

11. *Ibid.*, 130-31.

12. *Ibid.*, 138-39.

13. *Ibid.*, 140-41.

14. *Ibid.*, 159, 160-64.

15. Ashley to Schouler, Feb. 17, 1861, Schouler Papers; *Annals of Cleveland*, Vol. 44, Part 1, 383.

16. *Cong. Globe*, 36th Cong., 2 Sess., 378.

17. Chicago *Tribune*, Feb. 9, 1861.

18. *Cong. Globe*, 36th Cong., 2 Sess., 1263, 1327-30.

19. *Ibid.*, 1284-85, 1375.

20. Chase to Lincoln, Jan. 28, 1861, RTL; Toledo *Blade*, March 13, 1861; *O & S*, 700.

21. *Ibid.*, 743; Trefousse, *The Radical Republicans*, 158.

22. Toledo *Blade*, March 5, 13, 16, 18, 21, 1861; Roseboom, *Civil War Era*, 377.

23. Richard N. Current, *Lincoln and The First Shot* (Philadelphia, 1963), 192-94.

24. Trefousse, *The Radical Republicans*, 169-70; *O & S*, 195-96.

25. Toledo *Blade*, May 2, 10, 1861; 37th Cong., 3 Sess., House Report No. 47, 9; Ashley to Chase, May 5, 1861, Chase Papers, LC.

26. Ashley to Editor Toledo *Blade*, May 21, 24, 27, 1861, Toledo *Blade*, May 23, June 1, 4, 1861.

27. *Ibid.*, June 3, 7, 1861.

28. *Ibid.* Thaddeus Stevens is often associated with this theory, but he did not articulate it until Aug. 2, 1861; *Cong. Globe*, 37th Cong., 1 Sess., 414.

29. Toledo *Blade*, June 4, 8, 11, 1861.

30. Ashley to Editor Toledo *Blade* (June 7, 11, 1861), *Ibid.*, June 8, 11, 1861.

31. *Ibid.* (June 14, 18, 1861), *Ibid.*, June 19, 27, 1861.

32. *Ibid.* (June 21, 1861), *Ibid.*, June 29, 1861.

33. Roy P. Basler, ed., *The Collected Works of Abraham Lincoln* (New Brunswick, 1953), IV, 426-39; Allan Nevins, *The War for the Union* (New York, 1959), I, 187-91.

34. Herman Belz, *Reconstructing the Union, Theory and Policy during the Civil War* (Ithaca, 1969), 10-13; Trefousse, *The Radical Republicans*, 172-73; Ashley to Arnett, Nov. or Dec. 1892, in *O & S*, 360; *Ibid.*, 395.

35. *Cong. Globe*, 37th Cong. 1 Sess., 24, 32, 61, 99, 131, 205, 416, 431.

36. *Ibid.*, 222.

37. *Ibid.*, 223, 265; *O & S*, 697; Toledo *Blade*, July 27, 1861, Feb. 26, 1868; Toledo *Commercial*, Feb. 28, 1868.

38. *Cong. Globe.*, 37th Cong. 1 Sess., 248-49, 461; Nevins, *War for the Union*, I, 195-96; Leonard P. Curry, *Blueprint for Modern America: Nonmilitary Legislation of the First Civil War Congress* (Nashville, 1968), 153-58.

39. Trefousse, *The Radical Republicans*, 173-94; Ashley to James M. McKim, July 29, 1861, McKim-Maloney-Garrison Papers, NYPL.

40. Ashley to Editor Toledo *Commercial*, Jan. 1, 1863, in *O & S*, 245-46; Ashley to Editor Toledo *Blade* (June 18, 1861), *Ibid.*, June 27, 1861; *Ibid.*, Aug. 21, 1861, Aug. 22, 1862; Ashley to Editor Toledo *Commercial* (Feb. 6, 1863), *Ibid.*, Feb. 12, 1863; Roseboom, *Civil War Era*, 388-91; William B. Hesseltine, *Lincoln and the War Governors* (New York, 1948), 226.

41. Toledo *Blade*, Sept. 7, 1861; Voegeli, *Free But Not Equal*, 38; Roseboom, *Civil War Era*, 391-92.

42. Ashley to Chase, Sept. 6, 1861, Chase Papers, LC; Toledo *Blade*, Sept. 17, 1861.

43. Roseboom, *Civil War Era*, 397; Toledo *Blade*, Oct. 30, 31, Nov. 1, 22, 26, Dec. 17, 1861; *O & S*, 175, 176-77, 179, 181, 186, 190-91, 201, 204, 205, 206-207, 207-208, 211; *National Anti-Slavery Standard*, Jan. 11, 1862; *The Liberator*, Jan. 3, 1862.

VI: WARTIME CONGRESSMAN

1. Salmon P. Chase, *Inside Lincoln's Cabinet: The Civil War Diaries of Salmon P. Chase*, ed., David Donald (New York, 1954), 50-51.

2. Evans, *History of Scioto*, 289; Toledo *Blade*, Dec. 21, 1861.

3. *O & S*, 360; *Cong. Globe*, 37th Cong., 2 Sess., 168; *New York Times*, Dec. 28. 1861.

4. Docket, Dec. 15, 1857-Jan. 15, 1859; and Minutes, Feb. 23, 1860-Dec. 17, 1873, Committee on Territories, 35th Cong., 1 Sess.-43rd Cong., 1 Sess., House of Representatives, MS, National Archives, RG 233, Jan. 16., Feb. 6, 21, 24, 1862; Belz, *Reconstructing the Union*, 55; *Cong. Globe*, 37th Cong., 2 Sess., 986, 1084, 1117, 1193; New York *Tribune*, Feb. 26, 1862; *National Anti-Slavery Standard*, March 15, 1862.

5. *Cong. Globe*, 37th Cong., 2 Sess., 1193, 1198; New York *Tribune*, March 13, 1862; Chicago *Tribune*, March 13, 1862; *New York Times*, March 13, 1862.

6. *O & S*, 271-75; United States Congress, House of Representatives, 37th Cong., H.R. 356, preamble, sec. 1. The bills and resolutions are on microfilm prepared by the Library of Congress. Belz, *Reconstructing the Union*, 76-77, 93.

7. H. R. 356, sec. 2, 3; *O & S*, 361; Robert F. Horowitz, "Land to the Freedmen: A Vision of Reconstruction," *OH*, 86 (Summer 1977), 192-93; New York *Herald*, March 13, 1862, called the measure a "Universal Emancipation" bill.

8. H. R. 356, sec. 4, 6; Horowitz, "A Vision of Reconstruction," 193-95, 196-98; 37th Cong., Minority Reports of the Committee on Territories of a Bill to Establish Temporary Governments in Disloyal States, March 12, 1862, MS, National Archives, RG 233. One report was by James Cravens of Indiana, Aaron Harding of Kentucky, and George K. Shiel of Oregon. The other report was by Harding and Cravens.

9. H. R. 356, sec. 2, 5, 8.

10. Belz, *Reconstructing the Union*, 70-77, 80-81; *New York Times*, March 13, 1862; New York *Herald*, March 13, 1862.

11. 37th Cong., Minority Report of the Committee on Territories, Cravens, Harding, and Shiel; Toledo *Blade*, March 3, 1862; Belz, *Reconstructing the Union*, 79-81; *O & S*, 361. The radical New York *Tribune*, March 15, 1862, had one of the few favorable accounts of Ashley's bill.

12. *Cong. Globe*, 37th Cong., 2 Sess., 89-90; Curry, *Blueprint for Modern America*, 37; *O & S*, 329; John Y. Simon, "Congress under Lincoln," (Ph.D. dissertation, Harvard University, 1963), 422.

13. *O & S*, 702-703; Simon, "Congress under Lincoln," 428-29; *Cong. Globe*, 37th Cong., 2 Sess., 1192, Appendix, 101; Alfred G. Harris, "Slavery and Emancipation in the District of Columbia, 1801-1862," (Ph.D. dissertation, Ohio State University, 1946), 265; Toledo *Commercial*, March 23, 1863.

14. Harris, "Slavery and Emancipation," 266; Curry, *Blueprint for Modern America*, 38-42.

15. *O & S*, 214, 215, 221-22, 224, 703-704; *National Anti-Slavery Standard*, May 10, 1862; *Cong. Globe*, 37th Cong., 2 Sess., 3215-16.

16. Henry Wilson, *History of the Anti-Slavery Measures of the Thirty-seventh and Thirty-eighth United States Congresses, 1861-1865* (Boston, 1865), 93-97; 37th Cong., H.R. 374; *Cong. Globe*, 37th Cong., 2 Sess., 2030; Belz, *Reconstructing the Union*, 83.

17. *Cong. Globe*, 37th Cong., 2 Sess., 2069, 2769, 2871.

18. Minutes of the Committee on Territories, Feb. 12, March 6, 10, 1862; 37th Cong., H.R. 357; New York *Tribune*, March 17, 1862; Chicago *Tribune*, March 25, 1862; *Cong. Globe.*, 37th Cong., 2 Sess., 1193, 1341-42, 2027, 2028.

19. *Ibid.*, 2027-29, 2030; Jay J. Wagoner, *Early Arizona: Prehistory to Civil War* (Tucson, 1975), 470-71. The Senate passed the bill on Feb. 20, 1863; Boston *Journal*, Feb. 21, 1863; New York *Independent*, May 15, 1862.

20. *Cong. Globe*, 37th Cong., 2 Sess., 59-60, 958-59, 1179, 3795; *The Principia*, Feb. 23, 1863; Adam Gurowski to the Secretary of War, June 22, 1862, Adam Gurowski Papers, LC; Chicago *Tribune*, July 10, 1862.

21. Curry, *Blueprint for Modern America*, 78-92.

22. *Cong. Globe*, 37th Cong., 2 Sess., Appendix, 224, 225. One reason for Ashley's bitter attack on the administration was his disapproval of Lincoln's May 19, 1862, order revoking General David Hunter's abolition proclamation of early May.

23. *Cong. Globe*, 37th Cong., 2 Sess., Appendix, 225-27.

24. Curry, *Blueprint for Modern America*, 89-95.

25. *Cong. Globe*, 37th Cong., 2 Sess., 3267-68, 3400, Appendix, 412-13; Trefousse, *The Radical Republicans*, 221-22.

26. *Cong. Globe*, 37th Cong., 2 Sess., 349, 695, 901, 939, 1577, 2891, 3055.

27. *Ibid.*, 1035, 1971, 2158, 2769-70, 2905-2906.

28. Trefousse, *The Radical Republicans*, 177-98; Ashley to Greeley, March 25, 1862, Greeley Papers, LC; T. Harry Williams, *Lincoln and His Generals* (New York, 1952), 66, 83-84, 143, 177-78; *O & S*, 744; C. S. Ashley, "Governor Ashley's Biography," 170; B. A. Botkin, *A Civil War Treasury of Tales, Legends and Folklore* (New York, 1960), 224.

29. Ashley, "Memoir," chapter X, 41, 42; Richard Mott to Chase, Aug. 10, 1862, Chase Papers, LC; Ashley to Sumner, Aug. 2, 1862, SP; Ashley to Julian, Aug. 2, 1862, Julian-Giddings Papers; Toledo *Blade*, Aug. 9, 16, 17, 19, 20, 25, Sept. 1, 1862; *O & S*, 320-21.

30. Toledo *Blade*, Aug. 21, 25, 30, Sept. 3, 11, 12, 19, 20, 25, Oct. 2, 10, 11, 1862; Ashley to Editor Toledo *Blade* (Aug. 21, 1862), *Ibid.*, Aug. 30, 1862; Ashley, "Memoir," chapter X, 45-46; Latty to Chase, Sept. 10, 1862, Chase Papers, LC; Waggoner to Sumner, Sept. 17, 1862, SP; Chase to Latty, Sept. 17, 1862, Chase to Waggoner, Sept. 17, 1862, in Robert B. Warden, *An Account of the Private Life and Public Services of Salmon Portland Chase* (Cincinnati, 1874), 452-54.

31. *O & S*, 630-32; Ashley to His Constituents (Sept. 18, 1862), Toledo *Blade*, Sept. 19, 1862.

32. *Ibid.*, Sept. 2, 11, 20, 1862; Downes, *Lake Port*, 206; C.S. Ashley, "Governor Ashley's Biography," 172; Toledo *Commercial*, Dec. 24, 1862.

33. Downes, *Lake Port*, 205-207; Toledo *Blade*, Sept. 29, 1862; New York *Independent*, Oct. 2, 1862; Boston *Commonwealth*, Oct. 11, 1862.

34. H. B. Walbridge to Chase, Oct. 7, 1862, Chase Papers, LC; Waggoner, *History of Toledo*, 351; Downes, *Lake Port*, 207; Roseboom, *Civil War Era*, 401-402; *Congressional Quarterly's Guide to U.S. Elections*, 611.

35. Voegeli, *Free But Not Equal*, 62; Downes, *Lake Port*, 207; Toledo *Blade*, Oct. 17, 1862; Trefousse, *The Radical Republicans*, 259-60.

36. *Cong. Globe*, 37th Cong., 3 Sess., 10-11; Toledo *Blade*, Dec. 6, 1862. The members of the committee were Harrison G. Blake of Ohio, John P. Shanks of Indiana, S. L. Casey of Kentucky, Edward Haight of New York, and Jonathan W. Noell of Missouri.

37. 37th Cong., 3 Sess., House Report No. 47, 3-63.

38. *Ibid.*, 1, 2-3.

39. Toledo *Blade*, March 13, 1863; Toledo *Commercial*, March 20, 1863; *Annals of Cleveland*, Vol. 40, Part I, 1863, 2891.

40. Richard O. Curry, *A House Divided: Statehood Politics and the Copperhead Movement in West Virginia* (Pittsburgh, 1961), 69-84; *Cong. Globe*, 37th Cong., 2 Sess., 3307-20, 3377; *Ibid.*, 3 Sess., 59; Toledo *Commercial*, Jan. 16, 1863; *The Principia*, Dec. 18, 1862; Lincoln, *Works*, VI, 17, 26-28.

41. Trefousse, *The Radical Republicans*, 231-32. For the traditional interpretation see T. Harry Williams, *Lincoln and the Radicals* (Madison, 1941), 5-18.

42. Lincoln, *Works*, V, 529-32; Ashley to Dr. George Cheever, Dec. 23, 1862, George B. Cheever Papers, AASL.

43. Ashley to Editor Toledo *Commercial* (Jan. 1, 1863), *Ibid.*, Jan. 6, 1863.

44. *Ibid.*, Jan. 16, 1863.

45. *Cong. Globe*, 37th Cong., 3 Sess., 166, 294, 884-85, 914-15, 1592; Boston *Commonwealth*, Feb. 22, 1863. This territory was split into two parts in 1864, with one section adopting the name *Montana*. S. Edgerton to Col. W. F. Sanders, March 21, 1866, in C. S. Ashley, "Governor Ashley's Biography," 169-71.

46. *Cong. Globe*, 37th Cong., 3 Sess., 194; Boston *Commonwealth*, Jan. 10, 1863; Toledo *Commercial*, Jan. 9, 1863.

47. Belz, *Reconstructing the Union*, 105-15; Simon, "Congress Under Lincoln," 648, 649; Toledo *Commercial*, Feb. 27, 1863.

48. *Cong. Globe*, 640, 1148, 1293, 1479; Boston *Commonwealth*, Feb. 27, March 6, 1863; Chicgo *Tribune*, Feb. 9, March 7, 1863; Curry, *Blueprint for Modern America*, 67.

49. Frank L. Klement, *The Limits of Dissent: Clement L. Vallandigham and the Civil War* (Lexington, 1970), 125, 130; *Cong. Globe*, 37th Cong., 1410; Ashley to Editor Toledo *Commercial*, Feb. 12, 1863; Ashley to Gentlemen (Feb. 28, 1863), Toledo *Commercial*, March 2, 1863; *Ibid.*, March 19, 20, 21, 26, 30, April 1, 9, 1863; O & S, 248-56.

50. Roseboom, *Civil War Era*, 404-14; George Fort Milton, *Abraham Lincoln and the Fifth Column* (New York, 1942), 169-70.

51. Roseboom, *Civil War Era*, 414-16; Milton, *Lincoln and the Fifth Column*, 125-45.

52. Roseboom, *Civil War Era*, 416-18; Ashley to Chase, June 23, 1863, Chase Papers, LC; Christopher Dell, *Lincoln and the War Democrats: The Grand Erosion of Conservative Tradition* (Rutherford, N.J., 1975), 244.

53. Ashley to Chase, June 23, 1863, Chase papers, LC; Ashley to Lincoln, June 23, 1863, RTL.

54. *Ibid.*

55. Toledo *Commercial*, July 13, Aug. 19, 25, Sept. 28, Oct. 7, 1863; Findlay, *Hancock Jeffersonian*, July 3, 1863; Ashley to Sumner, Sept. 18, 1863, SP; Ashley to Gents, Sept. 28, 1863; Janney Family Papers, OHS; Chicago *Tribune*, Oct. 8, 1863; Ashley to Chase, Sept. 30, 1863, Chase Papers, LC.

56. Roseboom, *Civil War Era*, 421; Ashley to Dear Sir, Oct. 18, 1863, Toledo *Commercial*, Oct. 20, 1863.

VII: ACHIEVING A DREAM

1. Glydon, *Notable Men in the House*, 45-49.

2. Herman Belz, "The Ethridge Conspiracy of 1863: A Projected Conservative Coup," *JSH*, XXXVI (Nov. 1970), 549-52; Toledo *Commercial*, Jan. 9, 1863; Chicago *Tribune*, Dec. 8, 1863; *Cong. Globe*, 37th Cong., 3 Sess., 193-94, 1546-47.

3. *Ibid.*, 38th Cong., 1 Sess., 4-6, 6-8, 11; Chicago *Tribune*, Dec. 8, 12, 1863; Belz, "The Ethridge Conspiracy," 561-62, 566; Royal Cortissoz, *The Life of Whitelaw Reid* (New York, 1921)), I, 107-110. With the aid of fourteen border state Unionists led by Henry Winter Davis, the House later denied admission to the Louisiana members and had their credentials sent to the Committee on Elections.

4. New York *Tribune*, Dec. 14, 1863; Boston *Commonwealth*, Dec. 18, 1863; Howard K. Beale, ed., *The Diary of Edward Bates, 1859-1866, Annual Report of the American Historical Association*, IV (Washington, D.C., 1933), 347.

5. William E. Parrish, *Turbulent Partnership: Missouri and the Union, 1861-1865* (Columbia, 1963), 33-76; C.D. Drake to Lincoln, Aug. 11, 1863, R.G.Brown to Lincoln, Sept. 9, 1863, RTL; Tyler Dennett, ed., *Lincoln and the Civil War in the Diaries and Letters of John Hay* (New York, 1939), 101, 108; New York *Tribune*, Dec. 14, 1863.

6. Ashley to Robert C. Schenck, Nov. 4, 1863, Robert C. Schenck Papers, RHL; Joseph H. Barrett to William H. Smith, Nov. 10, Dec. 19, 1863, William H. Smith Papers, OHS; Michael Les Benedict, *A Compromise of Principle: Congressional Republicans and Reconstruction, 1863-1869* (New York, 1974), 67-68; Lincoln, *Works*, VII, 78-79.

7. *Cong. Globe*, 38th Cong., 1 Sess., 19-20; 38th Cong., H.R. 11, 12, 13, 14½, 15; H.R. Joint Resolution 6; Chicago *Tribune*, Dec. 11, 1863; Toledo *Commercial*, Dec. 18, 1863.

8. *Cong. Globe*, 38th Cong., 1 Sess., 19; 38th Cong., H.R. 14; Henry Wilson, *History of Antislavery Measures, 1861-1864*, 250; James G. Blaine, *Twenty Years of Congress* (Norwich, Conn., 1884), I, 505.

9. Henry Wilson, *The History of the Rise and Fall of the Slave Power in America* (Boston, 1876), III, 435-36.

10. Lincoln, *Works*, VII, 53-56.

11. Trefousse, *The Radical Republicans*, 283-84; Belz, *Reconstructing the Union*, 100-64, 169-73; Gerald S. Henig, *Henry Winter Davis: Antebellum and Civil War Congressman from Maryland* (New York, 1973), 192-93; Toledo *Commercial*, Dec. 19, 31, 1863; *O & S*, 258.

12. *Cong. Globe*, 38th Cong., 1 Sess., 33-34, 37.

13. *Ibid.*, 70; 38th Cong., H.R. 48, MS, National Archives, RG 233; Toledo *Commercial*, Dec. 29, 1863; Belz, *Reconstructing the Union*, 177-78.

14. H.R. 48, preamble, Toledo *Commercial*, Dec. 29, 1863.

15. H.R. 48, sec. 1, 2, 3; Herman Belz, *A New Birth of Freedom: The Republican Party and the Freedmen's Rights, 1861 to 1866* (Westport, Conn., 1976), 57-58.

16. H.R. 48, sec. 4, 5.

17. Belz, *Reconstructing the Union*, 181-82.

18. H.R. 48, sec. 6.

19. H.R. 48, sec. 7, 8; Belz, *Reconstructing the Union*, 184; Orestes Brownson, "The Presidential Message and Proclamation," *Brownson's Quarterly Review*, Nat. Ser., I (Jan. 1864), 103-111; *New York Times*, Jan. 19, 1864; Alexander C. Twining to Lincoln, Jan. 21, 1864, RTL.

20. H.R. 48, sec. 9, 10, 11. Other parts of the bill dealt with ports of entry, the appointment of customs collectors, and the stipulation that state laws inconsistent with the act were repealed.

21. New York *Evening Post*, Dec. 26, 1863; Chicago *Tribune*, Jan. 6, 1864; Toledo *Commercial*, Jan. 7, 1864; New York *Tribune*, Dec. 28, 1863; Lincoln to Nathaniel Banks, Dec. 24, 1863, in Lincoln, *Works*, VII, 89-90; Trefousse, *The Radical Republicans*, 284-85; *O & S*, 289; Fred Harvey Harrington, *Fighting Politician: Major General N. P. Banks* (Philadelphia, 1948), 113-15, 143-46; Belz, *Reconstructing the Union*, 193-95.

22. Toledo *Commercial*, Jan. 25, 1864; *Cong. Globe*, 38th Cong., 1 Sess., 1354.

23. Belz, *Reconstructing the Union*, 200-205.

24. Ashley to William Lloyd Garrison, March 22, 23, 1864, William Lloyd Garrison Papers, Boston Public Library; *O & S*, 266-75; also see *Cong. Globe*, 38th Cong., 1 Sess., 2069, for a similar Ashley view.

25. *O & S*, 266-67, 280-84, 286; *Cong. Globe*, 38th Cong., 1 Sess., 1357.

26. *O & S*, 277-78.

27. *Ibid.*, 288-93.

28. *Cong. Globe*, 38th Cong., 1 Sess., 2107-08, 3449-50, 3460, 3491, 3518; Belz, *Reconstructing the Union*, 220-21; Trefousse, *Wade*, 220-22.

29. Hay, *Diaries and Letters*, 204-209; Lincoln to Edwin M. Stanton, Feb. 5, 1864, in Lincoln, *Works*, VII, 169.

30. Wilson, *Rise and Fall of the Slave Power*, III, 430.

31. Henry V. Ames, *The Proposed Amendments to the Constitution of the United States During the First Century of Its History*, *Annual Report of the American Historical Association*, II (Washington, D.C., 1897), 217; *Cong. Globe*, 38th Cong., 1 Sess., 2993; Worcester *Daily Spy*, June 16, 1864; Blaine, *Twenty Years*, I, 507; *O & S*, 705.

32. *Cong. Globe.*, 38th Cong., 1 Sess., 3357; *O & S*, 707.

33. *Cong. Globe*, 38th Cong., 1 Sess., 1166-70, 1673, 2380, 2920, 2996, 3468; New York *Tribune*, Feb. 2, March 18, 1864; *National Anti-Slavery Standard*, March 26, 1864; Edward McPherson, *The Political History of the United States during the Great Rebellion* (Washington, D.C., 1865), 240, 262; Toledo *Commercial*, Nov. 23, 1863; Carl Sandburg, *Abraham Lincoln: The War Years* (New York, 1939), III, 172; Noah Brooks, *Washington in Lincoln's Time*, ed., Herbert Mitgang (New York, 1958), 132.

34. George Hoadly to Chase, Sept. 18, 1861, in Chase, *Diary and Correspondence*, 503, 505; Charles R. Wilson, "The Original Chase Organizational Meeting and *The Next Presidential Election*," *MVHR*, XXIII (June 1936), 61-70; William Frank Zornow, *Lincoln and the Party Divided* (Norman, 1954), 49; *New York Times*, Feb. 23, 1864; Toledo *Blade*, March 11, 1864; Ward Lamon to Lincoln, Feb. 6, 1864; Ashley to Lincoln, May 3, 1864, RTL; R. C. Parsons to Chase, March 2, 1864; Ashley to Chase, April 11, May 2, 1864, Chase Papers, LC; Ashley to R. K. Scott, May 3, 1864, R.K. Scott Papers, OHS; Lincoln, *Works*, VII, 200-201; Smith, *Chase and Civil War Politics*, 134-39; *Cong. Globe*, 38th Cong., 1 Sess., 1535.

35. Hay, *Diaries and Letters*, 180, 184; Howard K. Beale, ed., *Diary of Gideon Welles* (New York, 1960), II, 43; Toledo *Blade*, June 1, 1864; Ashley to George Lasky (May 6, 1864), Toledo *Commercial*, May 9, 1864.

36. Zornow, *Lincoln and the Party Divided*, 99-104; Baltimore *Daily Gazette*, June 9, 1864; John B. Bingham to Andrew Johnson, June 26, 1864, AJ, LC; John G. Nicolay and John Hay, *Abraham Lincoln: A History* (New York, 1890), IX, 62; Clarence Edward Macartney, *Little Mac: The Life of General George B. McClellan* (Philadelphia, 1940), 328.

37. Donald, *Diaries of Salmon P. Chase*, 230; Henig, *Henry Winter Davis*, 214-22; Trefousse, *The Radical Republicans*, 293. Some abolitionists were happy that Lincoln had vetoed the bill, since it had excluded Negroes from suffrage. James M. McPherson, *The Struggle for Equality: Abolitionists and the Negro in the Civil War and Reconstruction* (Princeton, 1964), 246.

38. New York *Tribune*, Aug. 5, 17, 1864; *Harper's Weekly*, VIII (Aug. 20, 1864), 530; Chicago *Tribune*, Aug. 11, 1864; Van Deusen, *Greeley*, 316; H. Winter Davis to Wade, July 19, 1864, Eldridge Collection, Henry E. Huntington Library and Art Gallery.

39. O & S, 738; Sandburg, *War Years*, IV, 136; Bruce Catton, *Grant Takes Command* (Boston, 1968), 340; *The War of the Rebellion: A Compilation of the Official Records of the Union and Confederate Armies* (Washington, D.C., 1880-1901), XLIX, 337.

40. Jessie Marshall Ames, ed., *Private and Official Correspondence of General Benjamin F. Butler* (Norwood, Mass., 1917), IV, 534, 535-36.

41. Ashley to Benjamin F. Butler, Aug. 5, 1864, Benjamin F. Butler Papers, LC; Ashley to Chase, Aug. 5, 1864, Chase Papers, LC.

42. J.W. Shaffer to Butler, Aug. 14, 17, 1864; J.K. Herbert to Butler, Sept. 13, 1864, Butler Papers; Winter Davis to Cheever, July 21, 1864; Smith Regina to Cheever, July 25, 1864, Cheever to E. Washburne, Sept. 10, 1864, Cheever Papers; Winter Davis to S. F. DuPont, Aug. 25, 1864, John D. Hayes, ed., *Samuel Francis DuPont: A Selection from His Civil War Letters* (Ithaca, 1969), III, 373; Zornow, *Lincoln and the Party Divided*, 110-18; Louis Taylor Merrill, "General Benjamin F. Butler in the Presidential Campaign of 1864," *MVHR*, XXXIII (March 1947), 555-70; James G. Randall and Richard N. Current, *Lincoln the President: Last Full Measure* (New York, 1955), 211-13.

43. Hans L. Trefousse, "Zachariah Chandler and the Withdrawal of Frémont in 1864: New Answers to an Old Riddle," *Lincoln Herald*, LXX (Winter 1968), 181-88; Elizabeth Yager, "The Presidential Campaign of 1864 in Ohio," *OAHQ*, XXIV (Oct. 1925), 571; Toledo *Commercial*, Sept. 17, 1864.

44. Ashley to George Lasky (May 6, 1864), *Ibid.*, May 9, 1864; *Ibid.*, April 19, May 16, 17, 23, 24, 25, 26, 28, June 3, 1864; Toledo *Blade*, May 11, 25, Oct. 8, 10, 11, 1864; H. B. Walbridge to Chase, May 16. 1864, Chase Papers, LC; Downes, *Lake Port*, 213.

45. Julian, *Political Recollections*, 234-36; Toledo *Commercial*, Sept. 8, 27, Oct. 3, Nov. 19, 22, 1864; Steedman to Waite, Sept. 28, 1864, in Toledo *Blade*, Oct. 3, 1864; *Ibid.*, Oct. 10, Nov. 22, 1864; Downes, *Lake Port*, 213; New York *Tribune*, Oct. 24, 1864. Within two years, differences over reconstruction and Ohio politics would divide Ashley from Sherman and Bingham.

46. Toledo *Commercial*, Nov. 2, 5, 7, 1864; *O & S*, 306-307; Ashley to Lincoln, Nov. 14, 1864, Edward Bates to Lincoln, Oct. 13, 1864, M. Waite to Lincoln, Oct. 22, 1864, Sumner to Lincoln, Oct. 24, 1864, J. S. Morrill to Lincoln, Nov. 2, 1864, RTL; Sumner to Francis Lieber, Oct. 14, 1864, SP; Schuckers, *Chase*, 487-88.

47. Toledo *Commercial*, Dec. 1, 1864; *O & S*, 309-314; *National Anti-Slavery Standard*, Dec. 24, 1864; *The Liberator*, Dec. 16, 1864; Charles Sumner, *The Works of Charles Sumner*, (Boston, 1870-83), IX, 139-40.

48. *O & S*, 706-708; Sumner to Cheever, Nov. 24, 1864, Cheever Papers; Boston *Commonwealth*, Dec. 4, 17, 1864; New York *Independent*, Dec. 22, 1864; *National Anti-Slavery Standard*, Dec. 24, 1864.

49. Lincoln, *Works*, VIII, 149; Randall and Current, *Last Full Measure*, 298-307; Carl Schurz to Elihu Washburne, Jan. 18, 1865, Elihu Washburne Papers, LC; Chicago *Tribune*, Jan. 12, 1865.

50. Ashley to John G. Nicolay, Dec. 25, 1864, RTL; Ashley to E. McPherson, Dec. 25, 1864, McPherson Papers; Ashley to John W. Longyear, Dec. 25, 1864, Michigan Historical Collections, University of Michigan.

51. *O & S*, 333-51, 355.

52. New York *Tribune*, Jan. 10, 14, 1865; Chicago *Tribune*, Jan. 12, 1865; Washington *National Republican*, Jan. 13, 1865; *Cong. Globe*, 38th Cong., 2 Sess., 257.

53. Albert G. Riddle, *Recollections of War Times: Reminiscences of Men and Events in Washington, 1860-1865* (New York, 1895), 324-25; Sandburg, *War Years*, IV, 13; George S. Boutwell, *Reminiscences of Sixty Years in Public Affairs* (New York, 1902), II, 36; Horace White, *The Life of Lyman Trumbull* (Boston, 1913), 28; Reinhard H. Luthin, *The Real Abraham Lincoln* (Englewood Cliffs, N.J., 1960), 572-73; Nicolay and Hay, *Lincoln*, X, 84-85; Fawn Brodie, *Thaddeus Stevens: Scourge of the South* (New York, 1959), 204; New York *Tribune*, July 30, 1867; John Hamilton to Chase, Jan. 27, 1865, Chase Papers, LC; *Cong. Globe*, 39th Cong., 1 Sess., 930; David Donald, *Charles Sumner and the Rights of Man* (New York, 1970), 193-94; LaWanda Cox and John H. Cox, *Politics, Principles & Prejudice, 1865-1866, Dilemma of Reconstruction in America* (New York, 1963), 3-30; Montgomery Blair to Johnson, June 16, 1865, AJ; David Lindsey, *"Sunset" Cox, Irrepressible Democrat* (Detroit, 1959), 95; Stephen B. Oates, *With Malice toward None: The Life of Abraham Lincoln* (New York, 1977), 439-41.

54. Ashley to Various Congressmen, Jan. 24, 1865, Michigan Historical Collections; Toledo *Commercial*, Jan. 31, 1865; *National Anti-Slavery Standard*, Feb. 4, 1865; *New York Times*, Jan. 31, 1865, was also predicting victory.

55. Ashley to Lincoln, Jan. 31, 1865, Lincoln to Ashley, Jan. 31, 1865, Lincoln, *Works*, VIII, 248; Ashley to William Herndon, Nov. 23, 1866, Herndon-Weik Collection of Lincolniana, LC; William H. Herndon and Jesse Weik, *Herndon's Life of Lincoln* (New York, 1930), 451; Samuel S. Cox, *Union-Disunion-Reunion, Three Decades of Federal Legislation* (Providence, 1885), 327-28. At the time Lincoln knew that peace commissioners were on the way to Fortress Monroe. Lincoln, the master politician, had answered Ashley's questions truthfully as the commissioners were not on the way to Washington.

56. Brooks, *Mr. Lincoln's Washington*, 408-409; Ralph Korngold, *Thaddeus Stevens: A Being Darkly Wise and Rudely Great* (New York, 1955), 231; New York *Independent*, Feb. 4, 1865; *O & S*, 709-711; *Cong. Globe*, 38th Cong., 2 Sess., 523-30.

57. *Ibid.*, 520-31; Luthin, *The Real Lincoln*, 573; "George Julian's Journal—The Assassination of Lincoln," *IMH*, XI (Dec. 1915), 327; Brooks, *Mr. Lincoln's Washington*, 410-11; Worcester *Daily Spy*, Feb. 2, 1865; New York *Tribune*, Feb. 1, 1865; Boston *Commonwealth*, Feb. 4, 1865; Toledo *Commercial*, Feb. 1, 3, 1865; *O & S*, 710-12; Frank A. Flower, *Edwin McMasters Stanton* (Akron, 1905), 190.

58. *National Anti-Slavery Standard*, Feb. 11, 1865; New York *Tribune*, Feb. 1, 1865; William Sheffield to Editor Toledo *Blade* (Feb. 2, 1865), Toledo *Blade*, Feb. 4, 1865; Toledo *Commercial*, Feb. 4, 1865; Blaine, *Twenty Years*, I, 536; Henry Dawes, Manuscript on the History of the Thirteenth Amendment, Henry Dawes Papers, LC. On this matter Clark Waggoner clearly showed that his opposition to Ashley was personal, for he refused to acknowledge that the congressman deserved credit for the passage of the amendment. Toledo *Blade*, Feb. 4, 9, 11, 1865; New York *Independent*, Feb. 9, 1865.

59. *Cong. Globe*, 38th Cong., 2 Sess., 53; 38th Cong., H.R. 602, Dec. 15, 1864, sec. 2, 7, 8, 10; a copy of the bill is also in the RTL Collection; *National Anti-Slavery Standard*, Dec. 24, 1864; New York *Tribune*, Dec. 17, 1864; Boston *Journal*, Dec. 19, 1864; Boston *Commonwealth*, Dec. 24, 1864; Worcester *Daily Spy*, Dec. 19, 1864; *New York Times*, Dec. 19, 1864; Benedict, *A Compromise of Principle*, 89.

60. Hay, *Diaries and Letters*, 245-46; Belz, *Reconstructing the Union*, 252-55.

61. *Ibid.*, H.R. 602, Dec. 20, 1864, amendments by Ashley, sec. 2, 4, 8, 10; *Cong. Globe*, 38th Cong., 2 Sess., 81; Winter Davis to S.F. DuPont, Dec. 20, 1864; Samuel F. DuPont Papers, Eleutherian Mills Historical Library.

62. Wendell Phillips to Moncure Conway, Jan. 8, 1865, McKim-Maloney-Garrison Papers; Boston *Commonwealth*, Dec. 24, 1864, Jan. 14, 1865; Belz, *Reconstructing the Union*, 258.

63. H.R. 602, Jan. 7, 1865, amendments by Ashley, sec. 12, 15; Belz, *Reconstructing the Union*, 259-60.

64. *Cong. Globe*, 38th Cong., 2 Sess., 280-81; Belz, *Reconstructing the Union*, 260-62. On the vote to postpone both Ashley and Davis voted no, but Stevens who did not think the bill went far enough voted yes. *Cong. Globe*, 38th Cong., 2 Sess., 301.

65. Gerrit Smith to General Ashley, Feb. 6, 1865, in *The Liberator*, Feb. 24, 1865; Springfield *Weekly Republican*, Feb. 18, 1865.

66. H.R. 602, Feb. 18, 1865, amendments by Ashley, sec. 3, 5, 11, 12, 13; Ashley to Theodore Tilton, Feb. 27, 1865, Garrison Papers. Ashley also pointed out that at the next session of Congress he would not consent to such a section.

67. *Cong. Globe*, 38th Cong., 2 Sess., 967-71; Belz, *Reconstructing the Union*, 263-65.

68. *Cong. Globe*, 38th Cong., 2 Sess., 1001-1002.

69. Edward L. Pierce, *Memoir and Letters of Charles Sumner* (Boston, 1878-1894), IV, 221, n4. Ashley to Tilton, Feb. 27, 1865, Garrison Papers; Ashley to Editor Boston *Commonwealth* (Feb. 27, 1865), Boston *Commonwealth*, March 4, 1865.

VIII: IMPARTIAL SUFFRAGE

1. Ashley to Sumner, April 15, 1865, SP; Ashley to Johnson, April 15, 1865, AJ.

2. Trefousse, *The Radical Republicans*, 305-308; "George Julian's Journal," 334-35; David Donald, *Lincoln Reconsidered* (New York, 1956), 4.

3. Toledo *Commercial*, April 20, 1865; Daniel J. Ryan, "Lincoln and Ohio," *OAHQ*, XXXII (Jan. 1923), 232.

4. Trefousse, *The Radical Republicans*, 309-311; Sumner to F. Lieber, May 2, 1865, SP.

5. J. K. Herbert to Butler, April 15, 1865, in Butler, *Correspondence*, V, 593-94; Wade to Butler, May 9, 1865, Butler Papers; Frederick Bancroft, ed., *Speeches, Correspondence and Political Papers of Carl Schurz*, I (New York, 1913), 254-55; Winter Davis to DuPont (May 21, 1865), DuPont Papers.

6. Toledo *Blade*, May 23, June 9, 14, 24, 1865; Toledo *Commercial*, June 8, 1865; New York *Herald*, June 17, 1865.

7. Toledo *Commercial*, June 8, 1865; Toledo *Blade*, June 9, 1865; New York *Herald*, June 17, 1865.

8. Kenneth M. Stampp, *The Era of Reconstruction, 1865-1877* (New York, 1966), 63-65; Eric L. McKitrick, *Andrew Johnson and Reconstruction* (Chicago, 1960), 49-51.

9. Toledo *Commercial*, June 8, 1865; Trefousse, *The Radical Republicans*, 315-18; Toledo *Blade*, June 9, 1865.

10. Toledo *Commercial*, Aug. 5, Sept. 9, Oct. 23, 1865; Montana *Post*, July 15, 22, 29, Aug. 3, 1865; Helena *Times*, Aug. 5, 12, 1865; Oregon *Statesman*, Aug. 26, 28, Sept. 4, 25, 1865; William H. Miller to Hezekiah L. Hosmer, July 14, 1865, Hezekiah Hosmer Papers, Western Americana Collection, Beinicke Library, Yale University.

11. *O & S*, 374-77. James M. McPherson has pointed out the meaning: *impartial* or *equal* suffrage, whether the franchise was qualified or unrestricted, it would apply equally to both races. *Universal* suffrage came to be understood as manhood suffrage for both races, with only residency and age requirements. Negro suffrage could mean either impartial or universal suffrage. McPherson, *The Struggle for Equality*, 327.

12. *O & S*, 380-81; Noah Brooks to McPherson, Sept. 19, 1865, McPherson Papers.

13. *O & S*, 389-91.

14. Toledo *Commercial*, Oct. 14, 1865; C. S. Ashley, "Governor Ashley's Biography," 187; Downes, *Lake Port*, 222.

15. Toledo *Blade*, Nov. 25, 1865; Stampp, *The Era of Reconstruction*, 62-82.

16. Charles R. Williams, ed., *Diary and Letters of Rutherford B. Hayes* (Columbus, 1922-1925), III, 6-7, 25.

17. Cox and Cox, *Politics, Principle and Prejudice*, 139-42; *Cong. Globe*, 39th Cong., 1 Sess., 3-6, 24-30; New York *Herald*, Dec. 11, 1865. On other occasions Ashley objected to the member-elect from Arkansas being admitted to floor privileges and to the introduction of a resolution for the admittance of a representative from Tennessee. *Cong. Globe*, 39th Cong., 1 Sess., 68-69, 11, 1552.

18. Bowers, *The Tragic Era*, 15, 157-58; Milton, *The Age of Hate*, 401, 412; Trefousse, *The Radical Republicans*, 339. A recent computerized study of congressional roll call votes has shown that during the Thirty-ninth Congress Ashley was more of a centrist than a radical. In the Fortieth Congress Ashley was a radical. John L. McCarthy, "Reconstruction Legislation and Voting Alignments in the House of Representatives, 1863-1869" (Ph.D. dissertation, Yale University, 1970), 225.

19. 39th Cong., 1 Sess., H.R. 54, preamble, sec. 1, 3, 5, 7, 8, in the William H. Seward Papers, University of Rochester.

20. *Ibid.*, sec. 10. The requirement for religious toleration clearly lays to rest the charge of Ashley's lifelong enemy Clark Waggoner that the congressman was anti-Catholic.

21. *Ibid.*, sec. 11.

22. *Ibid.*, sec. 13.

23. Ashley to William Seward, Dec. 19, 1865, Seward Papers.

24. Ashley to Addison C. Gibbs, Jan. 16, 1866, Addison C. Gibbs Papers, Oregon Historical Society.

25. *Ibid.* On Jan. 18, 1866, the House passed a bill granting suffrage without qualification to the Negroes of the District of Columbia. An amendment which restricted suffrage, regardless of race, to those who could read the Constitution and paid taxes, was offered by Robert S. Hale of New York. James Wilson, the mover of the measure, accepted this, although he indicated that he opposed the amendment and would vote against it. Opposition centered on the portion of Hale's amendment which read, "And to restrict such right of suffrage to the classes above named." Since this would have disenfranchised some loyal white citizens, who previously had the right of suffrage, and because an amendment to clear up the matter was rejected, Ashley and other radicals voted against the Hale amendment. The Senate did not act on an amended version of this bill until December, 1866. Chicago *Tribune*, Jan. 23, 1866; *Cong. Globe*, 39th Cong., 1 Session., 311.

26. Ashley to A. C. Gibbs, Jan. 16, 1866, Gibbs Papers.

27. Trefousse, *The Radical Republicans*, 330-33; Stampp, *The Era of Reconstruction*, 111-13; *Cong. Globe*, 39th Cong., 1 Sess., 1861, 3849-51. Ashley originally voted for the bills, then voted to override the vetoes.

28. 39th Cong., 1 Sess., H.R. Joint Resolution 89.

29. McKitrick, *Andrew Johnson and Reconstruction*, 349. Section 2 read:

> Representatives shall be apportioned among the several States which may be included within this Union according to their respective numbers, counting the whole number of persons in each State, excluding Indians not taxed. But whenever in any State the elective franchise shall be denied to any portion of its male citizens not less than twenty-one years of age, or in any way abridged, except for participation in rebellion or other crime, the basis of representation in such State shall be reduced in the proportion which the number of male citizens shall bear to the whole number of such male citizens not less than twenty-one years of age.

30. *Cong. Globe*, 39th Cong., 1 Sess., 2373, 2545, 3149; McKitrick, *Andrew Johnson and Reconstruction*, 352-55.

31. *O & S*, 392-93, 403, 412.

32. *Ibid.*, 396, 397-99, 403, 414; McKitrick, *Andrew Johnson and Reconstruction*, 350.

33. *Cong. Globe*, 39th Cong., 1 Sess., 2879.

34. *O & S*, 397; Downes, *Lake Port*, 391-92; C. S. Ashley, "Governor Ashley's Biography," 216.

35. *O & S*, 400-402, 406-412.

36. *Ibid.*, 403. This bill did not pass. When Congress adjourned no exact procedure for reconstruction had been established.

37. Trefousse, *The Radical Republicans*, 349-50; *Cong. Globe*, 39th Cong., 1 Sess., 1866, 3974-81.

38. Trefousse, *The Radical Republicans*, 355; *Cong. Globe*, 39th Cong., 1 Sess., 2372-74, 4205-4209. On May 15, Ashley guided through to passage a bill which declared that there could be no denial of the elective franchise on account of race or color in the territories. *Cong. Globe*, 39th Cong., 1 Sess., 2600-22.

39. During the session Ashley was also concerned with other matters. He was absent on the day of the Morrill tariff vote, but he announced that had he been present he would have voted no. Toledo *Commercial*, July 19, 1866. In a letter to the *Commercial*, March 23, 1866, he explained his yes vote on a preliminary roll call on the loan bill. "The only security and safety for the legitimate business of the country," he said, "is a return to the specie standard." *Ibid.*, March 30, 1866.

40. Ashley to A. C. Gibbs, July 6, 1866, Gibbs Papers.

41. Toledo *Blade*, June 6, Aug. 23, Sept. 24, 27, 28, 29, 1866; Worcester *Daily Spy*, Aug. 24, 1866.

42. Toledo *Blade*, June 12, Sept. 13, 15, 25, 27, 28, 1866; article from the Washington *Chronicle*, *Ibid.*, June 8, 1866; Toledo *Commercial*, Sept. 12, 15, 17, 29, 1866. During the campaign, Waggoner accused Ashley of not making sufficient effort to get federal funds for the Toledo harbor. This charge was false, as Ashley had presented petitions asking for improvement of the harbor on March 12, 19, and 22; on March 23 he presented a resolution for the same purpose. Congressman Thomas D. Eliot, chairman of the Committee on Commerce, in a public letter, defended Ashley's ardent efforts in behalf of the harbor. *Cong. Globe*, 39th Cong., 1 Sess., 1349, 1480, 1560, 1602; Thomas Eliot to Charles A. King (Oct. 1, 1866), Toledo *Blade*, Oct. 5, 1866; *Annals of Cleveland*, Vol. 48, Part 1, 3417; Ashley to James A. Garfield, Aug. 12, 1866, Garfield Papers; Ashley to Sumner, Aug. 25, 1866, SP; Ashley to William Endicott, Sept. 25, 1866, Ashley to Nathaniel Banks, Sept. 24, 1866, Nathaniel Banks Papers, LC; Joseph Schaffer, ed., *Intimate Letters of Carl Schurz, 1841-1869* (Madison, 1929), 369. John Sherman in an effort to build up his personal political machine in Ohio sided with Ashley's Toledo enemies. Benedict, *A Compromise of Principle*, 68-69; Felice Bonadio, *North of Reconstruction, Ohio Politics, 1865-1870* (New York, 1970), 116-20.

43. Toledo *Blade*, Sept. 5, 7, 1866; Mary Lincoln to Sumner, Sept. 10, 1866, SP; Edwin M. Stanton to Ashley, Sept. 14, 1866. A typewritten copy of this letter was given to the author by Congressman Thomas L. Ashley of Toledo. Schurz thought that Johnson was no longer sane. Schurz, *Letters*, 369.

44. Toledo *Commercial*, Sept. 25, 1866; Toledo *Blade*, Sept. 25, Oct. 12, 24, 1866; New York *Herald*, Oct. 18, 1866; Trefousse, *The Radical Republicans*, 348.

IX: LOYALTY BETRAYED

1. New York *Tribune*, Jan. 8, 1867; Boston *Commonwealth*, Jan. 12, 1867; Toledo *Blade*, Jan. 14, 1867; Chicago *Tribune*, Jan. 8, 1867; *Cong. Globe*, 39th Cong., 2 Sess., 319-20.

2. *Ibid.*, 310-20; *New York Times*, Jan. 8, 1867.

3. *Ibid.*; Toledo *Blade*, Jan. 10, 1867.

4. Milton, *The Age of Hate*, 382, 412-17; Bowers, *The Tragic Era*, 157, 159, 165; Allen W. Trelease, *Reconstruction, The Great Experiment* (New York, 1971), 78-81; McKitrick, *Andrew Johnson and Reconstruction*, 492; Woodward, "That Other Impeachment," 28.

5. *Impeachment Investigation*, House Report No. 7, 40th Cong., 1 Sess., serial No. 1314, 1198-99. Woodward also misread Ashley's statement to the Judiciary Committee. The Ohio radical never accused John Tyler or Millard Fillmore of having "done in" Presidents Harrison and Taylor, or of even having the slightest knowledge of the supposed conspiracy.

6. Woodward, "That Other Impeachment," 28; *Cong. Globe.*, 39th Cong., 2 Sess., 319-20; 40th Cong., 1 Sess., 18; *New York Times*, Nov. 24, 1867; New York *Tribune*, Nov. 25, 26, 1867; Chicago *Tribune*, June 4, 1867.

7. *Cong. Globe*, 40th Cong., 1 Sess., 68; Toledo *Blade*, Dec. 7, 1867; Carl Schurz to Wife, Oct. 29, 1867, Schurz, *Letters*, 409-410; New York *Independent*, Nov. 14, 1867; Michael Les Benedict, "The Rout of Radicalism: Republicans and the Elections of 1867," *CWH*, XVIII (Dec. 1972), 342-44; Hans L. Trefousse, *Impeachment of a President: Andrew Johnson, the Blacks and Reconstruction* (Knoxville, 1975), 106, 109-110.

8. Ashley to Johnson, April 15, 1865, AJ; Toledo *Blade*, June 9, 14, 24, 1865; Toledo *Commercial*, June 8, 1865; New York *Herald*, June 17, 1865; New York *Tribune*, July 30, 1867. In an interview Johnson explained how Ashley asked him to honor the agreement with Anson Herrick of New York, about his vote on the Thirteenth Amendment. Herrick's brother was supposed to be appointed internal revenue collector of New York City. The President said that he could not "be a party to any such bargain with Mr. Herrick or anyone else." On hearing this, Johnson continued, Ashley got "vexed" and "went off in a great rage." Toledo *Commercial*, Aug. 5, 1867.

9. *Annals of Cleveland*, Vol. 48, Part I,-3417; Ashley to Benjamin F. Wade, Feb. 17, 1867, Benjamin F. Wade Papers, LC; A.G. Clark to John Sherman, Feb. 25, 1866, John Sherman Papers, LC; Benedict, *A Compromise of Principle*, 69.

10. *O & S*, 439, 440, 442, 443-44, 451-53, 455, 457, 467, 486, 494-95, 497, 523, 524, 531; *Cong. Globe.*, 39th Cong., 2 Sess., 1075.

11. Welles, *Diary*, II, 395, 400, 552; Bates, *Diary*, 555; A Memorial to the House of Representatives of the United States in Regard to the Impeachment of President Johnson, Feb. 1866, Thaddeus Stevens Papers, LC; Chicago *Tribune*, Oct. 23, 1866; Edward B. Boutwell to Johnson, Sept. 16, 1866, A. H. Douglas to Johnson, Sept. 19, 1866, Henry Clay Dean to Charles Mason, Oct. 4, 1866, John W. Price to Johnson, Oct. 7, 1866, C. Knox to Johnson, Aug. 1866 [incorrectly dated, it should be Oct. 1866], AJ.

12. Downes, *Lake Port*, 224; Chicago *Tribune*, Oct. 8, 1866; Henry Clay Dean to Charles Mason, Oct. 4, 1866, Herman Ketchum to Johnson, Oct. 13, 1866, AJ; *New York Times*, Feb. 7, 1867; *The Nation*, IV (Feb. 28, 1867), 170-71; Toledo *Commercial*, Oct. 12, 1866.

13. *Ibid.*, Oct. 24, 1866; New York *Herald*, Oct. 18, 1866.

14. Toledo *Commercial*, Oct. 20, 1866; Toledo *Blade*, Oct. 23, Nov. 10, 16, 29, 1866; McPherson, *Struggle for Equality*, 369, 372; New York *Independent*, Oct. 4, 1866, Jan. 10, 1867; *The Nation*, III (Oct. 18, 1866), 310; Charles Halpine to Johnson, Nov. 26, 1866, AJ; J. W. Schaffer to Butler, Dec. 16, 1866, Butler Papers; *Cong. Globe*, 39th Cong., 2 Sess., 255, 1075.

15. *Ibid.*, 154, 1074-75; *The Nation*, III (Dec. 20, 1866), 485; Worcester *Daily Spy*, Dec. 18, 1866; New York *Tribune*, Dec. 18, 1866, Feb. 8, 1867; Chicago *Tribune*, Dec. 18, 1866, Feb. 2, 8, 1867; Baltimore *Gazette*, Feb. 5, 1867; *New York Times*, Feb. 5, 1867; Toledo *Commercial*, Dec. 20, 1866, Feb. 6, 13, 1867; Toledo *Blade*, Feb. 8, 1867; *Annals of Cleveland*, Vol. 50, Part I, 3168.

16. New York *Tribune*, Dec. 20, 1866, Jan. 1, 7, 1867; Toledo *Blade*, Dec. 27, 1866; James Garfield to Hinsdale, Jan. 1, 1867, in Theodore C. Smith, ed., *The Life and Letters of James Abram Garfield* (New Haven, 1925), I, 397; *The Nation*, III, (Dec. 27, 1866), 509; *New York Times*, Jan. 3, 6, 1867; Baltimore *Gazette*, Jan. 7, 1867; Chicago *Tribune*, Jan. 6, 1867; Toledo *Commercial*, Jan. 7, 10, 1867; Boston *Daily Advertiser*, Jan. 7, 1867; Trefousse, *Impeachment of a President*, 54-55; Michael Les Benedict, *The Impeachment and Trial of Andrew Johnson* (New York, 1973), 22-23. George Boutwell, Wendell Phillips, and the Loyal Southern Association also believed that reconstruction was impossible as long as Johnson was President. New York *Tribune*, Jan. 15, 19, Feb. 7, 1867; Chicago *Tribune*, Jan. 20, 1867. During 1867 Ashley was deeply involved in the struggle over reconstruction and the fight for Negro suffrage. These and other topics will be discussed in Chapter X.

17. Toledo *Blade*, Jan. 8, 10, 11, 21, 1867; *National Anti-Slavery Standard*, Jan. 12, 19, 1867; Worcester *Daily Spy*, Jan. 9, 14, 1867; New York *Tribune*, Jan. 8, 1867; *The Nation* IV (Jan. 10, 1867), 21, (Jan. 17, 1867), 41; *New York Times*, Jan. 8, 1867; Boston *Journal*, Jan. 14, 1867; Toledo *Commercial*, Jan. 18, 1867; Chicago *Tribune*, Jan. 19, 1867; Ebenizer W. Pierce to Johnson, Jan. 17, 1867, Thomas Miller to Johnson, Jan. 31, 1867, AJ; Charles G. Linny to Sumner, Jan. 31, 1867, SP. The New York *Herald* also supported impeachment. See the New York *Tribune*, Jan. 21, 1867; W. B. Phillips to Johnson, Jan. 25, 1867, AJ.

18. Welles, *Diary*, III, 8, 121; Baltimore *Gazette*, Jan. 9, 1867; Frank Smith to Johnson, Jan. 23, 1867, AJ; *New York Times*, Jan. 26, 1867; Toledo *Commercial*, Jan. 30, 1867; Washington *National Republican*, Jan. 9, 1867; Milton, *The Age of Hate*, 417; Ashley to R. K. Scott, Scott Papers.

19. New York *Tribune*, Jan. 9, 10, 24, Feb. 2, 1867; Toledo *Blade*, Jan. 9, 15, 1867; Worcester *Daily Spy*, Jan. 9, 14, 17, Feb. 4, 1867; *The Nation*, IV (Jan. 17, 1867), 41. On January 26, during a discussion on reconstruction, Ashley's feeling of betrayal was quite apparent when he angrily attacked the President and called him an apostate, who was joining with former Confederates. *Cong. Globe*, 39th Cong., 2 Sess., 781-89. Apparently, Johnson was doing some checking of his own during this period. He asked E. D. Townshed, the Assistant Adjutant General, to inquire into Ashley's military position during the war. E. D. Townshed to Robert Johnson, Jan. 17, 1867, AJ.

20. *Impeachment Investigation*, 2-15, 449-7 2, 858-59, 1189-94.

21. *Ibid.*, 159-62; Milton, *The Age of Hate*, 409-410.

22. David Miller DeWitt, *The Impeachment and Trial of Andrew Johnson* (New York, 1903), 156-58, 234; *Cong. Globe*, 39th Cong., 2 Sess., 1754-55; Toledo *Commercial*, March 5, 1867.

23. Worcester *Daily Spy*, March 7, 8, 1867; New York *Tribune*, March 6, 7, 1867; *New York Times*, March 6, 7, 1867; Toledo *Commercial*, March 3, 1867; Chicago *Tribune*, March 7, 1867.

24. *Cong. Globe.*, 40th Cong., 1 Sess., 18-19; *O & S*, 438-40.

25. *Cong. Globe*, 40th Cong., 1 Sess., 19; *O & S*, 440-41, 442, 443-44, 453; New York *Tribune*, March 8, 1867; Stanley I. Kutler, "Impeachment Reconsidered," *Reviews in American History*, I (Dec. 1973), 484-85. After the second impeachment attempt failed in 1868, Ashley quickly proposed a constitutional amendment which would have limited what he called *executive usurpation*. This clearly reinforces belief that fear of the growth of presidential power influenced Ashley's desire for impeachment. In a speech defending his amendment, Ashley accused Johnson of betraying the men who elected him Vice President. *O & S*, 464-68. Ashley had mentioned that he was against too much power being centralized in the hands of the President as early as 1859. *O & S*, 33-35.

26. *Cong. Globe.*, 40th Cong., 1 Sess., 19.

27. *Ibid.*, 19, 20, 22-25; *O & S*, 442-45; Chicago *Tribune*, March 8, 1867; Toledo *Blade*, March 8, 1867. Among the charges that Ashley lodged against Johnson were illegal use of the pardoning power and illegal use of the veto power. In February, 1869, he placed before the House another constitutional amendment looking toward subordination of the executive to the legislative authority. He specifically wished to limit the pardoning and veto powers of the President, to eliminate what he called the "Kingly prerogatives." He made similar statements in 1867 and 1868; and there can be no doubt that one of the motives for Ashley's first impeachment movement was fear that unchecked growth of presidential power would injure democracy. *O & S*, 451-53, 457, 486, 519-33; Ashley to Editor Toledo *Commercial* (May 29, 1868), Toledo *Commercial*, June 3, 1868. The Republican members of the Committee on the Judiciary were James F. Wilson of Iowa, chairman, George S. Boutwell of Massachusetts, Francis Thomas of Maryland, Thomas Williams of Pennsylvania, William Lawrence of Ohio, Frederick E. Woodbridge of Vermont, and John Churchill of New York. The Democratic members were Samuel S. Marshall of Illinois and Charles A. Eldridge of Wisconsin.

28. *Cong. Globe*, 40th Cong., 1 Sess., 447-55, 565-67, 592-93, 725; Chicago *Tribune*, March 25, April 2, June 4, 1867; New York *Herald*, May 7, 1867; Toledo *Blade*, May 9, 1867; *New York Times*, June 4, 17, 28, July 3, 1867; Worcester *Daily Spy*, April 1, 1867; Toledo *Commercial*, June 4, 1867; *The Nation*, IV (June 6, 1867), 445; New York *Tribune*, July 10, 11, 16, 1867; New York *Independent*, July 11, 1867.

29. Butler to J. W. Schaffer, April 8, 1867, Butler Papers; Ashley to Editor Toledo *Blade* (Dec. 13, 1867), Toledo *Blade*, Dec. 19, 1867. On July 8, Butler offered a resolution to set up a special committee to investigate the assassination of Lincoln. The resolution passed, with Ashley voting in the affirmative. *Cong. Globe*, 40th Cong., 1 Sess., 515-16.

30. Chicago *Tribune*, Aug. 21, 1867; DeWitt, *The Impeachment of Andrew Johnson*, 138-39.

31. Chicago *Tribune*, Aug. 21, 1867; DeWitt, *The Impeachment of Andrew Johnson*, 142; *New York Times*, Feb. 12, Aug. 15, 1867; Washington *Daily Chronicle*, Aug. 16, 1867; Toledo *Commercial*, Aug. 17, 1867.

32. *Ibid.*; Chicago *Tribune*, Aug. 21, 1867; New York *Times*, Aug. 15, 1867.

33. *Impeachment Investigation*, 1195, 1201-1202; DeWitt, *The Impeachment of Andrew Johnson*, 134; Memorandum of Robert Ball to W. G. Moore, May 10, 1867, Statement of Robert Walters, Aug. 1867, W. H. Chandler to Gideon Welles, Aug. 12, 1867, AJ. Chandler said that Ashley's first visit to the jail was not until March 30.

34. *Impeachment Investigation*, 1196, 1200-1203. Statement of Robert Walters, Aug. 1867, AJ.

35. *Impeachment Investigation*, 1204, 1206, 1207; W. H. Chandler to Welles, Aug. 12, 1867, [Unknown] to My Dear John, March 25, 1867, Memorandum of Robert Ball to W. G. Moore, May 10, 1867, T. B. Brown to Editor of the *Chronicle*, Aug. 1867, William J. C. Duhamel to Johnson, Aug. 6, 10, 1867, Captain Saville to [Unknown], Aug. 10, 1867, Ashley to Dunham, April 18, 1867, enclosed in Dunham to Johnson, July 29, 1867, AJ; Chicago *Tribune*, Aug. 21, 1867.

36. *New York Times*, April 26, June 10, 1867; William B. Matchett to Dunham, April 26, 1867, Ashley to Dunham, April 28, 1867, enclosed in Dunham to Johnson, July 29, 1867, Robert Ball to W. G. Moore, May 3, 1867, W. J. C. Duhamel to Col. Johnson, May 8, 1867, AJ; *Impeachment Investigation*, 1197, 1201, 1202-1203.

37. *Ibid.*, 1203. Riddle also asked Judge Fisher to delay Dunham's removal to Albany until after all the testimony had been given in the Surratt case. The testimony ended on July 26, 1867. A. G. Riddle to Seward, Aug. 15, 1867, in Toledo *Blade*, Aug. 19, 1867.

38. W. J. C. Duhamel to Johnson, Feb. 26, March 27, Aug. 10, 1867, AJ; Ashley to Butler, April, 1867, Butler Papers; Toledo *Commercial*, May 23, 1867.

39. *Impeachment Investigation*, 1189-95.

40. Ashley to W. P. Cutler, July 10, 1867, Misc. Mss. Collection, William Clements Library, University of Michigan.

41. Chicago *Tribune*, Aug. 21, 1867; Ashley to Riddle, Holt, July 22, 1867, Riddle to Johnson, July 23, 1867, Holt to Johnson, July 24, 1867, enclosed in Dunham to Johnson, July 29, 1867, AJ. Riddle to Seward (Aug. 15, 1867), Toledo *Blade*, Aug. 19, 1867; Holt to Editor *Chronicle* (Aug. 17, 1867), Washington *Daily Chronicle*, Aug. 20, 1867; *Impeachment Investigation*, 1195.

42. *New York Times*, July 28, 1867; Dunham to Johnson, July 29, 1867, AJ.

43. *Ibid.*

44. *Ibid.*

45. Welles, *Diary*, III, 143-46, 149, 152, 157, 161; James G. Randall and Theodore C. Pease, eds., *The Diary of Orville Hickman Browning* (Springfield, Ill., 1925, 1933), II, 152-54. The material appeared in the *New York Times*, Aug. 10, 1867; New York *Herald*, Aug. 10, 1867; Toledo *Blade*, Aug. 13, 1867; Toledo *Commercial*, Aug. 13, 1867.

46. Duhamel to Col. Johnson, May 8, 1867, Memorandum of Robert Ball to W. G. Moore, May 10, 1867, W. W. Moore to W. G. Moore, May 7, 1867, Duhamel to W. G. Moore, Aug. 11, 1867, Duhamel to Johnson, Aug. 21, 1867, Statement of Robert Walter, Aug. 1867, Chandler to Welles, Aug. 12, 1867, Brown to Editor *Chronicle*, Aug. 1867, AJ; Washington *Intelligence*, Aug. 26, 1867.

47. [Unknown] to My Dear John, March 25, 1867, William Rabe to Johnson, May 8, 1867, Memorandum of William Rabe to W. G. Moore, May 10, 1867, Chandler to Welles, Aug. 12, 1867, Rabe to W. G. Moore, Aug. 13, 19, 1867, AJ; Washington *Daily Chronicle*, Aug. 13, 1867. At one time it was rumored that Johnson had pardoned Rabe because the latter claimed he could supply information against Ashley. But this was never proved. *New York Times*, Aug. 12, 1867; Chicago *Tribune*, Aug. 12, 1867; New York *Tribune*, Aug. 12, 1867.

48. William H. Hughes to Johnson, Aug. 1867, Statement of Annie F. Ward, Sept. 9, 1867, Statement of F. S. Sarmiento [no date, but it appears to have been written in Aug. 1867], W. G. Moore, "The Small Diary," 33, AJ.

49. Dunham to W. G. Moore, Nov. 24, 1867, Dunham to My Dear Wife, Aug. 15, 1867, Dunham to My Dear Phebe, Dec. 15, 22, 1867, Feb. 16, March 1, June 7, 1868, AJ; *Record of Pardon Cases*, Vol. B, 576, Vol. C, 79, National Archives.

50. *New York Times*, Aug. 13, 15, 1867.

51. Toledo *Blade*, May 17, 1867; Ashley to Editor Toledo *Blade* (Dec. 13, 1867), *Ibid.*, Dec. 19, 1867; Ashley to D. W. H. Howard (Jan. 24, 1868), *Ibid.*, Feb. 5, 1868; Ashley to Editor New York *Tribune* (Dec. 15, 1867), New York *Tribune*, Dec. 23, 1867; *Impeachment Investigation*, 1197-1205.

52. Ashley to Editor Toledo *Blade* (Dec. 13, 1867), Toledo *Blade*, Dec. 19, 1867; *Ibid.*, Sept. 2, 1867; Chicago *Tribune*, Aug. 21, 1867.

53. Toledo *Blade*, Oct. 7, 1867; Roseboom, *Civil War Era*, 458-60.

54. *Ibid.*, *Civil War Era*, 462; Benedict, "The Rout of Radicalism," 342-44; New York *Independent*, Nov. 7, 1867; Schurz to Wife, Oct. 29, 1867, Schurz, *Letters*, 409-410. For a more detailed discussion of the 1867 election see Chapter X.

55. *Impeachment Investigation*, 1197-1208.

56. *Ibid.*, 1198-99.

57. *New York Times*, Nov. 24, 1867; New York *Tribune*, Nov. 25, 26, 1867; Toledo *Commercial*, Nov. 26, 1867. It was rumored that Churchill had changed his vote because he was paid $150,000, but no proof of this charge was ever established. Boston *Daily Advertiser*, Nov. 28, 1867; Welles, *Diary*, III, 238-39.

58. Johnson to Gentlemen of the Cabinet, Nov. 30, 1867, AJ; *New York Times*, Nov. 30, 1867.

59. Toledo *Blade*, Nov. 30, Dec. 7, 1867; New York *Tribune*, Dec. 2, 9, 1867; Excerpt from the Chicago *Tribune*, in Toledo *Commercial*, Dec. 2, 3, 1867; *Ibid.*, Dec. 3, 5, 6, 10, 1867; *New York Times*, Dec. 3, 1867; Garfield to Burke, Dec. 5, 1867, Garfield Papers; Frank Smith to Johnson, Nov. 30, 1867, William Thorpe to Johnson, Dec. 5, 1867, AJ; *Cong. Globe*, 40th Cong. 2 Sess., 68.

60. Toledo *Blade*, Dec. 7, 10, 1867; Ashley to Editor Toledo *Blade* (Dec. 13, 1867), *Ibid.*, Dec. 19, 1867. The letter also appeared in the New York *Herald*, Dec. 22, 1867, and the New York *Tribune*, Dec. 22, 1867. Ashley to Greeley, Dec. 19, 1867, Greeley Papers, NYPL; Ashley to Editor New York *Tribune* (Dec. 15, 1867), New York *Tribune*, Dec. 23, 1867.

61. *Ibid.*; Ashley to Editor Toledo *Blade* (Dec. 13, 1867), Toledo *Blade*, Dec. 19, 1867. In a letter to the *New York Times*, April 21, 1869, Ashley again denied that he had asked Dunham to lie. *New York Times*, April 29, 1869.

62. Ashley to Editor Toledo *Blade* (Dec. 13, 1867), Toledo *Blade*, Dec. 19, 1867.

63. George E. Welles to R. K. Scott, Dec. 6, 1867, Scott Papers.

CHAPTER X: RECONSTRUCTION AND DEFEAT

1. *O & S*, 416.

2. *Cong. Globe*, 39th Cong., 2 Sess., 7, 11.

3. New York *Tribune*, Dec. 6, 1866; Toledo *Commercial*, Dec. 7, 1866.

4. *New York Times*, Dec. 19, 1866; New York *Tribune*, Dec. 20, 1866, Jan. 1, 1867; Toledo *Blade*, Dec. 27, 1866; Ashley to Joseph Medill, Jan. 2, 1867, Misc. Mss, War 1861-1865, Box I, Letter A, New York Historical Society.

5. Stanley I. Kutler, *Judicial Power and Reconstruction Politics* (Chicago, 1968), 65-66; David Donald, *The Politics of Reconstruction, 1863-1867* (Baton Rouge, 1965), 57.

6. *Cong. Globe*, 39th Cong., 2 Sess., 250, 499.

7. *Ibid.*, 253. David Donald says that these officeholders were permanently disqualified, which is incorrect. Article four of section four read: "That no person who has held office, civil, military, or naval, under either of the recent revolutionary governments, State or confederate, shall be allowed to hold any office or honor or profit under said State governments until the Legislature thereof, by special act in each case, and by a two-third vote, shall have granted a full and unconditional pardon to such person." This procedure made reinstatment of political rights difficult but not impossible. Donald, *Politics of Reconstruction*, 65.

8. *Cong. Globe*, 39th Cong., 2 Sess., 253-54.

9. *Ibid.*, New York *Independent*, Jan. 10, 1867; Worcester *Daily Spy*, Jan. 10, 1867. On January 11, Ashley offered this bill, with minor changes, as a substitute for Stevens's bill, H.R. 882, which dealt with the reconstruction of North Carolina. This bill was referred to the Committee on Territories. Toledo *Blade*, Jan. 12, 1867; *National Anti-Slavery Standard*, Jan. 12, 1867; Docket of the Committee on the Territories, Jan. 10, 1867, 39th Cong., 2 Sess., H.R. 543.

10. Trefousse, *Wade*, 275, 276-77; *Cong. Globe*., 39th Cong., 2 Sess., 399-401; *New York Times*, Jan. 10, 1867; Toledo *Blade*, Jan. 11, 1867; Worcester *Daily Spy*, Jan. 14, 1867; Chicago *Tribune*, Jan. 15, 1867. Ashley's desire to have the two states in the Union in order to facilitate the battle for Negro rights throughout the country was attacked by radicals who felt his actions to be a betrayal. Ashley was not ready to sacrifice the ultimate goal of Negro suffrage, but he was ready to moderate immediate aims to achieve a long-time goal. *National Anti-Slavery Standard*, Jan. 26, 1867.

11. *Cong. Globe*, 39th Cong., 2 Sess., 480-81, 487, 1096, 1120-22; *New York Times*, Jan. 16, 1867; New York *Tribune*, Jan. 16, Feb. 11, 1867; Toledo *Blade*, Jan. 19, 1867; Donald, *Politics of Reconstruction*, 63.

12. 39th Cong., 2 Sess., H.R. 543, Sec. 2,3,16,17.

13. *Cong. Globe*., 39th Cong., 2 Sess., 500-505, 715-16; Donald, *Politics of Reconstruction*, 65, 67-68.

14. *O & S*, 420, 428-29, 432, 435.

15. *Ibid.*, 430-31.

16. Donald, *Politics of Reconstruction*, 69-81. During the discussion on this bill, Ashley presented an amendment, H.R. 1143, which contained the following section: "That whenever the people of any State government named in this act shall adopt a constitution of State government which shall secure to all citizens of the United States within said State, irrespective of race or color, the equal protection of the laws, including the right of elective franchise, and shall ratify the proposed amendment to the Constitution of the United States, then the provisions of this act shall cease to have any force and effect in such State." This was close to the positions of moderates like Bingham and Blaine, and again belies the idea that Ashley was an inflexible, doctrinaire ultraradical. *Cong. Globe*., 39th Cong., 2 Sess., 781, 782, 816, 817, 1106; Worcester *Daily Spy*, Feb. 12, 1867. On March 2, Congress also passed the Tenure of Office Act and the Command of the Army Act, both limiting Johnson's power.

17. John Hope Franklin, *Reconstruction: After the Civil War* (Chicago, 1961), 70-72; *Cong. Globe*, 40th Cong., 1 Sess., 314.

18. Stampp, *The Era of Reconstruction*, 129; Trefousse, *The Radical Republicans*, 369-70, 374; Georges Clemenceau, *American Reconstruction, 1865-1870*, ed., Fernand Baldensperger (New York, 1928), 40; Benedict, *A Compromise of Principle*, 242-43; Michael Perman, *Reunion Without Compromise: The South and Reconstruction: 1856-1868* (New York and London, 1973), 346-47.

19. Roseboom, *Civil War Era*, 457; Smith, *History of the Republican Party in Ohio*, I, 297; Ashley, "Memoir," chapter X, 57-58; Toledo *Blade*, June 22, 1867.

20. Roseboom, *Civil War Era*, 458; *Cong. Globe*, 40th Cong., 1 Sess., 565, 591-92, 691, 740; Clifford H. Moore, "Ohio in National Politics, 1865-1896," *OAHQ*, 38 (April-July 1928), 242-45.

21. *Ibid.*, 243; Roseboom, *Civil War Era*, 460; Toledo *Commercial*, Oct. 5, 8, 1867; Toledo *Blade*, Aug. 27, 29, 31, Sept. 7, 14, 17, 1867; G. E. Welles to Scott, Sept. 27, 1867, Scott Papers. The Toledo *Blade* said the opposition of the Democrats was "the outgrowth of the most detestable prejudice that ever warped the judgment of human beings." Toledo *Blade*, Sept. 14, 1867.

22. G. E. Welles to Scott, Sept. 27, 1867, Scott Papers; Roseboom, *Civil War Era*, 461-62. The greenback problem was also an important issue during the campaign. The Democrats supported George Pendleton's plan of paying off government bonds as they became due in greenbacks. Since the West had suffered a currency scarcity in the postwar period, this idea was popular with poor, debtor farmers and shopkeepers. The money issue contributed to the Democratic victory. Although Ashley realized that the Pendleton Plan had great voter appeal, he opposed it. He was basically a hard-money man; he had been so since the 1850s. The necessities of the Civil War made Ashley support the issue of greenbacks, and in 1866 and 1867 he voted for a proposal to prevent further reduction of greenbacks as a temporary measure. But at the same time he publicly stated his belief in hard money. Thus it appears that the Ohio radical was philosophically a hard-money man, but was not adamant about it, if the national interest called for soft money. Robert P. Sharkey, *Money, Class and Party: An Economic Study of Civil War and Reconstruction* (Baltimore, 1959), 111, 280; Toledo *Commercial*, March 30, 1866, Oct. 8, 1867; Chicago *Tribune*, Feb. 6, 22, 1867.

23. Trefousse, *The Radical Republicans*, 364, 372; *Cong. Globe*, 40th Cong., 2 Sess., 119.

24. *Ibid.*, 39th Cong., 1 Sess., 2879, 40th Cong., 1 Sess., 511, H.R. (Joint Resolution), 62, 40th Cong., 2 Sess., 117; Toledo *Blade*, Sept. 21, 1868; Toledo *Commercial*, July 16, 1867. G. E. Welles to Scott, Aug. 21, 1867, Scott Papers.

25. *Cong. Globe*, 40th Cong., 2 Sess., 117-19. It should be mentioned that when he first talked about this amendment in May, 1866, he indicated that he expected it to apply to women. *O & S*, 397.

26. Trefousse, *The Radical Republicans*, 361; Franklin, *Reconstruction*, 72.

27. 40th Cong., 2 Sess., H.R. 214; *Cong. Globe*, 40th Cong., 2 Sess., 264-67, 1417, 1453, 1861; New York *Tribune*, Dec. 9, 1867.

28. Fred L. Israel, ed., *The State of the Union Messages of the Presidents, 1790-1966* (New York, 1966), II, 1144-66; McKitrick, *Andrew Johnson and Reconstruction*, 499-503; Benjamin P. Thomas and Harold M. Hyman, *Stanton: The Life and Times of Lincoln's Secretary of War* (New York, 1962), 573.

29. Hans L. Trefousse, "The Acquittal of Andrew Johnson and the Decline of the Radicals," *CWH*, XIV (June 1968), 153-55; Blodgett to Sherman, Dec. 30, 1867, Sherman Papers; Franklin, *Reconstruction*, 75-76; *New York Times*, Feb. 28, 1868; *Cong. Globe.*, 40th Cong., 2 Sess., 1400.

30. *Ibid.*, 1102, 1360-62; *New York Times*, Feb. 25, 1868; *O & S*, 452-53, 455, 457.

31. Benedict, *The Impeachment and Trial of Andrew Johnson*, 26-36; Raoul Berger, "The President, Congress and the Courts," *The Yale Law Journal*, 83 (May 1974), 1137-53.

32. Toledo *Commercial*, Feb. 29, 1868.

33. Trefousse, *The Radical Republicans*, 385-86; Ashley to William H. Smith, March 21, 1868, Smith Papers; Worcester *Daily Spy*, April 20, 1868; Cincinnati *Gazette*, May 13, 1868; DeWitt, *Impeachment of Andrew Johnson*, 551-54; Toledo *Blade*, May 17, 1868.

34. Ashley to Denison Steele, May 16, 1868, in Toledo *Blade*, May 22, 1868; *Ibid.*, May 27, 1868; Ashley to Editor Toledo *Commercial* (May 29, 1868), Toledo *Commercial*, June 3, 1868; *New York Times*, May 27, 1868.

35. Ashley to Editor Toledo *Commercial* (May 29, 1868), Toledo *Commercial*, June 3, 1868. On May 20, U. S. Grant was nominated as the Republican presidential candidate and Schuyler Colfax was nominated vice presidential candidate. *New York Times*, May 22, 1868.

36. *Cong. Globe*, 40th Cong., 2 Sess., 2713; Toledo *Blade*, June 12, 27, 1868.

37. *O & S*, 463-502, 503. Ashley had been in favor of most of these ideas since 1854, and he continued to fight for them until his death. In 1891, for example, he made a speech in which he advocated a similar plan of constitutional change, which included direct election of senators and a secret ballot. *O & S*, 503, 766, 815.

38. G. E. Welles to Scott, Aug. 21, Sept. 27, Dec. 6, 1867, Scott Papers.

39. Toledo *Blade*, July 27, 1868.

40. *Ibid.*, Aug. 20, Sept. 21, 24, Oct. 12, 1868.

41. Ashley to Sumner, Aug. 22, 1868, SP; Ashley to Hassaurek, Sept. 15, 1868, Hassaurek Papers; Ashley to William E. Chandler, Sept. 8, 13, 30, 1868, William E. Chandler Papers, LC; Toledo *Blade*, Sept. 21, 26, Oct. 3, 6, 1868.

42. *New York Times*, Sept. 5, Oct. 14, 1868. In 1867, for example, Ashley had signed a petition in favor of women's suffrage. Chicago *Tribune*, Oct. 4, 1867. Ashley's wife Emma was the head of a women's suffrage group in Toledo. Toledo *Commercial*, May 18, 1869; Downes, *Lake Port*, 230, 392. Ashley to Sumner, Oct. 15, 20, 1868, SP; Ashley to Chandler, Oct. 15, 1868, Chandler Papers; C. S. Ashley, "Governor Ashley's Biography," 189-90, 196; *Congressional Quarterly's Guide to U.S. Elections*, 620; Ashley, "Memoir," chapter X, 52-55; Toledo *Blade*, Nov. 17, 1868.

43. Ashley to the Republicans of the 10th District, Oct. 15, 1868, in *Ibid.*, Oct. 17, 1868; Ashley to Sumner, Nov. 5, 1868, SP.

44. Ashley to Jacob M. Howard, Nov. 17, 1868, Jacob M. Howard Papers, Burton Collection, Detroit Public Library; Ashley to Sumner, Oct. 15, 1868, SP.

45. New York *Tribune*, Jan. 15, 1869; Toledo *Blade*, Jan. 19, Feb. 1, 1869; New York *World*, Jan. 26, 1869; 40th Cong., 3 Sess., H.R. 381; William Gillette, *The Right to Vote: Politics and the Passage of the Fifteenth Amendment* (Baltimore, 1965), 50, 67-69.

CHAPTER XI: GOVERNOR AND BUSINESSMAN

1. Members of the House of Representatives to Ulysses S. Grant, March 1869, Members of the Senate to Grant, March 1, 1869, Ohio Members of Congress to Grant [no date], R. K. Scott to Grant, March 3, 1869, Hayes to Grant, March 20, 1869, B. Butler to Grant, March 24, 1869, Julian to Grant [no date], Blaine to Grant, March 1869, William Clafin, William E. Chandler to Grant, March 1869, Logan to Hamilton Fish, March 24, 1869, Banks to Fish, March 27, 1869, Grant Adm., State Dept. App. Papers; Toledo *Blade*, March 29, April 13, 1869; New York *Tribune*, April 6, 1869; Montana *Post*, April 9, 1869; *New York Times,* April 18, 1869; Toledo *Commercial*, April 12, 1869. Ashley's appointment was opposed by both *The Nation* and the *New York Times*. Henry Raymond of *The Times* was a long-standing political opponent of the Ohioan. *New York Times*, April 18, 19, 21, 28, 1869; Ashley to Editor *New York Times* (April 21, 1869), *New York Times*, April 29, 1869; *The Nation*, VIII (April 15, 1869), 286, (April 22, 1869), 305, (April 29, 1869), 325-326, 328. When Ashley was nominated, General Benjamin F. Potts, who was aligned with the Sherman wing of the Ohio Republican party, let it be known that he too wanted to be territorial governor of Montana. Montana *Post*, April 16, 1869.

2. Ashley to H. Fish, April 27, 1869, Grant Adm., State Dept. App. Papers; Ashley to J. C. B. Davis, July 23, 1869, H. Chase to Grant, Dec. 20, 1869, State Dept. Terr. Papers, Montana; Ashley to Sumner, Dec. 19, 1869, SP; Toledo *Blade*, June 4, 1869.

3. Ashley to J. C. B. Davis, July 23, 1869, State Dept. Terr. Papers, Montana; Ashley to Sumner, July 18, 1869, SP.

4. Ashley to Benno Speyer [no date], Toledo *Blade*, May 21, 1869; *Ibid.*, Aug. 18, 30, Oct. 4, 1869; Seymour Dunbar, ed., *The Journals and Letters of Major John Owen, Pioneer of the Northwest, 1850-1871* (New York, 1927), II, 142.

5. Merrill G. Burlingame and K. Ross Toole, *A History of Montana* (New York, 1957), I, 219, 222; James M. Hamilton, *From Wilderness to Statehood, A History of Montana, 1805-1900* (Portland, 1957), 281; Stanley R. Davidson and Dale Tash, "Confederate Backwash in Montana Territory," *MMWH*, XVII (Oct. 1967), 50-54, 58; Thomas F. Meagher to Seward, Dec. 11, 1865, State Dept. Terr. Papers, Montana.

6. New York *World*, Oct. 1, 1869; Toledo *Commercial*, Oct. 22, 1869; *The Nation*, IX (Oct. 7, 1869), 282-83.

7. Toledo *Commercial*, Nov. 17, 1869; Toledo *Blade*, Nov. 17, 1869.

8. See Chapters III, IV; Hans L. Trefousse, "Ben Wade and the Negro," *Ohio Historical Quarterly*, LXVIII (April 1959), 161-76; Foner, *Free Soil, Free Labor, Free Men*, 295-97; Toledo *Commercial*, Nov. 17, 1869.

9. Clark C. Spence, "Spoilsman in Montana," *MMWH*, XVIII (Spring 1968), 30-31; Ashley to Fish, Jan. 23, 1870, State Dept. Terr. Papers, Montana; *House Journal of the Sixth Session of the Legislative Assembly of the Territory of Montana*, Dec. 6, 1869-Jan. 7, 1870, 14-15; C. S. Ashley, "Governor Ashley's Biography," 252, Appendix F, "Message of Governor Ashley."

10. *Ibid.*, 252-67, 268-71, 282-83, 286-87.

11. *Ibid.*, 267, 271-74.

12. *Ibid.*, 274-77, 280, 283-84.

13. Spence, "Spoilsman in Montana," 31, 32; Helena *Daily Herald*, Dec. 31, 1869; *House Journal, Sixth Session*, 47-49, 108-109, 124, 129, 133, 164, 166-70; Hamilton, *From Wilderness to Statehood*, 307-310; Ashley to Sumner, Dec. 16, 1869, SP.

14. Ashley to Greeley, Dec. 18, 1869, Greeley Papers, NYPL; Ashley to Sumner, Dec. 19, 1869, SP; Ashley to Sherman, Dec. 20, 1869, Sherman Papers; Ashley to Garfield, Dec. 24, 1869, Garfield Papers; Ashley to Banks, Jan. 30, 1870, Banks Papers; Ashley to Colfax, Feb. 28, 1870, Colfax Papers; Ashley to Columbus Delano, Dec. 27, 1869, R.E. Fisk to Grant, March 29, 1870, Montana Territorial Republican Committee to Grant, Dec. 1869, H.L. Hosmer to Fish, Dec. 25, 1869. Republicans of Montana to Grant, Jan. 1870, Grant Adm., State Dept. Appt. Papers; New York *Tribune*, Dec. 17, 1869; Ashley to Fish, Dec. 17, 1869, Ashley to Grant, Dec. 20, 1869, State Dept. Terr. Papers, Montana; Helena *Daily Herald*, Dec. 17, 1869, Jan. 24, 1870; Toledo *Blade*, Dec. 28, 1869.

15. Donald, *Charles Sumner and the Rights of Man*, 434, 436.

16. Toledo *Blade*, March 24, 1870; Toledo *Commercial*, July 25, 1870; Ashley to Sumner, March 4, July 29, 1870, SP.

17. C. S. Ashley, "Governor Ashley's Biography," 194; Donald, *Charles Sumner and the Rights of Man*, 433-34, 436-45.

18. Allan Nevins, *Hamilton Fish, The Inner History of the Grant Administration* (New York, 1937), 311; Spence, "Spoilsman in Montana," 33; Ashley Interview, Toledo *Commercial*, Dec. 29, 1870; Ashley to Sumner, July 29, 1870, with clippings from the Toledo *Blade* concerning Sherman's opposition to Ashley, SP; Tom Stout, ed., *Montana Its Story and Biography* (Chicago, 1921), I, 314; Bonadio, *North of Reconstruction*, 119, 136.

19. C. S. Ashley, "Governor Ashley's Biography," 194-95; Benjamin F. Potts to R. B. Hayes, Nov. 29, 1870, Ashley to Hayes, May 20, 1871, Hayes Papers; Ashley to Sumner, Dec. 26, 1870, SP; Ashley to Schurz, Dec. 26, 1870, Carl Schurz Papers, LC; Toledo *Commercial*, Dec. 8, 1870, Jan. 2, 6, 1871; Toledo *Blade*, Jan. 4, Aug. 17, Dec. 16, 1871; Cincinnati *Commercial*, Jan. 6, 1871; Jay Cooke to Sherman, Aug. 22, 1871, Sherman Papers.

20. C. S. Ashley, "Governor Ashley's Biography," 195; Cincinnati *Gazette*, Dec. 14, 1871; H. D. Cook to Sherman, Aug. 21, 1871, Sherman Papers; Roseboom, *Civil War Era*, 478.

21. *Ibid.*, 478-80; Ashley to Whitelaw Reid, Dec. 21, 1871, Whitelaw Reid Papers, LC; Ashley to D. W. H. Howard (Dec. 21, 1871), Toledo *Blade*, Dec. 27, 1871; Cincinnati *Gazette*, Dec. 29, 1871, Jan. 2, 4, 1872; Rush R. Sloan to Sherman, Dec. 5, 1871, Sherman Papers; Toledo *Commercial*, Dec. 20, 1871; *Ohio State Journal*, Jan. 1, 1872; John Sherman, *Recollections of Forty Years in the House, Senate and Cabinet* (Chicago, 1895), I, 474-80; Moore, "Ohio in National Politics," 272-73.

22. William E. Parrish, *Missouri under Radical Rule, 1865-1870* (Columbia, 1965), 296-326; Trefousse, *The Radical Republicans,* 440-45; John G. Sproat, *The Best Men,* (New York, 1965), 73-81; Bently Brinkerhoff Gilbert, "Some Aspects of Ohio's Part in the Liberal Republican Movement," *Ohio Archaeological and Historical Society Bulletin,* 13 (July 1955), 191-92; Donald, *Charles Sumner and the Rights of Man,* 449-53, 498-501; Ashley to Sumner, March 12, 1871, SP.

23. Samuel Bowles to Sumner, March 18, 1872, Edward Atkinson to Sumner, March 25, 1872, SP; Atkinson to Schurz, March 20, 1872, Schurz Papers; Ashley to Reid, April 2, 7, 1872, Reid to Ashley, March 17, 1872, Reid Papers; *New York Times*, March 27, 1872.

24. Donald, *Charles Sumner and the Rights of Man*, 540-44; New York *Tribune*, May 1, 1872; Toledo *Commercial*, May 2, 1872; George Seldon Henry, Jr., "Radical Republican Policy toward the Negro during Reconstruction, 1862-1872," (Ph.D. dissertation, Yale University, 1963), 331; Van Deusen, *Greeley*, 404-420.

25. W. Phillips to Sumner, July 19, 1872, SP; Patrick W. Riddleberger, "The Break in the Radical Ranks: Liberals vs. Stalwarts in the Election of 1872," *JNH*, XLIV (April 1959), 137-48, 156; James M. McPherson, "Grant or Greeley? The Abolitionists' Dilemma in the Election of 1872," *AHR*, LXXI (Oct. 1965), 41-50.

26. Ashley to Reid, May 14, 1872, Reid Papers; Ashley to Sumner, July 15, 1872, SP; Ashley to Lyman Trumbull, Oct. 14, 1872, McCormick Family Papers, Wisconsin Historical Society; Toledo *Commercial*, July 18, 19, Oct. 2, 9, 1872; New York *Tribune*, July 5, Aug. 8, 1872.

27. *O & S*, 566, 569, 570, 571-73, 575-76; Trefousse, *The Radical Republicans*, 462-63; Toledo *Blade*, June 29, 1872; McPherson, "Grant or Greeley?" 57-61.

28. *Historical Hand Atlas* (Chicago & Toledo, 1882), 215; C. S. Ashley, "Governor Ashley's Biography," 197, 214-15; Paddock, "An Ohio Congressman," 3; Sunderland, "Introductory Address," 2.

29. Henry E. Riggs, *The Ann Arbor Railroad Fifty Years Ago* (Ann Arbor, 1947), 17-18; Toledo *Blade*, July 7, 1877.

30. John M. Morgan, "The Ashleys Build a Railroad," *NOQ* (Spring 1958), 84-94; Willis F. Dunbar, *All Aboard: A History of Railroads in Michigan* (Grand Rapids, 1969), 166-67.

31. *Ibid.*, 167-68; Downes, *Lake Shore*, 228; John M. Morgan, "The Ann Arbor Strike of 1893," *NOQ*, 30 (Summer 1958), 173, 175; C. S. Ashley, "Governor Ashley's Biography," 207.

32. *O & S*, 661-66, 687-88; Ashley to Benjamin F. Arnett, Dec. 19, 1892, in *Ibid.*, 598-99; C. S. Ashley, "Governor Ashley's Biography," 206.

33. *O & S*, 667-74; Morgan, "The Ann Arbor Strike of 1893," 174.

34. Toledo *Blade*, Sept. 22, 23, 25, 30, Oct. 4, 10, 16, 20, 22, 23, 25, 29, 31, Nov. 5, 1890, Sept. 8, 12, Oct. 11, 19, 31, Nov. 7, 9, 10, 1892; *O & S*, 675-80; Clark Waggoner, "Seventh Congressional District, J. M. Ashley and His Record," Nov. 1, 1890, Waggoner to Hayes, Nov. 21, 1890, Hayes Papers.

35. C. S. Ashley, "Governor Ashley's Biography," 218-19; New York *Tribune*, Sept. 17, 1896.

36. *O & S*, Appendix.

BIBLIOGRAPHY

MANUSCRIPT COLLECTIONS

James M. Ashley File, Toledo Public Library
James M. Ashley "Memoir," University of Toledo Library
Nathaniel P. Banks Papers, Library of Congress
Benjamin F. Butler Papers, Library of Congress
Salmon P. Chase Papers, Library of Congress
Salmon P. Chase Papers, Ohio Historical Society
Salmon P. Chase Papers, Historical Society of Pennsylvania
William E. Chandler Papers, Library of Congress
George Cheever Papers, American Antiquarian Society Library
Schuyler Colfax Papers, University of Rochester
Henry L. Dawes Papers, Library of Congress
Samuel F. DuPont Papers, Eleutherian Mills Historical Library
Eldridge Collection, Henry E. Huntington Library and Art Gallery
James A. Garfield Papers, Library of Congress
William Lloyd Garrison Papers, Boston Public Library
Addison C. Gibbs Papers, Oregon Historical Society
Joshua R. Giddings Papers, Ohio Historical Society
Horace Greeley Papers, Library of Congress
Horace Greeley Papers, New York Public Library
Adam Gurowski Papers, Library of Congress
Friedrich Hassaurek Papers, Ohio Historical Society
Rutherford B. Hayes Papers, Rutherford B. Hayes Library
Herndon-Weik Collection of Lincolniana, Library of Congress
Hezekiah L. Hosmer Papers, Beinicke Library, Yale University
Jacob M. Howard Papers, Burton Collection, Detroit Public Library
Janney Family Papers, Ohio Historical Society
Julian-Giddings Papers, Library of Congress
Andrew Johnson Papers, Library of Congress
Robert Todd Lincoln Collection, Library of Congress
John W. Longyear Papers, Michigan Historical Collections,
    University of Michigan
McCormick Family Papers, Wisconsin Historical Society
McKim-Maloney-Garrison Papers, New York Public Library
Edward McPherson Papers, Library of Congress
Miscellaneous Manuscripts, War 1861-1865, Box I, Letter A,
    New York Historical Society
Miscellaneous Manuscripts, William Clements Library,
    University of Michigan

Whitelaw Reid Papers, Library of Congress
William Schouler Papers, Massachusetts Historical Society
Carl Schurz Papers, Library of Congress
Robert K. Scott Papers, Ohio Historical Society
Robert C. Schenck Papers, Rutherford B. Hayes Library
William H. Seward Papers, University of Rochester
John Sherman Papers, Library of Congress
Wilbur H. Siebert Papers, Ohio Historical Society
William Henry Smith Papers, Ohio Historical Society
Edwin M. Stanton Papers, Library of Congress
Thaddeus Stevens Papers, Library of Congress
Charles Sumner Papers, Houghton Library, Harvard University
Benjamin F. Wade Papers, Library of Congress
Elihu Washburne Papers, Library of Congress
Gideon Welles Papers, Connecticut Historical Society

NEWSPAPERS

Boston *Commonwealth*
Boston *Daily Advertiser*
Boston *Journal*
Baltimore *Gazette*
Chicago *Tribune*
Cincinnati *Commercial*
Cincinnati *Gazette*
Cleveland *Leader*
Findlay *Hancock Jeffersonian*
Helena *Daily Herald*
The Liberator
Montana Post
National Anti-Slavery Standard
New York *Evening Post*
New York *Herald*
New York *Independent*
New York Times
New York *Tribune*
New York *World*
Ohio State Journal
Oregon *Statesman*
The Principia
Springfield *Weekly Republican*

Toledo *Blade*
Toledo *Commercial*
Washington *Daily Chronicle*
Washington *Daily Intelligencer*
Washington *National Republican*
Worcester *Daily Spy*

MAGAZINES AND JOURNALS

Brownson's Quarterly Review
Harper's Weekly
The Nation

PUBLIC DOCUMENTS

Congressional Globe, 36th-40th Congress.
Grant Administration, 1869-1877, State Department Appointment Papers, Box 2, James M. Ashley, National Archives.
House Journal of the Sixth Session of the Legislature of the Territory of Montana, Dec. 6, 1869-Jan. 7, 1870. Helena, 1870.
Record of Pardon Cases—Andrew Johnson, Vol. B., Vol. C, National Archives.
The War of the Rebellion: A Compilation of the Official Records of the Union and Confederate Armies. 128 vols. Washington, D.C., 1880-1901.
U.S. Congress. House of Representatives. Docket, Dec. 15, 1857-Jan. 15, 1873; Minutes, Feb. 23, 1860-Dec. 17, 1873, Committee on the Territories, 35th Cong., 1 Sess.-43rd Cong., 1 Sess., MS, National Archives.
U.S. Congress. House of Representatives. 36th-40th Congress. *Bills and Resolutions*. Microfilm, Library of Congress.
U.S. Congress. House of Representatives. 37th Congress. Minority Reports of the Committee on the Territories of a Bill to Establish Temporary Governments in Disloyal States. MS, National Archives.
U.S. Congress. House of Representatives. *Select Committee to Investigate Charges against the Hon. J. M. Ashley*. House Report No. 47. 37th Cong., 3 Sess., 1863.
U.S. Congress. House of Representatives. *Impeachment Investigation*. House Report No. 7. 40th Cong., 1 Sess., 1867.
U.S. Department of State Territorial Papers, Montana, 1864-1872, National Archives.

PUBLISHED CORRESPONDENCE AND SPEECHES

Arnett, Benjamin W., ed., *Duplicate Copy of the Souvenir from the Afro-American League of Tennessee to Hon. James M. Ashley of Ohio*. Philadelphia, 1894.

Bancroft, Frederick, ed., *Speeches, Correspondence and Political Papers of Carl Schurz*. 6 vols. New York, 1913.

Basler, Roy P., ed., *The Collected Works of Abraham Lincoln*. 8 vols. New Brunswick, N. J., 1953-1955.

Hayes, John D., ed., *Samuel Francis DuPont: A Selection from His Civil War Letters*. 3 vols. Ithaca, N.Y., 1969.

Marshall, Jessie Ames, ed., *Private and Official Correspondence of Gen. Benjamin F. Butler during the Period of the Civil War*. 5 vols. Norwood, Mass., 1917.

Schafer, Joseph, ed., *Intimate Letters of Carl Schurz, 1841-1869*. Madison, Wisc., 1928.

AUTOBIOGRAPHIES, DIARIES, MEMOIRS AND OTHER PRIMARY SOURCES

Annals of Cleveland, 1818-1935: A Digest and Index of the Newspaper Record of Events and Opinions. Cleveland, 1936-1938.

Beale, Howard K., ed., *The Diary of Edward Bates, 1859-1866. Annual Report of the American Historical Association for 1930*. Vol. IV. Washington, D.C., 1933.

————, *Diary of Gideon Welles*. 3 vols. New York, 1960.

Blaine, James G., *Twenty Years of Congress: From Lincoln to Garfield*. 2 vols. Norwich, Conn., 1884-1886.

Bourne, Edward G., ed., *Diary and Correspondence of Salmon P. Chase. Annual Report of the American Historical Association for 1902*. Vol II. Washington, D.C. 1903.

Boutwell, George S., *Reminiscences of Sixty Years in Public Affairs*. 2 vols. New York, 1902.

Brooks, Noah, *Washington in Lincoln's Time*. Edited by Herbert Mitgang. New York, 1958.

Cox, Samuel, *Union—Disunion—Reunion, Three Decades of Federal Legislation*. Providence, R.I., 1885.

Dennett, Tyler, ed., *Lincoln and the Civil War in the Diaries and Letters of John Hay*. New York, 1939.

Donald, David, ed., *Inside Lincoln's Cabinet: The Civil War Diaries of Salmon P. Chase*. New York, 1954.

Glydon, Howard [Laura Searing], *Notable Men in the House*. New York, 1862.

Gurowski, Adam, *Diary*. 3 vols in 2. New York, 1868.

Israel, Fred L., ed., *The State of the Union Messages of the Presidents, 1790-1966*. 3 vols. New York, 1966.

Julian, George W., *Political Recollections, 1840-1872*. Chicago, 1884.

McPherson, Edward, *The Political History of the United States of America during the Great Rebellion*. Washington, D.C., 1872.

————, *The Political History of the United States of America during the Period of Reconstruction*. Washington, D.C., 1880.

Memorial Address at the Unitarian Church of Ann Arbor, Jan. 10, 1897. Ann Arbor, 1897.

Official Proceedings of the Republican Convention Convened in the City of Pittsburgh, Pennsylvania on the Twenty-Second of February, 1856. New York, 1856.

Owen, John, *The Journals of Major John Owen, Pioneer of the Northwest, 1850-1871*. Edited by Seymour Dunbar. 2 vols. New York, 1927.

Pierce, Edward L., ed., *Memoir and Letters of Charles Sumner*. Boston, 1878-1894.

Poore, Ben Perley, *The Federal and State Constitutions, Colonial Charters and Other Organic Laws of the United States*. 2 vols. Washington, D.C., 1894.

Porter, Kirk H., and Donald B. Johnson, *National Party Platforms, 1840-1956*. Urbana, Ill., 1956.

Proceedings of the First Three Republican National Conventions, 1856, 1860, 1864. Minneapolis, 1893.

Randall, James G., and Theodore C. Pease, eds., *The Diary of Orville Hickman Browning*. 2 vols. Springfield, Ill., 1925-1933.

Riddle, Albert G., *Recollections of War Times: Reminiscences of Men and Events in Washington, 1860-1865*. New York, 1885.

Sherman, John, *Recollections of Forty Years in the House, Senate and Cabinet*. 2 vols. New York, 1895.

Scribner, Harvey, ed., *Memoirs of Lucas County and the City of Toledo*. 2 vols. Madison, Wisc., 1910.

Williams, Charles R., ed., *Diary and Letters of Rutherford B. Hayes*. 5 vols. Columbus, Ohio, 1922-1925.

Wilson, Henry, *History of the Rise and Fall of the Slave Power in America*. 3 vols. Boston, 1876.

————, *History of the Anti-Slavery Measures of the Thirty-Seventh and Thirty-Eighth United States Congresses, 1861-1865*. Boston, 1865.

UNPUBLISHED MATERIAL

Bradford, David, "The Background and Formation of the Republican Party in Ohio, 1844-1861." Ph.D. dissertation, University of Chicago, 1947.

Harris, Alfred G., "Slavery and Emancipation in the District of Columbia, 1801-1862." Ph.D. dissertation, Ohio State University, 1946.

Henry, George Selden, Jr., "Radical Republican Policy toward the Negro during Reconstruction,1862-1872." Ph.D. dissertation, Yale University, 1963.

McCarthy, John Lockhart, "Reconstruction Legislation and Voting Alignments in the House of Representatives, 1863-1869." Ph.D. dissertation, Yale University, 1970.

Paddock, Margaret Ashley, "An Ohio Congressman in Reconstruction." M.A. thesis, Columbia University, 1916.

Simon, John Y., "Congress Under Lincoln." Ph.D. dissertation, Harvard University, 1963.

Spencley, Kenneth J., "The Original Impeacher, James M. Ashley in the Civil War and Reconstruction." M.A. thesis, University of Illinois, 1962.

SECONDARY WORKS

Ames, Henry V., *The Proposed Amendments to the Constitution of the United States during The First Century of Its History. Annual Report of the American Historical Association.* Vol. II, Washington, D.C., 1897.

Ashley, Charles S., "Governor Ashley's Biography and Messages." *Contributions to the Historical Society of Montana,* VI (1907), 143-289.

Baringer, William, *Lincoln's Rise to Power.* Boston, 1937.

Belz, Herman, *Reconstructing the Union: Theory and Policy During the Civil War.* Ithaca, N.Y., 1969.

———, "The Etheridge Conspiracy of 1863: A Projected Conservative Coup." *JSH,* XXXVI (Nov. 1970), 549-67.

———, *A New Birth of Freedom: The Republican Party and Freedmen's Rights, 1861 to 1865.* Westport, Conn., 1976.

Benedict, Michael Les, "The Rout of Radicalism: Republicans and the Elections of 1867." *CWH,* XVIII (Nov. 1972), 334-44.

———, *The Impeachment and Trial of Andrew Johnson.* New York, 1973.

———, *A Compromise of Principle: Congressional Republicans and Reconstruction, 1863-1869.* New York, 1975.

Berger, Raoul, "The President, Congress, and the Courts." *The Yale Law Journal,* 83 (May 1974), 1111-55.

Bernstein, Leonard H., "Convention in Pittsburgh." *WPHM,* XLIX (Oct. 1966), 289-300.

Biographical Dictionary of American Congress, 1774-1949. Washington, D.C., 1950.

Bonadio, Felice A., *North of Reconstruction: Ohio Politics, 1865-1870.* New York, 1970.

Botkin, B. A., *A Civil War Treasury of Tales, Legends and Folklore.* New York, 1960.

Bowers, Claude G., *The Tragic Era: The Revolution after Lincoln.* Cambridge, 1929.

Brand, Carl F., "History of the Know-Nothing Party in Indiana." *IMH*, XVIII (March, June 1922), 47-81, 177-206, 266-80.

Brodie, Fawn M., *Thaddeus Stevens: Scourge of the South*. New York, 1959.

Brownson, Orestes, "The President's Message and Proclamation." *Brownson's Quarterly Review*, Nat. Ser., I (Jan. 1864), 85-112.

Burlingame, Merrill G., and K. Ross Toole, *A History of Montana*, 3 vols., New York, 1957.

Carpenter, John A., *Sword and Olive Branch: Oliver Otis Howard*. Pittsburgh, 1964.

Catton, Bruce, *Grant Takes Command*. Boston, 1968.

Clemenceau, Georges, *American Reconstruction, 1865-1870*. Edited by Fernand Baldensperger. New York, 1928.

Cochran, William C., "The Western Reserve and the Fugitive Slave Law." Western Reserve Historical Society *Collections*, CI (1920), 118-204.

Cortissoz, Royal, *The Life of Whitelaw Reid*. 2 vols. New York, 1921.

Cox, LaWanda, and John H. Cox, *Politics, Principle, and Prejudice, 1865-1866: Dilemma of Reconstruction America*. New York, 1963.

Cox, LaWanda, "The Promise of Land for the Freedmen." *MVHR*, XLV (Dec. 1958), 413-40.

Crandall, Andrew W., *The Early History of the Republican Party, 1854-1856*. Gloucester, Mass., 1960.

Current, Richard N., *Lincoln and the First Shot*. Philadelphia, 1963.

Curry, Leonard P., *Blueprint for Modern America: Nonmilitary Legislation of the First Civil War Congress*. Nashville, 1968.

Curry, Richard O., *A House Divided: Statehood Politics and the Copperhead Movement in West Virginia*. Pittsburgh, 1961.

Davidson, Stanley R., and Dale Tash, "Confederate Backwash in Montana Territory." *MMWH*, XVII (Oct. 1967), 50-68.

Dell, Christopher, *Lincoln and the War Democrats: The Grand Erosion of Conservative Tradition*. Rutherford, N.J., 1975.

DeWitt, David Miller, *The Impeachment and Trial of Andrew Johnson*. New York, 1903.

Dictionary of American Biography. 22 vols. New York, 1928-58.

Donald, David, *Lincoln Reconsidered*. New York, 1956.

——, *The Politics of Reconstruction, 1863-1867*. Baton Rouge, 1965.

——, *Charles Sumner and the Coming of the Civil War*. New York, 1961.

——, *Charles Sumner and the Rights of Man*. New York, 1970.

Downes, Randolph C., *Lake Port*. Toledo, 1951.

——, *History of Lake Shore Ohio*. Toledo, 1952.

Dunbar, Willis F., *All Aboard: A History of Railroads in Michigan*. Grand Rapids, Mich., 1969.

Evans, Nelson W., *A History of Scioto County, Ohio, Together with a Pioneer Record of Southern Ohio*. Portsmouth, Ohio, 1903.

Filler, Louis, *The Crusade Against Slavery, 1830-1860*. New York, 1960.

Flower, Frank A., *Edwin McMasters Stanton*. Akron, Ohio, 1905.

Foner, Eric, *Free Soil, Free Labor, Free Men: The Ideology of the Republican Party before the Civil War*. New York, 1970.

Fortune, Alonzo W., *Origins and Development of the Disciples*. St. Louis, 1944.

Franklin, John Hope, *Reconstruction after the Civil War*. Chicago, 1961.

Frederickson, George M., "A Man but Not a Brother: Abraham Lincoln and Racial Equality." *JSH*, XLI (Feb. 1975), 39-58.

Gilbert, Bentley B., "Some Aspects of Ohio's Part in the Liberal Republican Movement." *Ohio Archaeological and Historical Society Bulletin*, 13 (July 1955), 191-200.

Gillette, William, *The Right to Vote: Politics and the Passage of the Fifteenth Amendment*. Baltimore, 1965.

Going, Charles B., *David Wilmot, Free Soiler*. New York, 1924.

Hamilton, James M., *From Wilderness to Statehood, A History of Montana, 1805-1900*. Portland, Ore., 1957.

Harriman, H., "Address Upon Governor Ashley." Address at a Memorial Service, Ann Arbor, Michigan, January 10, 1897.

Harrington, Fred Harvey, *Fighting Politician: Major General N. P. Banks*. Philadelphia, 1948.

Hart, Albert Bushnell, *Salmon Portland Chase*. New York, 1899.

Henig, Gerald S., *Henry Winter Davis: Antebellum and Civil War Congressman from Maryland*. New York, 1973.

Herndon, William H. and Jesse W. Weik, *Herndon's Life of Lincoln*. New York, 1930.

Hesseltine, William B., *Lincoln and the War Governors*. New York, 1948.

Hewitt, Edward R., *Those Were the Days*. New York, 1943.

Hirshson, Stanley P., *Grenville M. Dodge, Soldier, Politician, Railroad Pioneer*. Bloomington, 1967.

Historical Hand-Atlas. Chicago & Toledo, 1882.

Holt, Michael F., *The Political Crisis of the 1850s*. New York, 1978.

Horowitz, Robert F., "James M. Ashley and the Presidential Election of 1856." *OH*, 83 (Winter 1974), 4-16.

———, "Land to the Freedmen: A Vision of Reconstruction." *OH*, 86 (Summer 1977), 187-99.

Howard, Victor B., "The 1856 Election in Ohio: Moral Issues in Politics." *OH*, 80 (Winter 1970), 24-44.

Hyman, Harold M., *A More Perfect Union: The Impact of the Civil War and Reconstruction on the Constitution*. New York, 1973.
———, ed., *The Radical Republicans and Reconstruction 1861-1870*. Indianapolis, 1967.
Jacobs, Donald M., and Raymond H. Robinson, *America's Testing Time: 1848-1877*. Boston, 1973.
Johnson, Thomas H., and Harvey Wish, eds., *The Oxford Companion to American History*. New York, 1966.
Julian, George W., "George W. Julian's Journal—The Assassination of Abraham Lincoln." *IMH*, XI (Dec. 1915), 324-37.
Kahn, Maxine Baker, "Congressman Ashley in the Post-Civil War Years." *NOQ*, 36 (Summer, Autumn 1964), 116-33, 194-210.
Klement, Frank L., *The Limits of Dissent: Clement L. Vallandigham and the Civil War*. Lexington, Ky., 1970.
Korngold, Ralph, *Thaddeus Stevens: A Being Darkly Wise and Rudely Great*. New York, 1955.
Krug, Mark M., *Lyman Trumbull: Conservative Radical*. New York, 1965.
Kutler, Stanley I., *Judicial Power and Reconstruction Politics*. Chicago, 1968.
———, "Impeachment Reconsidered." *Reviews in American History*, I (Dec. 1973), 480-87.
Lindsey, David, *"Sunset" Cox: Irrepressible Democrat*. Detroit, 1959.
Luthin, Reinhard H., "Salmon P. Chase's Political Career before the Civil War." *MVHR*, XXIX (Jan. 1943), 517-40.
———, *The Real Abraham Lincoln*. Englewood Cliffs, N.J., 1960.
Lynch, William O., "Anti-Slavery Tendencies of the Democratic Party in the Northwest, 1848-1850." *MVHR*, XI (Dec. 1924), 319-31.
Macartney, Clarence E., *Little Mac: The Life of General George B. McClellan*. Philadelphia, 1940.
McKitrick, Eric L., *Andrew Johnson and Reconstruction*. Chicago, 1960.
McPherson, James M., "Grant or Greeley? The Abolitionist Dilemma in the Election of 1872." *AHR*, LXXI (Oct. 1965), 41-61.
———, *The Struggle for Equality: Abolitionists and the Negro in the Civil War and Reconstruction*. Princeton, 1964.
Mantell, Martin E., *Johnson, Grant, and the Politics of Reconstruction*, New York, 1973.
Merrill, Louis Taylor, "General Benjamin F. Butler in the Presidential Campaign of 1864." *MVHR*, XXXIII (March 1947), 537-70.
Meyer, Leland W., *The Life and Times of Colonel Richard M. Johnson of Kentucky*. New York, 1932.
Milton, George Fort, *The Age of Hate: Andrew Johnson and the Radicals*, New York, 1930.

Milton, George Fort, *Abraham Lincoln and the Fifth Column*. New York, 1942.

Moore, Clifford H., "Ohio in National Politics, 1865-1896." *OAHQ*, XXXVII (April-July 1928), 220-427.

Morgan, John M., "The People Choose Freedom: The Congressional Election of 1860 in Northwest Ohio." *NOQ*, 22 (Summer 1950), 106-119.

———, "The Ashleys Build a Railroad." *NOQ*, 30 (Spring 1958), 82-99.

———, "The Ann Arbor Strike of 1893." *NOQ*, 30 (Summer 1958), 164-75.

Nevins, Allan, *The Emergence of Lincoln*. 2 vols. New York, 1950.

———, *Hamilton Fish, The Inner Story of the Grant Administration*. New York, 1937.

———, *Ordeal of the Union*. 2 vols. New York, 1947.

———, *The War for the Union*. 2 vols. New York, 1959-60.

Nicolay, John G., and John Hay, *Abraham Lincoln: A History*. 10 vols. New York, 1890.

Oates, Stephen B., *With Malice Toward None: The Life of Abraham Lincoln*. New York, 1977.

Paludin, Phillip S., *A Covenant with Death: The Constitution, Law, and Equality in the Civil War Era*. Urbana, Ill., 1975.

Parrish, William E., *Missouri Under Radical Rule, 1865-1870*. Columbia, Mo., 1965.

———, *Turbulent Partnership: Missouri and the Union, 1861-1865*. Columbia, Mo., 1963.

Perman, Michael, *Reunion without Compromise: The South and Reconstruction, 1865-1868*. Cambridge and New York, 1973.

Pike, James S., *First Blows of the Civil War*. New York, 1879.

Potter, David M., *Lincoln and His Party in the Secession Crisis*. New Haven, 1942.

———, *The Impending Crisis, 1848-1861*. Completed and edited by Don E. Fehrenbacher. New York, 1976.

Preston, Delorus, "The Underground Railroad in Northwest Ohio." *JNH*, XVII (1932), 409-436.

Randall, James G., and Richard N. Current, *Lincoln the President: Last Full Measure*. New York, 1955.

Rawley, James A., *The Politics of Union: Northern Politics during the Civil War*. Hinsdale, Ill., 1974.

Riddleberger, Patrick W., "The Break in the Radical Ranks: Liberals vs. Stalwarts in the Election of 1872." *JNH*, XLIV (April 1959), 136-57.

Riggs, Henry E., *The Ann Arbor Railroad Fifty Years Ago*. Ann Arbor, 1947.

Roseboom, Eugene H., *The Civil War Era.* The History of the State of Ohio, edited by Carl Wittke, vol. IV. Columbus, Ohio, 1944.

————, "Salmon P. Chase and the Know-Nothings." *MVHR*, XXV (Dec. 1938), 335-50.

Ryan, Daniel J., "Lincoln and Ohio." *OAHQ*, XXXII (Jan. 1923), 7-281.

Sandburg, Carl, *Abraham Lincoln, the War Years.* 4 vols. New York, 1939.

Schuckers, Jacob William, *The Life and Public Services of Salmon Portland Chase.* New York, 1874.

Sefton, James E., *The United States Army and Reconstruction, 1865-1877.* Baton Rouge, 1967.

Sewell, Richard H., *Ballots for Freedom: Antislavery Politics, 1837-1860.* New York, 1976.

Sharkey, Robert P., *Money, Class, and Party: An Economic Study of Civil War and Reconstruction.* Baltimore, 1959.

Shipherd, Jacob R., compiler, *History of the Oberlin-Wellington Rescues.* New York, 1969.

Smith, Donald P., *Chase and Civil War Politics.* Columbus, Ohio, 1931.

Smith, Joseph P., ed., *History of the Republican Party in Ohio.* 2 vols. Chicago, 1898.

Smith, Theodore Clark, *The Life and Letters of James Abram Garfield*, 2 vols. New Haven, 1925.

Smith, William, *The Francis Preston Blair Family in Politics.* 2 vols. New York, 1933.

Spence, Clark C., "Spoilsman in Montana." *MMWH*, XIV (Spring 1968), 24-35.

————, *Territorial Politics and Government in Montana, 1864-89.* Urbana, Ill., 1975.

Sproat, John G., *The Best Men, Liberal Reformers in the Gilded Age.* New York, 1965.

Stafford, Dorothy, "Men Who Made Toledo, James M. Ashley—Slavery and a Railroad." Toledo *Blade*, March 26, 1950.

Stampp, Kenneth M., *The Era of Reconstruction, 1865-1877.* New York, 1966.

Stevens, Robert L., ed., "John Brown's Execution—An Eye Witness Account." *NOQ*, 21 (Autumn 1949), 140-48.

Stewart, James Brewer, *Joshua R. Giddings and the Tactics of Radical Politics.* Cleveland, 1970.

————, *Holy Warriors: The Abolitionists and American Slavery.* New York, 1976.

Stout, Tom, ed., *Montana Its Story and Biography.* 2 vols. Chicago, 1921.

Sunderland, J. T., "Introductory Address." Jan. 10, 1897. Pamphlet, University of Michigan Library.

Thomas, Benjamin P., *Abraham Lincoln: A Biography.* New York, 1952.

——, and Harold M. Hyman, *Stanton: The Life and Times of Lincoln's Secretary of War.* New York, 1962.

Thomas, Sister M. Evangeline, *Nativism in the Old Northwest.* Washington, D.C., 1936.

Trefousse, Hans L., "The Acquittal of Andrew Johnson and the Decline of the Radicals." *CWH,* XIV (June 1968), 148-61.

——, "Ben Wade and the Negro." *Ohio Historical Quarterly,* LXVIII (April 1959), 161-76.

——, *Benjamin Franklin Wade: Radical Republican from Ohio.* New York, 1963.

——, *The Radical Republicans: Lincoln's Vanguard for Racial Justice.* New York, 1969.

——, *Impeachment of a President: Andrew Johnson, the Blacks and Reconstruction.* Knoxville, 1975.

——, "Zachariah Chandler and the Withdrawal of Frémont in 1864: New Answers to an Old Riddle." *Lincoln Herald,* LXX (Winter 1968), 181-88.

Trelease, Allen W., *Reconstruction, the Great Experiment.* New York, 1971.

Unger, Irwin, *The Greenback Era: A Social and Political History of American Finance, 1865-1879.* Princeton, 1964.

Van Deusen, Glyndon G., *Horace Greeley: Nineteenth Century Crusader.* Philadelphia, 1953.

——, *The Jacksonian Era, 1828-1848.* New York, 1959.

——, *William Henry Seward.* New York, 1967.

Voegeli, V. Jacque, *Free But Not Equal: The Midwest and the Negro During the Civil War.* Chicago, 1967.

Wagoner, Jay J., *Early Arizona; Prehistory to Civil War.* Tucson, Ariz., 1975.

Waggoner, Clark, *A History of the City of Toledo and Lucas County, Ohio.* New York & Toledo, 1888.

Warden, Robert B., *An Account of the Private Life and Public Services of Salmon P. Chase.* Cincinnati, 1874.

White, Horace, *The Life of Lyman Trumbull.* Boston, 1913.

Whiting, William, *The War Powers of the President, and the Legislative Powers of Congress in Relation to Rebellion, Treason and Slavery.* 3rd ed. Boston, 1863.

Williams, T. Harry, *Lincoln and the Radicals.* Madison, Wisc., 1941.

——, *Lincoln and His Generals.* New York, 1952.

Wilson, Charles R., "The Original Chase Organization Meeting and *The Next Presidential Election.*" *MVHR,* XXIII (June 1936), 61-79.

Winter, Nevin O., *A History of Northwestern Ohio.* 2 vols. Chicago, 1919.

Woodward, C. Vann, "That Other Impeachment." *The New York Times Magazine*, (Aug. 11, 1974), 9, 26-32.

Yager, Elizabeth, "The Presidential Election Campaign of 1864 in Ohio." *OAHQ* (Oct. 1925), 548-64.

Zornow, William Frank, *Lincoln & the Party Divided*. Norman, Okla., 1954.

INDEX